Changes in Care

Global Perspectives on Aging

Series editor, Sarah Lamb

This series publishes books that will deepen and expand our understanding of age, aging, ageism, and late life in the United States and beyond. The series focuses on anthropology while being open to ethnographically vivid and theoretically rich scholarship in related fields, including sociology, religion, cultural studies, social medicine, medical humanities, gender and sexuality studies, human development, critical and cultural gerontology, and age studies. Books will be aimed at students, scholars, and occasionally the general public.

Jason Danely, *Aging and Loss: Mourning and Maturity in Contemporary Japan*

Parin Dossa and Cati Coe, eds., *Transnational Aging and Reconfigurations of Kin Work*

Sarah Lamb, ed., *Successful Aging as a Contemporary Obsession: Global Perspectives*

Margaret Morganroth Gullette, *Ending Ageism, or How Not to Shoot Old People*

Ellyn Lem, *Gray Matters: Finding Meaning in the Stories of Later Life*

Michele Ruth Gamburd, *Linked Lives: Elder Care, Migration, and Kinship in Sri Lanka*

Yohko Tsuji, *Through Japanese Eyes: Thirty Years of Studying Aging in America*

Jessica C. Robbins, *Aging Nationally in Contemporary Poland: Memory, Kinship, and Personhood*

Rose K. Keimig, *Growing Old in a New China: Transitions in Elder Care*

Anna I. Corwin, *Embracing Age: How Catholic Nuns Became Models of Aging Well*

Molly George, *Aging in a Changing World: Older New Zealanders and Contemporary Multiculturalism*

Cati Coe, *Changes in Care: Aging, Migration, and Social Class in West Africa*

Changes in Care

....

Aging, Migration, and Social Class in West Africa

CATI COE

Rutgers University Press

New Brunswick, Camden, and Newark, New Jersey, and London

Library of Congress Cataloging-in-Publication Data

Names: Coe, Cati, author.
Title: Changes in care: aging, migration, and social class in West Africa / Cati Coe.
Description: New Brunswick: Rutgers University Press, 2021. | Series: Global perspectives on aging | Includes bibliographical references and index.
Identifiers: LCCN 2021004402 | ISBN 9781978823242 (paperback) | ISBN 9781978823259 (hardcover) | ISBN 9781978823266 (epub) | ISBN 9781978823273 (mobi) | ISBN 9781978823280 (pdf)
Subjects: LCSH: Older people—Care—Ghana. | Older people—Services for—Ghana. | Church work with older people—Ghana. | Ghana—Social conditions—21st century.
Classification: LCC HV1487.G42 C64 2021 | DDC 362.609667—dc23
LC record available at https://lccn.loc.gov/2021004402

A British Cataloging-in-Publication record for this book is available from the British Library.

All photos by the author

∞ The paper used in this publication meets the requirements of the American National Standard for Information Sciences—Permanence of Paper for Printed Library Materials, ANSI Z39.48-1992.

www.rutgersuniversitypress.org

Manufactured in the United States of America

For caregivers everywhere

Contents

Changes in Care

Introduction

• •

After an absence of four years, in June 2013 I returned to Akropong, the town in southern Ghana where I had done research since 1997, to catch up with friends still living and mourn those who had passed. Behind the main Presbyterian church called Christchurch, an imposing white building on the hill, the foundation of a new building was being laid, cement block by cement block (fig. I.1).

"What is that building?" I asked. To my surprise, the response was that it would be a senior day center. One woman on the church's aged program committee explained to me that the problem in Akropong is that the children of older adults have traveled for work, leaving their parents alone, without anyone to help them. The minister had traveled to America seven years before, saw the residential facilities there, and brought the idea back with him. Other organizers explained to me that although older adults in Akropong might be living with their children or grandchildren, they were left alone during the day when the other household members went to school or work. As a result, they had the idea for a senior day program where older adults could meet their friends, have a hot meal, and consult with a nurse on staff.

While waiting for the senior day center to be completed, the church was in the meantime engaged in several activities to support aging congregants. It regularly organized quarterly gatherings of older parishioners where they received Holy Communion from the minister. The church had also arranged the part-time services of a government nurse to visit parishioners at home to consult on health issues and provide routine health checks (for example, of blood pressure and resting blood sugar levels). The minister himself explained to me that part of the reason for these programs came from the number of bedridden adults to whom the church was providing Holy Communion at home; there were so many that visiting homebound congregants took up much of the time of the senior and

1

FIG. I.1 Day center being built, Akropong, June 5, 2013.

junior ministers. Such visits also gave church leaders a sense of the needs of their aging congregants.

I was astonished by the building and the reasons for it. Ghanaians had always told me that those in Europe and America "threw away" their old people by putting them into nursing homes, whereas they themselves took care of them in their extended families (*abusua*). Although a day program was certainly not a full-time residential facility or nursing home, the construction of the senior day center and the ongoing initiatives in Christchurch spoke to changes in attitudes and new concerns about aging in Akropong. In fact, once I was sensitized to the issue, everywhere I looked people seemed to be engaged in creating new institutions and programs for older adults, some inspired by ideas or experiences outside of Ghana, and others more homegrown, spreading laterally as people shared ideas about aging and elder care with one another.

Four years later, by the end of December 2016, the day center for older adults was finally completed. It was beautiful, a striking addition to the landscape with its aquamarine paint. Its metallic fixtures shone brightly. A balcony graced the second floor. To my eyes, the building looked more like the mansions being built in the capital Accra or along the hillsides around the town of Akropong than an institutional facility, making me wonder about its ultimate purpose. My doubts turned out to be justified: despite the completion of the building three years earlier, the building had still not been formally opened by September 2019, and the organizers had given up on the idea of a day program. Instead, they had decided that the church could use the building for other purposes. The quarterly gatherings for older adults remained popular, and the pressure of Holy Communion services at home had increased, but the home visits by the nurse had ended, with her retirement. The nurse's former assistant remained on staff, and she occasionally visited people at home. I will return (in chapter 4) to the specific reasons why the aged center did not open after years of preparation; for now, I discuss the larger implications of the senior day center.

This book is about social change, albeit one of fits and starts, in episodic and contingent ways. I argue that this is one way social change occurs, and that in order to understand social change, we also need to understand the ways in which it does not occur and what remains the same. Things may be started but never get off the ground. The inconsistencies speak to the limits of social change, to the ways that ideas fail to become routine practice because of the lack of shared understanding about goals or the use of resources. And yet, in the sputtering, the idea also takes shape and may gather resources. Furthermore, some of those sputterings last a long time, sparking initiatives by others and causing the idea to spread. Some initiatives continue by adapting and morphing in response to conflicts, adapting to others' concerns, resources, and period in the life course. Even an unused building like the Akropong senior day center can become a seed that germinates in spreading the idea or practice to others. This is a way by which ideas and practices travel and become enacted. This book is therefore about fragile processes, illustrating the contingent nature of social life in general and social change in particular.

Anthropologists have moved away from grand theories and toward more indeterminate, nuanced conceptualizations. We have discarded terms like "culture," "globalization," and "kinship systems" (Abu-Lughod 1991), replacing them with more processual and contingent terms like "repertoire" (Coe 2013b), the "traveling model" (Behrends, Park, and Rottenburg 2014), "assemblage" (Ong and Collier 2005), and "kinning" (Howell 2006). In the study of aging, too, we need concepts to study the emergence of new practices and discourses that are shared by more than one individual but have not become institutionalized.

In order to capture an indeterminate and possibly transitional level of social change, I proposed in earlier work with Erdmute Alber the concept of *inscription* (Coe and Alber 2018).[1] Inscription falls within the continuum between shared norms, on the one hand, and individual actions, on the other. Inscription, always in the making, is more standardized than individual behavior. It emerges when some people are doing, believing, and feeling in similar ways. However, it is not, and often not yet, as standardized and shared within society as a norm. Norms, in contrast, are discussed in patterned, formulaic discourse, although usually they are evoked at moments of norm violation. They are shared knowledge about how people should behave. Inscription, in contrast, is not dominant or hegemonic.

Inscriptions are based on individual and familial emotions, experiences, and restrictions, as well as on actions of reflecting on and responding to processes of institutional and societal change. Inscriptions are social experiments, as people begin feeling and thinking their way through a problem to which existing norms do not propose adequate answers. As an experimental practice, it can be contested and negotiated, competing against other understandings and even against social norms, but it is sometimes so invisible and unarticulated as to escape social censure or commentary. In these experiments, discourses and practices may be disconnected from or even contradictory to one another. Instead, there may be a swirl of discourses—as in the example of the aged center, about lonely older adults and working, migrant adult children; about the pressures of Holy Communion on church staff; and about the neglect of older persons by their kin. These discourses mobilize resources and change infrastructures, leading to the construction of a prominent building behind the church, and the hiring of a nurse, for example, but also to unused buildings, unsatisfying meetings, and both slow and abrupt shifts in plans. They have effects on persons in that they can become embodied in everyday habits and routines; they can have material effects as in building construction and the mobilization of social, emotional, and financial resources.

Processes of inscriptions are happening due to the fact that every society is in motion. They often take place when discrepancies between norms and behavior occur: if there were neither change nor conflicting norms, inscriptions would not happen. Inscriptions are responses to the practical conflicts and problems caused by conflicting or increasingly irrelevant norms. This is why they always indicate processes of change. Conceptualizing inscription as a processual moment in between norms and individual behavior implies possible dynamics in all directions: it could start as an individual practice that is gradually shared by others. If it spreads, it could gradually develop into a social norm. Of course, this dynamic could, and does, happen in the other direction, as when shared norms come to contradict one another and become less dominant and less shared. What is an inscription today can, in the future, become more articulated and even dominant and hegemonic as a social norm, or it might fade into the background as part of the transition to yet another social norm. The concept of inscription is needed to indicate a level of articulation and practice that is not socially normed and, even more importantly, not necessarily discursively organized.

The term "inscription" derives from "kin-scripts," which Carol Stack and Linda Burton (1993) developed some decades ago to theorize the ways that kin create scripts for the life courses of their members. Through this concept, they emphasize the temporality of multiple life courses and the ways that each life course affects the life courses of others. In extending Stack and Burton's discussion of kin-scripts, however, unlike them I emphasize the ways scripts are coming into being and being made and formed, rather than the ways that existing scripts are being negotiated in practice. As a result, "inscription" is used rather than "script," to emphasize the processual quality by which scripts are made in practice and negotiation with others.[2]

In my earlier work with Erdmute Alber, we were particularly interested in inscriptions around age and stages in the life course. In addition to the age-scripts and the aforementioned kin-scripts Stack and Burton have discussed, other kinds of inscriptions are possible, such as gender-inscriptions. This book is concerned with new practices and discourses of care for older adults in Ghana and thus focuses on both age inscriptions and care inscriptions.

Although many other topics could serve as the jumping-off point, care and aging particularly lend themselves to an analysis of social change. Age, age norms, and age scripts are critical to social organization, undergirding a particular social order and the domination of particular groups (Bourdieu 1977). Because age is a key component of the social order, including the distribution of power, wealth, and property, aging trajectories—in their institutionalization, restrictions and constraints, social meaning, and social roles—are highly sensitive to social change. Jennifer Cole and Deborah Durham argue that "periods of pronounced social change have often seen increased concern with age" (2007, 6). All social change affects aging and age categorization.

Furthermore, care organizes social relations in particular ways because it is central to the process of social reproduction of persons across the life course, within households and society at large. The nature of care is defined around normative understandings of need (Thelen 2015), whether assistance with "activities of daily living" or companionship to stave off loneliness, as we will see. These understandings of care mobilize social and material resources, including labor (Buch 2015; Chen 2015; Held 2005). Because of its centrality to the social reproduction of persons, care also indexes belonging. Lisa Stevenson (2014) defines care as the way in which people come to matter in a particular way. Care is the product of a moral imagination situating people within a moral universe (Livingston 2005); some people become deserving of care (as kin members or fellow citizens, for example) within this moral community, and others are excluded from care. For example, in southern Ghana, those who looked after their own children in defined ways and maintained their marriages are constructed as deserving the care of their children as they age (Apt 1996; Van der Geest 1997, 2002b). In the discussion below, I elaborate on the concept of inscription, highlight the processes by which inscription occurs, and illuminate some of the reasons why it is happening now.

Inscriptions, Social Norms, and Hegemonies

Since early debates on age-grade societies, anthropologists have documented the variety of norms, rituals, and practices around the stages in the life course and the ways that age-grade-related norms are central to the construction of political power and social organization in those societies (Bernardi 1985; for an overview of the literature, see also Alber and Häberlein 2010). Additionally, mainly focused on Euro-American societies, sociologists have analyzed changes in normative expectations of different age stages or, more generally, within life course regimes. These age norms work in hegemonic ways and are often implicit in social organization, verbal expressions, and cognitive categories. Sometimes they are not even articulated but rather are what Pierre Bourdieu (1977) called *doxa*, to refer to what is so taken for granted that it can be assumed without saying, as "common sense."

Silence about the norm, as well as its alternatives, can be an indicator as well as a maintainer of doxa. John Borneman argues that the "inability or refusal to name a practice relates directly to the severity with which it breaches the norm; silence keeps practice in the realm of doxa, defined by Bourdieu as 'that which is beyond question' (1977, 169). Bestowing a name would objectively recognize a practice that is best regulated by keeping it unmentionable; namelessness thus prevents the development of a language for description that might bring individual practices into public discourse" (1992, 295). In Ghana, one doxa, although it is occasionally articulated, as in rumors about witchcraft or complaints about remittances, is the notion of balanced reciprocity: that is, those who received care should return care at some point in time. This doxa is the rationale for adult children's care of their parents and is articulated in a Twi proverb, told to me by an older man in this way: "If your mother or father or someone looks after you while your teeth are coming in, when it comes to the time where his or her teeth are falling out, you look after him or her."[3] As I illustrate below, this doxa can then be extended to justify care beyond the adult children. To the extent that older adults have contributed to their church or the nation of Ghana, they make the case that the church or state ought to reciprocate by caring for them in their own time of need.

Another doxa concerns the meaning of care. Good care is primarily associated with food and evaluated through discussions about the quality and quantity of food. Secondarily, bathing daily is considered important. Medical care is much less important and is indexed through food and cleanliness. Care is often expressed symbolically through remittances and the provision of money to enable an older person's daily life (Coe 2011).

At other times, norms around age and care are articulated in formulaic and conventional discourses, what Bourdieu (1977) called *orthodoxy*. Social norms that are articulated as orthodoxy are weaker than doxa, which are taken for granted and not subject to debate. One example of orthodoxy comes from Madagascar where older persons monopolize and manipulate knowledge about kinship relations in order to affect decisions about new marital relations (Astuti 2000). Although their knowledge is articulated as orthodox, it is important to note that there is scope for contestation even using orthodox discourses, as people can present different opinions, all of which they frame as based on orthodox norms.

In Ghana, kin care for older adults is the orthodox position, in the terminology of Bourdieu (1977), meaning that it is the conventional, formulaic, and normative position. For example, when I told young or middle-aged Ghanaians about my research, they dismissed it, saying that in Ghana adult children took care of their aging parents. It is the only position articulated and promoted by the state in its policy about aging. As I discuss in chapter 1, the government of Ghana's Aged Policy articulates the orthodox position of "family" care that coincides with local discourse. It also aligns with neoliberal social and economic policies in which the state does not assume responsibility for the care of older adults. However, it is important to note that the orthodoxy can shift over time without people realizing it. Furthermore, the fact that this stance is articulated strongly is a sign of its weaker position; it is not doxa, so commonsensical as not needing articulation. Even the Aged Policy's promotion of kin care suggests that "the traditional family" needs help in caring for its older members. In the discussion to come, I address the disconnect between this orthodox stance and actual practices, which leads to inscriptions around age and care such as the senior day center in Akropong.

What is articulated as orthodoxy can also be challenged by alternative constructions, which Bourdieu called *heterodoxies*. These are positions that are not shared by all and not even intended to be legitimized as such but are nevertheless shared by several actors. They could be articulated as positions of minority groups or as emerging, not yet articulated, norms. In contrast to the orthodoxy espoused by younger Ghanaians or by the state, those with older parents or those who were themselves aging told more complicated stories of kin care, in which kin care led to tension or neglect, or of their need for paid care in one way or another. Those whose children were living up to their obligations were content with the orthodoxy, but some older adults perceived the reliance on adult children's support to be precarious—they were alert to the potential disconnect between the orthodoxy of kin care and its actual enactment. They urged acceptance of children's financial and emotional limitations and expressed openness to alternative arrangements, including residential facilities, paid care, and self-reliance.

Both quiet, unnoticed transformations and highly visible changes in the orthodoxy of kin care for older adults are happening in different social circles. With regard to Bourdieu's terminology, some care inscriptions met the criteria of heterodoxy; that is, they were in direct opposition to the orthodoxy of kin care and were regarded with suspicion and alarm by proponents of the orthodoxy. The most criticized heterodox inscription was residential facilities for older adults, viewed by the government of Ghana and nongovernmental organizations (NGOs) that advocate for aging policies as anathema due to their foreign origin, expense, and unsuitability for the Ghanaian context. Residential facilities were in some ways a token, in the conception of Behrends, Park, and Rottenburg (2014), representing a particular social order and set of arrangements, in this case of foreignness. This heterodoxy was articulated strongly by Dr. J. B. Asare, a psychiatrist, one of the founders of a local NGO affiliated with the international NGO HelpAge International, based in the United Kingdom. Dr. Asare expressed his reasons for his dislike of the idea of residential facilities in Ghana: "To remove the old people, segregate them and put them into a place [like a nursing home]: One, you are going to put them in an unnatural environment. Number two, we think that they cannot be looked after very well [in these environments]. Thirdly, they will have to pay a lot of money to do it, unless government supports it, and we are against even government providing such facilities, unless that person is severely ill and infirm and has to be in a facility. Even that one: we would still want the person to manage at home" (taped interview, June 28, 2013). At the same time, this heterodoxy is active in people's imaginations and discussed frequently because those who have traveled abroad become familiar with it, and it contrasts so strikingly, symbolically, with the orthodoxy of kin care. Only a few small nursing homes with small numbers of residents are currently in operation in Accra (discussed in chapter 5). Residential facilities serve as the primary heterodoxy.

Others found problematic the growth of commercial nursing agencies, which are increasingly popular among the urban middle class and elite, particularly those who have lived abroad or have children abroad. The heterodoxy that has been gaining traction among the policy elite in Ghana, including among lower-level civil servants at the local level, and which may become the new orthodoxy, is what Christchurch in Akropong proposed but failed to achieve: a senior day center to cater to older adults during the day, focused on providing social interaction for relatively active and well older adults rather than everyday care for those who are bedridden and disabled in residential facilities. Ghanaian sociologist of aging Delali Dovie (2019) describes several "archetypes" or models by which aged care in Ghana is being organized. One is "the adult day center archetype": "In this context, older adults eat, interact with other facility users as well as play games such as ludo, cards and a host of others during the day and then depart to their respective homes at the end of the day. This archetype more extensively keeps older adults busy and away from boredom and loneliness" (6). This approach also has the longest institutional history in Ghana, with the first adult day center set up in 1993 in Accra by the Catholic Church. That center, currently defunct, garnered media attention over the years, allowing the concept to travel, that is, to be picked up by other institutions, like Christchurch. As an inscription, senior day centers exist both in practice and in discourse in the circles of aging advocates, but have not become a widely established norm.

Another approach with which the mainline churches, including the Presbyterian Church in Akropong, are experimenting is with voluntary and social associations like aged fellowship groups. Sometimes this takes the form of occasional gatherings, which Dovie (2019) describes as the occasional archetype: "First, the occasional archetype which takes the form of a rare phenomenon entails the bringing together of older adults to a social gathering by a lead individual, where they are feted and socially interacted with. It serves as a means of reducing boredom and loneliness, albeit for a short while. It is a form of respite particularly for those who have no one to depend on in terms of social interaction" (6). Within some churches, these occasional gatherings have become more regular and more organized by older adults themselves. In these contexts, older adults are not fêted: rather than sitting in rows of chairs as the objects of instruction and charity, they are organizing activities for their own enjoyment and economic needs. In these cases, these older adults also become more oriented to advocacy on behalf of aging within their social worlds.

Other possibilities are more discursive, floated as ideas that may gain traction as practice one day—or not. For example, some older adults within the church fellowship groups advocated for balanced reciprocity with the state or church, rather than with their adult children: because they have contributed to the development of the nation or the institution, these institutions should reciprocate. Another idea floated is a more individualistic approach, in which older adults are encouraged to plan for their own retirement, rather than relying on their children to provide for them. This approach has major advocates among retirement planners, including advisors within the pension funds who provide workshops to civil servants (Dovie 2018). The private market in insurance is growing across Africa (Bähre 2012; Golomski 2015).

However, not all emergent care inscriptions need to be heterodoxies set in contrast to orthodoxies; some are just emerging without being in direct opposition to other, more dominant norms. Some emergent inscriptions were not censured or stigmatized; some were noticed not as deviant from kin care, but rather as extensions of it. These inscriptions include more quiet changes negotiated among kin. For instance, rather than middle-aged daughters moving to care for their mothers in the hometown, sometimes the mothers move in with the daughters, negotiating new relationships with their sons-in-law in a place where they are strangers and have no church or neighborly community. Sometimes, adult children arrange for someone (whether an adult woman for hire or a foster child in exchange for schooling) to live with an aged person in the daughter's stead. Neighbors also look out for older adults. These practices pass under the radar; not discussed, they are enacted at the level of practice. These less visible adjustments in practices are *alterodox inscriptions*. Despite their lack of discussion in the public realm, they represent changes for those involved in care giving and receiving.

The Need for Inscription

When enacted, social norms—whether as doxa or orthodoxy—are put into use in a particular situation, to help interpret what is going on (as in Goffman's notion of "frame" [1986]) and guide subsequent action. They provide people with goals in relation to such action and help them understand their emotional responses to such situations. However, a dominant discourse or social norm may be insufficient to justify or explain a particular response, causing another script to be mobilized (Swidler 2001). The friction between a social norm and the "balky world" (Sewell 2005, 179) in which it is mobilized is one of the causes of inscriptions.

Max Gluckman's Manchester School provided influential theorization about social change in Africa. Manchester School anthropologists focused on atypical events that expressed conflict and crisis, known as situation analysis. These illustrated the hidden social and political tensions in a society: "They revealed what ordinary and routine social practices of a repeated, ongoing kind tended to obscure" (Kapferer 2010, 3). Such conflicts tended to reveal doxa, when what was silently understood was articulated in the midst of confrontations. At the same time, situation analysis often highlighted singular events or significant performances when the course of history was changed (Marx 1963; Sahlins 1980) or when "the intransigencies and irresolvable tensions ingrained in social and personal life (the two being inseparable) boiled to the surface and became, if only momentarily, part public awareness for the participants as well as for the anthropologist" (Kapferer 2010, 3). In contrast, my analysis focuses on how the ordinary routines of everyday life—such as the care of an aging parent—create ordinary problems, for which people mobilize the social and economic resources available. In line with the Manchester School, I see these everyday moments as indicative of social tension and as generating social change. Coping with these ordinary problems may bring to consciousness how the existing doxa or orthodoxy is insufficient to resolve these dilemmas, problematizing life as lived and allowing new ideas and practices to be adopted.

Confronting a situation that problematizes received wisdom is often an emotional experience. Raymond Williams used the term "structures of feelings" to refer to emergent feelings and thoughts, born of lived experience, that do not fit a doxa or orthodoxy. Because of the patterned ways that experience does not match a social norm, the resulting feelings, thoughts, and actions are also patterned. These can be confused and unarticulated, manifesting themselves as "an unease, stress, a displacement, a latency: the moment of conscious comparison has not yet come, often not yet coming" (Williams 1977, 130). Jean and John Comaroff describe the same process: "It is the realm of partial recognition, of inchoate awareness, of ambiguous perception, and, sometimes, of creative tension: that liminal space of human experience in which people discern acts and facts but cannot or do not order them into narrative descriptions or even into articulate conceptions of the world; in which signs and events are observed, but in a hazy, translucent light; in which individuals or groups know that something is happening to them but find it difficult to put their fingers on quite what it is" (1991, 29). When people respond to existing social norms about aging with chaotic feelings and thoughts, they change their practices and behavior. Through this process, new social relations emerge. Although a new vision of society, personhood, and social roles are implicit in these practices, they are not necessarily a kind of resistance in the way hidden transcripts are (Scott 1985).

Inscriptions may remain here in this unstable, chaotic state, and yet be shared by numerous people. However, in some cases, people may then begin to try to make such "unease" coherent and organized, finding new language to talk about their new patterns of behavior. This is the next stage of inscription.

The Types of Processes in the Formation and Generation of Inscription

In this book, I highlight several processes by which social change occurs in relation to age and care inscriptions. Here, I identify processes based on *substituting adjacent relations, mixing of discourses in which heterodoxy becomes orthodoxy, organizing unease discursively*, or *maintaining a social norm through alterodox care inscription*.

1   *Substitution of adjacent relations.* Changes in the organization of caring for the older person can occur through the substitution of similar persons, without discourses reflecting these organizational changes in practice. In earlier work on conflicts concerning whether children were slaves, pawns, or foster children in the colonial Gold Coast, I argued that care norms could change through the substitutions of adjacent relations (Coe 2012, 2013a). The work of Heather Rae-Espinoza (2011) provides another example: when grandmothers in Ecuador take care of grandchildren whose mothers have migrated abroad, the children tend to normalize this difference by representing their grandmothers as their mothers to their friends, schoolmates, and teachers. As I discuss later on in the book (in chapters 2 and 7), among wealthier families in both rural and urban areas, adult daughters are being replaced or helped by hired caregivers, to provide daily care to older adults. The slippage between categories of persons seen as similar—younger, poorer women—thus allows people to maintain a discourse that conforms to the social norm of kin care, even as they enact an alterodox age inscription in practice and behavior.

2   *A mix of discourses, in which sometimes heterodoxy becomes orthodoxy.* People can mix orthodox and heterodox discourses. The amalgamation of different explanations for disease is common in the development of scientific thought (Fleck [1935] 1979). Similarly, Laura Ahearn (2001a, 110) shows how "newer" ideals of love and personal compatibility co-exist with "older" notions that marriage is determined by fate in Nepal. For example, a Nepalese woman mixes the two idioms of fate and choice in explaining her marriage, "We didn't dislike each other enough to break up. This is my fate, I said, see? . . . Well, for myself it was written that

I would marry; if it hadn't been, I would have left him, see?" Mixing discourses leads to the elision of the differences between the new and the old. In these processes, formerly heterodox discourses or practices may also become the dominant or orthodox discourse or practice. Erdmute Alber, Tabea Häberlein, and Jeannett Martin (2010; Alber 2011) showed how the trousseau was introduced among peasant Lokpa in northwest Benin about forty years ago, when some of them saw this practice among neighboring ethnic groups. As these trousseaus of modern consumer goods such as beds, "modern" pots and other household things were highly attractive, little by little, girls started to leave their home region in order to work in the cities as domestic workers. Today, the contemporary norm of youth is to work in urban households to acquire a trousseau, which almost all girls of the Lokpa region fulfill. The heterodoxy, namely girls acquiring a trousseau through migration, has become the new orthodoxy, and a former age inscription has become a dominant norm, namely that a girl needs to migrate to become an adult. In the case of Ghana, a heterodoxy of senior day centers seems to be becoming an orthodoxy in aging advocacy circles, as a way of supporting kin to take care of their older adults, in a less institutional way than a complete residential facility.

3   *Organization of unease discursively through comparisons and temporal hierarchies.* When people generate new practices, they may begin to name, justify, and organize those practices. One strategy by which they can order their experiences is by creating hierarchies, comparisons, and dichotomies. For example, "this was the way of the past, this is now," or "we do this, they do that" (Sewell 2005; see also Douglas 1986). Dualisms are "forms of ordering that entail particular social practices" (Yarrow 2008, 429). In Tatjana Thelen's work in Romania (2015), she noted how Romanians tended to criticize Germans for putting their older relatives into institutions while the Romanians tried to keep them at home. Lawrence Cohen (1998) similarly noted Indian evaluations of the "bad family"—the modernized and Western-oriented Indian family—that did not take care of their aging parents. While seemingly intransigent in criticism of an Other time or society, these hierarchies can be easily inverted and seem to be a step in the process of integrating new ideas and practices. Thus, ten years after the original research, Thelen noted that with the out-migration of Romanian women to care for Germans in their homes, Romanians began to place their older relatives in institutions and praised the Germans for their use of home care rather than institutional care. Similarly, two decades after Cohen's original research, Sarah Lamb (2009) showed that Indians were far more open to nonfamilial care environments and had adapted institutional care homes associated with the Western family to concepts like the

ashram and the joint family household. As noted above, Ghanaians often contrast what is happening in the West with what is happening in Ghana through the use of phrases like "the Ghanaian traditional family" and modernity. The notion that family life changes with modernity, becoming more nucleated and with narrower relations of solidarity, is a central tenet of modernization theory (see Apt 1996 for an extensive discussion of this view in Ghana). Because the institutionalization of the aged is considered one outcome of modernization, care practices for the aged are a key symbolic distinction between "modern" and "traditional" societies in everyday discussions and policy documents (Thelen and Coe 2019). However, these contrasts, made in the attempt to close off options, in fact open new possibilities in practice. Even when negatively evaluated through contrasting dichotomies, as in "this is traditional and that is modern," such dichotomies can introduce heterodoxies that can become incorporated as possible solutions when "tradition" or an orthodoxy no longer seems to be viable or reliable. Arjun Appadurai expresses, "Lives today are as much acts of projection and imagination as they are enactments of known scripts or predictable outcomes" (1996, 205). Cultural resources in the form of ideas and practices are necessary for the acts of projection and imagination that Appadurai discusses. Ideas and institutions travel and are translated. In Ghana, the resources for inscriptions include representations from societies constructed as Other and different. As I argue in chapter 2, the heterodox token of institutional facilities is transformed in older Ghanaians' imagination to address their needs. In particular, they imagine these institutions as promoting their goals for a comfortable and happy old age, in which they receive food, medical care, friendship, and public recognition. Furthermore, they are using these foreign institutions symbolically, to critique the current state of affairs, and as a lament to incite others to action. Thus, although these dichotomies and hierarchies of age trajectories seem rigid and can be articulated quite passionately, they can collapse or be inverted quite rapidly.

4 *Maintenance of a social norm through alterodox inscription.* People might maintain a social norm through new practices. Tabea Häberlein (2018) argues that the intergenerational contract between young and old is maintained through migrants sending gifts and foodstuffs to their parents in the villages in northern Togo, who are cared for, on a daily basis, by nonmigrants. Erdmute Alber (2018) shows that in Benin, the old and dominant norm that children should take care of their aging parents can be fulfilled in a new way. Those who have lived a middle-class lifestyle, including the expectation of living independently, do not always want to move into the households of their children when they age. Alber mentions the case of a retired man who was unable to afford

finishing the construction of his house. Instead of taking him into his own household, as the dominant norm would suggest, his son helped him financially to finish building his own house. With this action, he enabled his father to continue living independently, at the same time as he fulfilled the social norm of caring for the parent. In Ghana, care for older adults has two different meanings: providing daily care through feeding, dressing, and cleaning and sending financial assistance for others to provide care on a daily basis. As I discuss in chapter 1, the hiring of paid caregivers by adult children allows them to live up to the expectations of kin care; this is also an example of *the substitution of adjacent relations* as poorer women substitute for the care work of adult daughters.

These four types—the substitution of adjacent relations, the mixture of discourses in which heterodoxy becomes orthodoxy, the organization of unease discursively, and the maintenance of a social norm through alterodoxy—constitute the major ways by which inscription occurs. Triggered by often very small modifications in the social order, both heterodox and alterodox age and care inscriptions occur and sometimes rapidly become social norms, as they are shared within social networks and become more coherent and stable, a process that may result in a new dominant codification around care. Other inscriptions float into disuse, unable to capture the imagination of other people.

Actors and Institutions

The making of new age and care inscriptions can be driven by practices of older people themselves, through their agency or "the socially mediated capacity to act" (Ahearn 2001b, 112) As Jennifer Cole has discussed, we have a "synoptic illusion" that views young people as a source of social change and newness, and older adults more engaged in cultural preservation and conservation (2013). Yet, as she notes, "the movement toward old age is a profoundly innovative process" for those who are aging and encountering new circumstances of bodily decline and changing social networks (226). As this stage of life becomes more extensive—lasting a decade or more—new questions about its meaning and practices need to be answered by those who are encountering aging (see Thelen and Coe 2019). There are many examples in the literature. For instance, Martine Segalen (2016) has noted that grandparents in France feel compelled to invent new terms of address for themselves such as Papi and Mami, responding to changes in the values and roles associated with grandparenthood and generating new possibilities for the performance of grandparenting. In China, older, uneducated women position themselves as important for national development by fostering disabled children (Raffety 2017). The literature illustrates a high level of older people's agency in shaping age inscriptions, but in situations constrained by larger structural forces shaped by social norms. The inscriptions being generated in Ghana highlight the agency of older adults in imagining their futures, criticizing the status quo, and pragmatically adjusting their strategies.

Older persons draw on the cultural and social resources available to them, including orthodox age and care narratives, in making the personal transitions of aging. They also create new social forms and possibilities as they undergo personal and social transformation and encounter new life problems. Sometimes, older people seem more open to possibilities that differ from the orthodoxy precisely because they acknowledge that kin care seems uncertain. In my conversations with younger people, they were often categorical and judgmental about the heterodoxy, such as saying, "In Ghana, we do not use old age homes" and "We take care of our aged." Although I heard laments and complaints in my visits with Ghanaian older adults, I also heard resignation to the existing circumstances that led to pragmatic solution-oriented approaches and political critique, particularly from older women who sympathized with the economic struggles of their children. This line of thinking prompted age and care inscriptions. The state's relative silence about and lack of attention to aging creates a weak orthodox discourse about aging solutions. As a result, older people in Ghana have the space to construct heterodox and alterodox discourses and practices, however tentative and disconnected, and engage in advocacy with those around them in promoting these new inscriptions.

However, it is not older people's agency alone that create inscriptions. Inscriptions can also be socially mediated by cohort members (Riley and Riley 1986), including friends and acquaintances at church. Caring others, including adult children and neighbors, also play a role. Inscriptions also come from institutions, to the extent that institutionalized norms generate unexpected and unsought-for practices. In this study, key institutions include churches, the government, and academics and NGOs that are involved in advocacy about state policy. Laws and regulations of aging through retirement policies and social security measures directly regulate the social and economic conditions through which aging is framed and can generate alterodox age inscriptions in response. For instance, the introduction of a pension system for all older people in South Africa has led to the emergence of an age inscription of investing a portion of the pensions of older persons into household food security and the schooling of the children (Case and Menendez 2007). In the United States, the age at which one is eligible to receive Social Security is not meant to push people into retirement, and yet people make retirement decisions around the age markers set by the Social Security Administration. Alber (2018) observes that for many state officials from northern Benin working in the capital in the south, retirement from state employment is associated with the inscription of moving back to northern Benin and thus relocating the household.

Inscriptions, then, emerge from state policies, individuals, kin, and cohorts and are negotiated by older persons and others in everyday contexts and in relation to social norms. An inscription is therefore not always a sign of an older person's agency. Both individuals and other institutions like states construct narratives, and these exist dynamically and dialogically with each other (Borneman 1992, 285). These dialogues are sometimes with other scripts and discourses from the present and the past, including those of different societies or different levels of societal organization, whether kin networks, the state, or other social organizations such as religious entities. This is especially true in situations where transnational migration and media make available images of aging institutions and care practices from unfamiliar social contexts.

Persons, including older persons, affect the social order in which they live, as they pursue their own projects (Ortner 2006). This is especially visible in the case of relatively wealthy older people in the Global North who are part of the "do-it-yourself generation" (Gambold 2018), but also true in other contexts. If, for instance, South African older people decide to invest parts of their pensions into the education of their grandchildren, they are also affecting the social order in which they live (Case and Menendez 2007). However, as in other matters of social life, power and wealth affect the ability to generate and share age inscription. Thus, an examination of inscription is a crucial way to understand otherwise unnoticed and unremarked-upon processes of social change.

Personal Subjectivity, the Body, and the Material World in Age Inscription

Dominant norms are not simply expressed verbally but also affect personal subjectivity, the physical body, and the landscape. The term "habitus," proposed first by Marcel Mauss (2006) in 1935 and further developed by Pierre Bourdieu (1977), seeks to explain the ways that dominant norms become felt and embodied by individuals. Habitus, in Mauss's conception, comprises the everyday routines or bodily techniques of a person such as habits of brushing one's teeth or style of walking. Inculcated through previous experiences, these habits and routines are embedded in the body, a set of tastes and dispositions perhaps not even available to a person's consciousness, although Bourdieu thinks the habitus may be available to consciousness or undergirded by ideals that are discussed more explicitly within a community (like honor). For Bourdieu, the habitus is "the cultivated disposition, inscribed in the body schema and in the schemas of thought," which disposes a person to act a particular way in a situation (1977, 15). The habitus is "a system of lasting, transposable dispositions which, integrating past experiences, functions at every moment as a *matrix of perceptions, appreciations, and actions* and makes possible the achievement of infinitely diversified tasks, thanks to analogical transfers of schemes, permitting the solution of similarly shaped problems" (82–83, emphasis original). The habitus disposes people to act in a certain way but is flexible enough to be applied, through analogy, to new situations people face (Sewell 2005).

The past experience that Bourdieu attributes as the source of bodily inscription is one's childhood (Bourdieu and Passeron 1990). Because Bourdieu conceptualized the habitus as formed most strongly in childhood by kin, the habitus seems resistant to historical analysis, or an exploration of how it changes through time, both within the course of a person's life course and across generations. Some theorists, and Bourdieu himself, have recognized that the habitus is inscribed through various social contexts. Jay MacLeod, for instance, in his study of adolescent boys growing up in a public housing complex in the United States, reworked the notion of the habitus, considering it to be multilayered, not only constituted through the boys' family life but structured through their subsequent experiences with peers and school (1995, 137–138). This book argues that embodied practice can be reinscribed through shifting norms or even more transient, liminal age inscription at any stage in the life course.

Habitus emphasizes bodily and unconscious dispositions, an important point to make, but which slights the moments when such dispositions become visible and discussed. As Jean and John Comaroff (1991) have argued, the historical moments when something commonsensical becomes the subject of commentary or when topics of debate become naturalized into bodily responses and reactions are important because they signal change.

However, there can be various levels of habitual embodiment also; in other words, embodiment does not simply signal doxa, or what is so dominant as to be commonsensical. Instead, some bodily and material practices may be so fragile that they have not yet obtained a discourse with patterned terms and representations; this is what inscription means. Buildings can be constructed, but not opened, or not used for their intended purpose. Policies about the aged can be written, but not made into legislation and not enacted. Inscription is more flexible and fragile than the ways that the habitus or regimes of the body are normally conceived, in which dominant discourses and norms shape persons (Bourdieu 1977; Foucault 1980). Inscription is meant to capture this sense of indeterminacy, at the level of discourse, in the body, in the built landscape, and in policy.

Inscriptions in Times of Global Aging, Migration, and Inequality

Three contemporary factors result in a need for inscriptions and thereby shape actual ways of experiencing care in older adulthood: the increasing length of the life course and the aging of the population as a whole; migration and mobility, which is rearranging social roles and obligations between the generations; and changing relations of inequality. These processes are resulting in the creation of new meanings and temporalities.

Global Aging

The latest UN report on "World Population Ageing" (2013) documents not only that people are living longer around the world, but that there is a shift in populations as a whole, in which the share of older persons has increased as a result of reduced fertility and mortality. The global share of older people (aged sixty years or over) increased from 9 percent in 1990 to 12 percent in 2013, with the share of older persons aged eighty years or over within the older population at 14 percent (up from 7 percent in 1950). The report predicts the proportion of older people to continue to grow, reaching 21 percent of the world population by 2050. Older persons are projected to exceed the number of children for the first time in 2047, mainly due to changes in life expectancy in less developed regions. African countries are also undergoing this "longevity revolution" (Hoffman and Pype 2016, 1), although they remain primarily youthful at the current moment. Furthermore, these demographic changes are happening much more quickly in the Global South than occurred historically in Europe and the United States: the doubling of the older population from 10 to 20 percent happened over a hundred years in France, and in twenty to thirty years in China, Brazil, and India (Bloom and Luca 2016). Africa is expected to proceed similarly through a rapid demographic transition, in which its older population is projected to grow fourfold by 2050, to 160 million people (United Nations, Population Division 2012). This anticipated demographic shift will require new social responses (Mba 2010) and is prompting inscriptions.

Ghana is an ideal place to study this phenomenon: it has one of the highest proportions of persons over the age of sixty in sub-Saharan Africa (Mba 2010). Between 1960 and 2010, the population of older Ghanaians increased by over 400 percent, from about 200,000 to 1.6 million (World Health Organization 2015). According to the 2010 population census in Ghana, those sixty and above constitute 6.5 percent of the population, or about 1.6 million people out of a total population of 24.7 million (Ghana Statistical Service 2012). Of those 1.6 million older adults, 56 percent are women, 44 percent are men. The overwhelming majority of those older adults are in their sixties. Like other unequal societies, Ghanaians experience vast inequalities in life expectancies and quality of life in aging, as a result of poverty and differential access to health care.

Chronic diseases have rapidly increased in Ghana, as deaths from infectious diseases, such as malaria, cholera, and typhoid, decline. Cardiovascular diseases have become a leading cause of death in Accra (de-Graft Aikins 2007). By 2003, one of four conditions—stroke, hypertension, diabetes, and cancer—was in the top ten causes of death in all the regional health facilities (de-Graft Aikins 2007). In a large-scale survey of those over the age of fifty, 33 percent reported hypertension, 14 percent arthritis, 7 percent diabetes, 6 percent a cardiovascular condition, and 4.9 percent treatment for stroke (Ayernor 2012). These diseases, except for stroke, do not necessarily cause physical weakness and frailty, except when not treated well, but lack of consistent treatment and medication is common among aging adults in Ghana (see also Moran-Thomas 2019). Debility and frailty from unregulated diabetes, a stroke, or dementia require long-term, ongoing assistance with daily activities, without any expectation of a rapid end for such need for care (de-Graft Aikins 2005). Scholars anticipate these conditions will increase with the aging of Ghana's population: "The prevalence rates of chronic non-communicable diseases (NCDs) (like diabetes, hypertension, and stroke), neurodegenerative diseases (like dementia and Alzheimer's disease) and disability (all forms) are expected to rise among the older populations with implications for health systems and health and social care at the community and family levels" (de-Graft Aikins and Apt 2016, 37). Both the changing age demographics and the increase in these noncommunicable diseases have created greater needs for care. The World Health Organization (2015) estimates that 50 percent of those aged sixty-five to seventy-five in Ghana required some assistance with their daily activities, while 65 percent of those older than seventy-five did. For the most part, given the lack of state support, this burden has fallen on kin.

Every aging person encounters the many physiological, emotional, and social changes of aging as if they were new because they are new to the individuals going through aging processes. Cole and Durham (2007) elaborate on this point, using Karl Mannheim's notion of "fresh contact." Mannheim's groundbreaking essay was written in 1928, affected by his impression of World War I, rapidly changing societies in Europe, and extremely distinct generational experiences. His main argument is that every new generation has a completely different worldview, knowledge, and experience of historical events. He suggests that there is a special historical force to the fresh contact of groups of people who come of age at the same time. Cole and Durham expand his concept to suggest that "every individual undergoes 'fresh contact' throughout his life" (18), not just in youth, but also, for example, through a change of residence or status.

Because of increasingly longer life spans in Europe over the past century, Peter Laslett argued, "Our situation remains irreducibly novel; it calls for invention rather than imitation" (1980, 181). As people live longer, and with less risk of death at younger ages, they experience more overlap with the lives of their children and grandchildren and more accumulated experiences in general (Alber, Geissler, and Whyte 2004; Hagestad 1986; Hareven 1982). People may experience four or five generations alive simultaneously (Hagestad and Burton 1986; Hoffman and Pype 2016). Although frailty and death were once experienced as human conditions, their possibility looming at any point in the life course, particularly for women in their childbearing years, it is now more tightly associated with aging. Longer life spans have consequences not only for the construction and perception of old age but also for intergenerational relations.

Independent of his or her cohort, each person encounters aging as new to him or her and has to cope with those changes (Cole 2013). To the extent that aging is not elaborated institutionally or socially, then older adults have to generate their own meanings, perhaps with the help of their social networks, in the form of age inscriptions. Aging's lack of elaboration made it ripe for institutionalization (Riley and Riley 1986). The aging transition in Europe was accompanied by a greater attention to chronological age and a standardization of the life course, which also led to greater individualization (Kohli 2009). The structuring of the life course was a major factor in organizing industrial society as a whole.

Africans are known for their respect of their elderly; this representation makes them valued care workers when they migrate abroad (Coe 2019a). The concept of elderhood is well established and elaborated in Ghana. J. B. Danquah ([1944] 1968), writing in the 1940s, waxes eloquent about the Akan respect for the elder: the ɔpanyin or Nana. So does C. K. Brown (1999), writing fifty years later. However, Danquah also notes that an elder needs to be "of the right sort and served his age and his community by living well and aiding them also to live well" ([1944] 1968, 126). Thus, not all those who age become elders deserving of respect. Sjaak van der Geest (2001) also talks about the qualities of an ɔpanyin: wisdom, self-restraint, and dedication to his family. In order to do the vital work of mediating disputes and organizing funerals in the family, an elder must reside in the hometown (Apt 1996). The literature overwhelmingly indicates that respect is given only to older adults who were successful in life (Apt 1996; Miescher 2005; Stucki 1995; Van der Geest 1997, 1998). One key sign of success is building a house; another is having children and raising them to successful adulthood. Being wealthy is not enough; sharing wealth is also important (Miescher 2005). The life stage of ɔpanyin or Nana does not correspond to age: a fifty-year-old woman may be a grandmother or childless. As a result, an aging migrant may postpone a return to his hometown because he has not put in place the conditions of successful elderhood by building a house there (Stucki 1995). One careful study of older adults in northern Togo and Benin showed that in fact the "young old"— those who were in positions of authority—ironically received more in the way of remittances than those who were older, poorer, and frailer; these aging adults redistributed those remittances as a way to maintain their power and authority (Häberlein 2018).

Living elders are "almost ancestors" (Van der Geest 2002a, 17). The respect given them is also due to their power, like ancestors, to generate prosperity and well-being or, in contrast, misfortune. They have the power to bless and curse those who are younger, making them liable to be called witches (Van der Geest 2002c). Van der Geest (2003, 59) argues that the performance of respect by younger people to older people is a "compromise, a strategy to deal with the disappearance of practical reciprocity. It is a strategy because it allows both generations to retain their dignity and—to some extent—their relatedness. Behind that appearance of mutual respect, however, resentment and loneliness may lie." Thus, ethnographic research conducted in Ghana suggests that *elders* are respected, but that not all older people become elders, and thus may be resented as a burden or a witch, pitied as "worthless" or "useless," or simply tolerated. One national survey, from 1991, corroborated this finding: it found that 43 percent of older respondents considered being old to be "a period of hardship and misery," in comparison to only 3.4 percent finding it a time of being "respected by society" (Brown 1999, 112).

New categories for aging are emerging beyond the highly developed cultural category of elderhood. Age from birth is used by some institutions to differentiate older adults as a social category. Those in the civil service—including teachers, police, and medical personnel—tend to use the age of sixty as the definition of old age because it is both the compulsory retirement age and the age at which one can receive a pension. However, only about 10 percent of the working population in Ghana is contributing to the state pension scheme (Obiri-Yeboah and Obiri-Yeboah 2014) and only 14 percent are employed in the public sector and subject to compulsory retirement (Ghana Statistical Service 2015). At the same time, the retirement and pensions of civil servants may serve as fodder for non–civil servants to plot their life course (Alber 2018). For example, a seamstress in Akropong told me that she would be "retiring" in January 2020 as she was nearing the age of sixty and would be "getting a pension." When I questioned her further, she admitted that she was not enrolled in the state pension program. Instead, she was planning to sell her shop to someone who would pay her a monthly income, which she framed as a pension (fieldnotes, August 25, 2019). The Presbyterian Church of Ghana also uses age to define who is eligible for its aged programs, but uses seventy years old instead of sixty. Matilda Riley and John Riley note, "Age is built into the changing organization of institutions and roles through formal or informal criteria for entry and exit, through expectations of how roles are to be performed, and through sanctions for role performance" (1986, 55). Although institutions in Ghana tend to rely on age-driven social categories, generally, outside these institutional settings, years or age do not define a person.

Contemporary older people with whom I spoke put great emphasis on their physical strength as a sign of aging. For many the marker of aging is physical condition, with frailty and disability more significant than birthdays. For example, people distinguish between older people who are "strong" or "weak" physically. Strength means being able to walk, work on one's farm, and engage in daily, physical activities, in contrast to those who are weak (wɔn honam yɛ mmɛrew). For example, one woman in the town of Begoro in Akyem in the Eastern Region used both age and strength as markers to indicate her aging: "In a few months, I will be seventy-three years old. When I was a young woman, I was strong. I could go anywhere. I could go to farm and then return to go to school; I could do everything. When I reached the age of sixty, I became weak and feeble, in my knee, my back, my whole body. Getting up in the morning, I am as tired as if I had worked all night, and if I try to work, I make no headway. That's how weak I have become."[4] Similarly, at a pensioners' meeting in Akropong, Akuapem, a retired teacher crossed the room, and the president of the association, a retired nurse, made fun of how she was walking, in a friendly way. The retired teacher joked back, "I want to show that I am an old woman."[5] Many older adults expect to continue to engage in income-generating activities and generally engage in farming or petty commerce, which allow them some flexibility in their activity level, in relation to their health and strength (Apt 1996; Brown 1999; Grieco, Apt, and Turner 1996). Aging is associated with physical weakness, but this marker, like elderhood, is not a universal phenomenon, in that some older adults become more disabled than others.

Through its aged program (discussed further in chapter 4), the Presbyterian Church of Ghana has institutionalized a new "aged" category for providing programs and services. "The aged" distinguishes older adults from adult men and women, young adults, youth, and children. This category of "aged" overlays other notions of aging, whether becoming an ancestor worthy of respect or experiencing physical frailty.

Outside the context of the Presbyterian Church, aging seems to be a category of vulnerability for the purposes of charity. Elite women are involved in high-profile charity work, with individuals starting foundations and programs, and some of these programs focus on older women. Thus, in 2015 I attended the seventh annual National Widows Alliance conference at the Convention Center in La, a suburb of Accra. This event had been advertised on TV and was sponsored by the Mama Zimbi Foundation, and Mama Zimbi herself cut a flamboyant and colorful figure. She promised at the conference to build a vocational center for widows and the children of widows to learn gari making, bead making, and other crafts. The event included speeches by important people, advertisements from an herbal medicine sponsor, a health check, dancing, and the distribution of food. Although some widows are young women, in general they are considered to be older women. As a result of these initiatives, older people become characterized alongside other "vulnerable groups" in public discourse. These events by patrons are often mentioned in the media (e.g., Amenuveve 2015). When I mentioned my research to one young woman who was doing her national service (after completing university) in a bank in New Tafo, in Akyem in the Eastern Region, she responded that it was good that I was helping those in need like orphans and widows even though I had not mentioned widows particularly and was doing research, rather than providing assistance (fieldnotes, August 15, 2019). The Constitution of the Fourth Republic, enacted in 1993, also mentions older people as a vulnerable group: one of the social objectives of the state is "the protection and promotion of all other basic human rights and freedoms, including the rights of the disabled, the aged, children and other vulnerable groups" (Government of Ghana 1993, Article 37b). Although older men and women retain decision-making power and responsibility over solving family conflicts and supervising family rituals as family heads, seniority is becoming less significant. The new inscriptions of aging present older adults as passive recipients of assistance of aid and worthy of compassion from patrons. At this point in time, perhaps because of its newness, it is not clear whether this new identity of "the aged" is a sign of empowerment or marginalization or possibly both simultaneously.

The institutionalization of the life course has created and is creating new rituals and rites of passage for aging, such as retirement and returning to one's hometown. Thus, not only are individuals adjusting to the longer life spans they are experiencing, but so too are societies and states adapting to a larger share of older adults. Inscriptions respond to the new experiences and related challenges of these new life course expectations.

Mobility and Migration

Migration and mobility are an important aspect of the contemporary world, affecting the lifeworlds of migrants and nonmigrants alike, through an expansion of "the global horizon" in which people imagine themselves emplaced (Graw and Schielke 2012). Migration and mobility affect state as well as kin forms of intergenerational support. Because of migration, the coordination and synchronization of multiple life courses—from the care and schooling of the youngest generation to parenting and employment of the middle generation and to the aging and activities of the older generation—need to be reworked (Dossa and Coe 2017) because lives are highly interdependent (Hagestad 1986; Hareven 1982) and lifetimes are intertwined (Alber, Geissler, and Whyte 2004). "New models of both personhood and intergenerational care" may need to be generated (Cole and Durham 2007, 13). For example, mothers of migrant women may be kin-scripted to fill "the care slot," provide child care to grandchildren, and take care of the family house in the hometown (Leinaweaver 2010). New financial resources, such as remittances from migrants, may contribute to the outsourcing of the care of older adults to non-kin caregivers. The loss of the migrant's kin-work may result in new fragility and uncertainty for older people, and the migrant's remittances create new class dynamics as non-kin paid workers take on significant roles in care.

Ghana has, and has had, a considerable amount of both internal and international migration. International migration became prominent in the 1980s and intensified in the 1990s, with the amount of remittances increasing rapidly, constituting more than a third of Ghana's gross domestic product in 2005 and 10 percent of household income in 2000 (International Organization for Migration 2009), although it has dropped since (World Bank 2019a). Estimates of those abroad range from 3 to 7 percent of the population resident in Ghana (Twum-Baah 2005; World Bank 2011). Urban migration is also an important phenomenon. Urban migration has been happening since the 1950s in Ghana. Drawing on the 1960 census and surveys he did in 1962, John Caldwell (1969) estimated that a third of the rural population in southern Ghana had taken part in some form of urban migration, with males, young adults (aged fifteen to twenty-four), and the more educated more mobile than their contemporaries. Urban migration resulted in major metropolitan areas becoming more youthful, and rural areas and towns becoming naturally occurring retirement communities where older adults resided. In 2003, 68 percent of those over the age of sixty lived in rural areas, 32 percent in urban areas (Mba 2010). The Greater Accra Region, where the capital and largest city Accra is located, has the lowest proportion of older people in Ghana (Mba 2010).

International migration has helped sustain commercial care services in urban areas. Many of the commercial nursing services I discuss in chapter 5 were founded by return migrants, who are using capital earned abroad to start care businesses in Ghana. Many of the users of commercial nursing services in urban middle-class and elite circles are parents of migrants abroad and rely on their remittances to pay for the services. Another major subset of users of commercial nursing services is return migrants, some of whom returned to live in Ghana when they became ill.

However, migration is not the sole cause of age and care inscriptions. The increased importance of women's formal work—which urban and transnational migration intensifies—is another major stimulus in age and care inscriptions, making women experience more time pressure and less incentive to begin a period of underemployment in the rural hometown to care for a mother or father. The historical increase in the felt needs required by children—in which children are no longer a major source of household labor but have rights to many years of expensive education—also makes children's and their parents' labor less available for elder care. These issues are related to class, in that middle-class and elite households are more likely to feel these changes connected to women's and children's roles as well as have the resources to find alternative solutions.

I will illustrate how both migrants and nonmigrants are the source of inscriptions in response to situations affected by migration. Migrants are not more agentive than nonmigrants, as is so commonly discussed in the migration literature. Even those who stay at home in the context of ongoing migration adjust, change, and take on new scripts and have their doxa challenged (Baldassar and Merla 2014; Hirsch 2003). Sarah Lamb (2009) discusses how changes in aging institutions in Indian were being driven by those abroad as well as a domestic middle class that had international connections. Thus, an examination of age and care inscriptions is a key window into understanding how migration and mobility affect social change. The somewhat unformulated, experimental, and tentative practices around aging and care signal how high rates of internal and international migration lead to transformations in care.

Inequality

Inscriptions are also emerging because two axes of inequality are also shifting in Ghana. One axis is a gerontocratic one, in which people gain authority and power through seniority and in which children and young adults are the main providers of household labor. This axis of inequality is temporal, associated with a stage in the life course, and therefore temporary: children without status can potentially grow into elders with power and authority. Seniority is a key measure of inequality within households composed of kin.

As noted above, a truism on the African continent is that older people are respected, by virtue of their seniority. However, only some older people obtain the status of *elder*, with men, grandparents, and the wealthy most eligible. The orthodoxy of the respected elder is changing. As mentioned previously, not only do older women lament (or make fun of) their frailty and weakness, downplaying that they are elders worthy of respect, but increasingly they, like orphans, are becoming the object of pity and intervention in contemporary Ghana and subject to patronage by wealthy men and women.

A new axis organized around social class, in which status is a permanent condition rather than dependent on the life course, seems to be becoming more prominent in care decisions. Social class is one way of assessing the differential status, finances, and social positions of people. Such differences may also mark self-conscious affiliations, as social classes distinguish themselves from others through their practices and social networks. In the gerontocratic model, domestic labor (including the work of care) is associated with age, particularly with adolescent girls. Within a social class system, care becomes a class-based relation of domestic servitude in which poorer women perform care work in more prosperous and educated households. Often these more prosperous and educated households have access to remittances from abroad, which enable them to hire this labor. Care becomes a prominent site of boundary work between different classes, as I discuss in chapter 7. Focusing on care as labor allows us to consider the internal differentiation of households, whether by age or by class.

Inscription is an indicator of pressure points for social change. In this context, it suggests that dominant trajectories of aging and caring are not or no longer working for everyone. Although these processes are continuously occurring in everyday social life, three social conditions are particularly generative of inscriptions around age and care in contemporary Ghana: first, the longer life spans of populations around the world, including in large parts of the Global South; second, migration and mobility, both international and regional, which are affecting the lifeworlds of both migrants and nonmigrants alike; and third, changing processes of inequality, which affect conditions of labor and social relations.

Looking Ahead: The Structure of the Book

This study is based on research carried out since 2013 in short visits (comprising thirty-three weeks or about eight months in all) to track emergent social change in Ghana. Its focus is southern Ghana, particularly the rural towns of the Eastern Region and the combined metropolitan area of the capital city Accra and its neighboring port city of Tema (map 1). As such, the older population discussed tends toward the Christian, the educated, and the middle class and elite. The research builds on relationships and insights from my previous ethnographic work on schools and transnational families, mainly conducted in Akuapem and Accra, beginning in 1997.

This study also relies on the many pioneers who have come before me. Ghana has been a major site of anthropological and historical research, including on

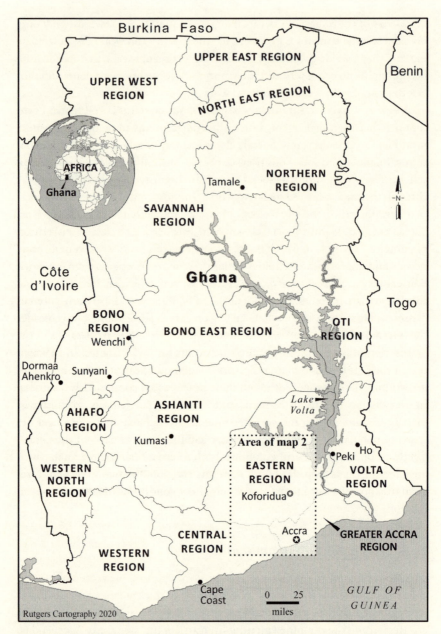

MAP 1 Ghana and its regions. Created by Michael Siegel, Rutgers Cartography.

aging. Ghanaian sociologist Nana Araba Apt (1996) was the first to produce a major book-length study of aging, using research in the Central Region from 1988 to 1989. Barbara Stucki (1995) wrote a dissertation on aging based on anthropological research in a rural area of the Ashanti Region in 1990–1991. Sjaak van der Geest used his long-term ethnographic research in the town of Tafo in Kwawu to understand older people's lives, particularly those of older men, from 1994 to 2000, which he detailed in a slew of publications (1997, 1998, 2002a, 2002b, 2002c, 2003, 2004a, 2004b). Historian Stephan Miescher (2005) studied masculinity through oral histories with older men in Kwawu. Ghanaian sociologist C. K. Brown (1999) conducted a national survey of almost fifteen hundred older adults in 1991. Isabella Aboderin also wrote a book about aging in Ghana based on research in Accra in 2004. A newer generation of Ghanaian scholars, like Delali Dovie (2018, 2019), Sarah Dsane (2013), and Daniel Doh (2012), and a spate of master's theses (Addo 2003; Ani 2002; Nelson-Cofie 1998) have also illuminated aging in Ghana. I am indebted to these works for helping me place my research within a larger historical and social context.

Chapter 1 lays out the orthodoxy of kin care, as illustrated in state policy documents and public discourse. This orthodox narrative is troubled by the unacknowledged history that I lay out in the 1860s, including the use of domestic slaves in care. Care by adult daughters did dominate in the 1990s, a pattern I discuss. This chapter focuses on the substitution of adjacent relations, in which women in different roles and at different stages of the life course provided elder care. This substitution is a way of providing continuity, even as practices change.

Chapter 2 illustrates the ways that older Presbyterians in rural towns in the Eastern Region of Ghana are attracted to the heterodox idea of residential facilities, although they have no experience with them. What they are actually doing is engaging in alterodox practices to delay or avoid a migrant daughter's return to the hometown to live with her parent. These practices include hiring a paid care worker, as discussed in chapter 2, or an aging mother moving into her daughter's household in a different town or relying on neighbors, as discussed in chapter 3. These two chapters illustrate how the heterodoxy becomes available as a possible idea for the care of older Ghanaians, precisely because it is set in opposition to the orthodoxy, and how the social norm of kin care is maintained through alterodox inscriptions.

Chapter 4 examines the inscriptions among various congregations in rural towns in southern Ghana that focus on social gatherings for older congregants to mitigate their loneliness. These efforts at organizing and advocating for the aging within the churches are fragile, and yet despite their evanescence, these practices spread, so that even some government officials consider these practices to be models for state interventions to support Ghana's rapidly aging population.

Chapters 5, 6, and 7 turn to the sprawling metropolitan area of Accra-Tema, where commercial responses are emerging to support wealthier and middle-class Ghanaians and those with access to remittances from abroad. Commercial care services primarily take the form of private nursing agencies, although a few small residential facilities have also opened. Chapter 5 examines the effect of transnational migration on the creation and use of these commercial care services, looking specifically at the experiences of owners, consumers, and employees of these agencies. Chapter 6 discusses the education of care workers, including relations between private and public healthcare sectors in the context of neoliberalism. Chapter 7 explores more fully the class dimensions of care work, discussing how those who do care work—mainly moderately educated young women—position themselves as nurses, despite being perceived by their employers as mainly domestic servants. Rather than care being associated with age, particularly the work of children, care becomes a class-based relation of servitude.

This book examines processes of social change, in the context of aging in Ghana where kin care is constructed as both traditional and ideal. There has simultaneously been a quiet revolution and a more vocal, self-assertive one in addressing the problems with kin care. The quiet one, taking place in rural households with access to urban and transnational remittances, is that women are hired to care for older adults, replacing their daughters or fostered grandchildren. Older women move in with their daughters rather than the other way around, neighbors and tenants fill in the gaps, and older adults are encouraged to plan for their retirement. More visible and discussed changes are taking place within the context of religious institutions and commercial markets, although even here in fits and starts. Mainline churches and individual ministers within them are beginning to recognize the difficulties faced by their aging congregants and are initiating various programs to combat their social isolation. However, these are constrained by financial difficulties and priorities to raise the stature of the church that focus on middle-aged people. Commercial care services—particularly the use of home care services, but also nursing homes—are offered to urban middle-class and elite households. These services are stigmatized and expensive, making their use limited, but home care services that supplement kin care and househelp have become common and accepted in elite circles, more so than residential care facilities, in part because of their similarity to domestic service, a long-standing practice in elite, urban households.

The ways these changes are playing out speak to the absence of the state's interest in aging issues. Using the ideology of kin care, the Ghanaian government pays little attention to its older population. Families' struggles to provide care create room for individual initiatives, what I call inscriptions. Despite their fragile and short-lived nature, these practices are patterned as individuals face similar struggles and share their strategies. I argue that these innovations in care are happening in episodic and scattered ways, visible in certain circles more than others. Ultimately, through a focus on elder care, the book illustrates the uncertain and contingent nature of social change.

1

The Orthodoxy of
Family Care

• •

In July 2014, in a church in a town in southern Ghana, I observed a rehearsal for a play about elder care. The play was performed by members of an aged fellowship group organized by the Presbyterian Church of Ghana in Obo, Kwawu.[1] The play featured two couples who raised their children well—that is, to be educated and Christian. Despite their exemplary parenting, including selling off their cloth to pay for their children's education, only one couple's children remembered them and sent remittances from the city, while the second couple was abandoned by their migrant children who accused them of witchcraft, perhaps as an excuse to stop supporting them.

The play presented several orthodoxies about elder care in Ghana—that is, the publicly acknowledged truth that one hears over and over again.[2] Subsumed under the umbrella of kin care, one orthodoxy concerns the central role of adult children in providing elder care: they are deemed responsible because of the care they have received previously from their parents. A parent's investment in children's education and morality ought to make them successful and grateful, both qualities necessary to support their parent in their elder years (Aboderin 2006; Coe 2011). Second, care for older adults is understood as financial support.[3] I call the sending of remittances a care manager role, whereas daily assistance with household chores and personal care, which I call care provision, was overlooked in this drama. Indeed, in my discussions with older Presbyterians in rural towns of the Eastern Region, financial difficulties came up extremely frequently as a problem of aging. One of children's major care roles was to provide financial assistance. For example, giving the opening prayer for an aged fellowship meeting in a Presbyterian Church in Obomeng (Kwawu), the older participant said, "Lord God, take pity on me. My children, wherever they have gone, let them be people of high status. Look after them for me, so if they get something [i.e., money], they will do what? They will bring it to you so you will eat."[4] "Money thus becomes a vehicle for love and respect," notes Sjaak van der Geest (1997, 555). In his research in Kwawu in the 1990s, remittances from migrants were particularly important to older adults for buying food and paying for health care.

In their work on care in African American families in the United States, Carol Stack and Linda Burton (1993) usefully introduce the concept of kin-work, by which they mean all the labor that is necessary to keep families alive from generation to generation, from paid employment to child and elder care and household work. Kin-work would include both care management and care provision roles (Dossa and Coe 2017). In the scripts of contemporary southern Ghana, as the play illustrates, adult children are expected to provide elder care, which is framed as economic support. However, as the play also illustrates, they also might renege on their responsibilities, leaving their parents bitter and impoverished. Who provides daily care to aging adults is unaddressed in the play, suggesting that it is less important.

The orthodox script, which focuses on adult children's role in elder care, aligns with a view of "tradition" in which families care for their elderly. In this narrative, "modernity" is set in direct opposition to "tradition." It is modernity that creates the motivations, institutions, and markets that prompt families to shift kin-work to the state and paid workers, as in the heterodoxy that is represented by Western residential facilities. This modernization narrative is prominent in scholarly studies of aging in Ghana, notably by the Ghanaian sociologist Nana Araba Apt (1996), in which she argues that migration and education lead to lack of respect and care of older adults. Much scholarship in Africa has noted the invention of tradition, with seminal work on the use of tradition by colonial officials as part of indirect rule and by migrants to control women in their hometowns in Southern Africa (Ranger 1983; Vail 1989). Most of Ghana's state efforts to document and revive "tradition" have been directed at the performing arts and children and young adults (Coe 2005; Schauert 2015). However, building on popular discourses regarding intergenerational expectations, state and scholarly responses to the problems of aging in Ghana have invented the "traditional family" as an orthodoxy.

Articulations of the Orthodoxy: Ghana's Aged Policy and Popular Discourses

Beginning in the early 1990s, the government of Ghana began to craft a policy about aging. These efforts were in conjunction, and very much in alignment, with the African Union's initiative to compose a protocol on older persons, fueled by international agreements such as the 1991 UN Principles for Older Persons, the 1992 UN Proclamation on Ageing, and the 2002 Madrid International Plan of Action on Ageing. The African Union was assisted in its efforts at policy writing by HelpAge International. Similarly, the Ghanaian government has been encouraged to adopt and maintain its policy on aging by advocates from the local affiliate of this international NGO, HelpAge Ghana, and the Ghanaian scholarly community, which have been involved in writing the government's policy.[5]

The government of Ghana drafted its policy on aging around an image of a traditional, idealized family. Although it acknowledges that older adults are "no longer able to rely on the family for support" (Government of Ghana 2010, section 3.5.2, 22), it presents "the family" as the proper site for the care of older adults: "Effort will be made to uphold the traditional family structures and norms such that it will be able to provide the needed support to older relatives. The family will be encouraged to develop plans and incorporate in these plans strategies to support older people in the family. The family will be assisted to identify, support and strengthen traditional support systems to enhance the ability of families and communities to care for older family members" (Government of Ghana 2010, section 4.6.3, 36). Ghana's emphasis on "the traditional family" differs from the African Union's Draft Protocol on Older Persons (2014), which instead highlights the role of adult children. The African Union recommends that member states "adopt policies and legislation that provide incentives to all stakeholders including adult children, to support Older Persons in their communities, ensuring that they remain at home for as long as possible." In other places, the language is almost identical across the two policies.[6] In contrast to Ghana's Policy on Ageing, the African Union Draft Protocol recommends that residential facilities be provided optionally for older persons and be regulated to provide quality care. In this, the African Union Draft Protocol cleaves more closely to the World Health Organization recommendations on aging (2015) and the UN Convention on the Rights of Persons with Disabilities (2008), both of which are agnostic on the issue of residential facilities, privileging the older or disabled person's agency and choice in making a decision about his or her care. Thus, Ghana's aging policy diverges from African Union and international aging policies in being more emphatic about the role of "the traditional family."

In Ghana, care by "the family" is thus the orthodox position, meaning that it is the conventional, formulaic, and normative position. As Sjaak van der Geest (2016) has argued, this approach seems to ignore the plight of older adults in Ghana and presents the government as needing to do little to support senior citizens: the family will take the primary role in care, and the government will support the family in doing so. Writing about elder care in northern Ghana, Kelsey Hanrahan similarly posits, "Relying on misleading assumptions that traditional values *ensure* the support of older persons, especially in areas that already rely so heavily on informal care provision, will only serve to perpetuate inequitable support of the aging populations" (2018, 76). To the extent that the family becomes the medical agent of the state, then decisions about deciding which lives are worth caring for occur in domestic spaces and are affected by the conflicts and exchanges of intimate social relations (Biehl 2005, 22). Overlooked in the term "family" are the differences between family members: the kin-work of elder care in Africa mainly falls on women and girls of all ages (World Health Organization 2017). One indication of the government's lack of concern for older adults is that although it drafted an aged policy in 2003, which was then updated in 2010, Parliament has still not passed this policy as of 2021 (Citinewsroom 2018).

Isabella Aboderin and Monica Ferreira (2008) note the ineffectiveness of and lack of action resulting from the African Union's aging protocol and argue this is due to older adults being seen as inconsequential for national economic development. The government of Ghana, like its African counterparts, seems to approach the "problem" of aging through an economic and financial perspective. Ghana's Ageing Policy is primarily concerned with the impact of a rapidly aging population on economic growth (Government of Ghana 2010). A civil servant at the Ministry of Gender, Children, and Social Protection tasked with shepherding the aged policy told me that the challenge to enacting the policy is that the state sees aging as solely a matter of fiscal spending, whereas budgetary investments that see "returns" (his word) were considered more favorably (fieldnotes, August 4, 2014). In practice, state resources in Ghana are concentrated on the futures of the young (Doh 2012), which are viewed as resulting in "returns" to economic development over the long term.

In addition, Lauren Morris MacLean (2002), in her comparative analysis of social welfare initiatives in Ghana and its neighbor Côte d'Ivoire, suggests that the hands-off approach of the Ghanaian government is due to the British colonial government's decentralized approach. "Social policy in colonial Ghana was seen as supplementing 'traditional' systems of social welfare in the community, while in Côte d'Ivoire, administrators aimed to supplant these 'inadequate' systems with more activist policies for individuals" (70). Although chiefs in Ghana did not in fact provide social welfare in the form of elder care per se, other than in mediating family conflicts, old-age pensions were dismissed by British colonial officials in 1945. "Colonial documents clearly indicate the view that social welfare should be promoted in collaboration with the private sector, including churches, voluntary societies, and members of the local communities" (71). Thus, the disengagement of the Ghanaian government from elder care is supported not only by the orthodoxy of "family" care and the focus on economic growth under the influence of neoliberalism since the 1980s, but also by more long-standing governmental practices that have cemented the state's weak responsibility for its citizens' well-being and its reliance on other important social institutions as partners.

The orthodoxy of "family" care—whether in local discourse, state aged policy, or advocacy organizations—constructs institutional facilities as the heterodoxy to kin care. It considers them heterodox because they are Western and thus foreign and "modern," inappropriate to Ghanaian "tradition." Nana Araba Apt, *the* sociologist of aging in Ghana, considers residential facilities to be antithetical to Ghanaian kinship, as well as too expensive for government budgets (1991, 1996; interview, July 2, 2013). Professor Apt was active in shaping government policy and HelpAge's advocacy during the 1990s and early 2000s. In an early report to the Department of Finance and Economics (Apt 1991), she argued that the institutionalization of older adults in residential facilities should be the last alternative and that emphasis instead should be placed on options that support family care and keep older adults in their households.

Mrs. Alberta Akoley Ollennu, a cofounder of HelpAge Ghana, was similarly adamant against residential facilities in an interview with me, but in a more understated way: "HelpAge is not keen to establish homes; rather, they should stay with their families, whatever family is available" (interview, May 30, 2013). A civil servant at the Ministry of Gender, Children, and Social Protection dismissed senior residential facilities as something that people in Ghana would never use (fieldnotes, June 22, 2015). Ghanaian governments since the 1990s, across various parties and administrations, as well as the NGOs that have advised them, have explicitly advocated against institutional facilities. With institutional facilities appearing to be the only alternative to "the traditional family," the range of policy options to support the aged narrowed substantially.

The orthodoxy of care by the family, set against the heterodoxy of institutional facilities, is also articulated in popular discourses. It is often stated by educated people involved in aging advocacy, like religious ministers and NGO staff. At an aged fellowship group meeting in a Presbyterian Church in Akwasiho (Kwawu), the orthodoxy was expressed in this way:

> The minister then gives a speech in Twi contrasting Ghana with Germany,
> which he visited: Germany has aged homes where people go, and the
> government helps the old people. But in Ghana, we do not do that; there is
> an extended family, not just the nuclear family (the man, woman, and the
> children only). The children migrate to look for work, but perhaps they cannot
> send money back. The church is helping a little. But he does not think they will
> ever adopt homes for older adults. Later, he talks about "the cultural divide"
> between those with the extended family system and the nuclear family system.
> (fieldnotes, July 21, 2014)

A minister at Abetifi Ramseyer, also in Kwawu, made a similar statement to that of the Akwasiho minister: he said that in Europe they constructed buildings for the old people. But here, according to our culture (*ammamrɛ*), families have the time ("*abusua wɔ bere*") to look after older people. Let us hold onto our custom ("custom *so mu yiye*") in order to exert ourselves to look after the old women ("*bɔ yɛn ho mmɔden ahwɛ mmarewa*") (fieldnotes, July 22, 2014). The owner of a residential facility in Accra discussed how she had been vilified on social media as trying to "disintegrate the family" by bringing in something "foreign to our culture" (fieldnotes, June 10, 2014). In state and public discourses in Ghana, the orthodoxy constructs Africa as the site of "tradition" or culture—where older adults are cared for by the extended family system—and contrasts it with the heterodoxy of the "modernity" of Western Europe and North America with their supposed institutional facilities for older adults.

It is important to note that the Ghanaian image of the West as relying on residential facilities is badly distorted because most elder care in the West is currently provided by kin (for the United States, see U.S. Department of Health and Human Services 2003). Furthermore, governments in the West have been moving away from institutional care and promoting aging in place or home-based initiatives instead. As a result of the ascendance of neoliberalism as an ideology promoting a reduced government role in social welfare, policies in favor of deinstitutionalization and community care accelerated during the 1980s and 1990s in the West and Latin America (Han 2012; Muehlebach 2012). Currently, in many OECD countries, between half and three-quarters of older people receive long-term care at home (World Health Organization 2015). Thus, although articulated in relation to "tradition" against a Western modernity, family care in Ghana is in fact aligned with international norms, based on more recent changes in care in the West and circulating ideologies about a limited state role.

Furthermore, the orthodoxy relies on an opposition between the traditional—extended—family associated with Ghana and the nuclear family associated with the West. However, as the play suggests, it is children—that is, members of the nuclear family—who are given primary responsibility for the care of older adults. The children of an older person may or may not be members of a family (*abusua*) in Ghana. In a matrilineal society, prominent in my research sites of Kwawu and Akyem and to a lesser extent in Akropong, a man's children are not members of his *abusua*, whereas the children of his sisters are; the children of a woman would be members of her family. Although the Ageing Policy expounds on the significance of "the family,"[7] the play emphasizes the care of the children, not the *abusua*, which includes siblings and their children. This shrinking of the network of responsibility for care from "the extended family" to adult children has been particularly noted by Isabella Aboderin (2004, 2006) in a study of older adults and their children and grandchildren in Accra, a change that she links to a transformation in inheritance. The intestate Succession Law of 1985 (PNDC Law 111) made spouses and children the major beneficiaries of the wealth of the deceased (Apt 1996; see also Van der Geest 1997, 2002b). Because children are privileged over members of extended kin such as the deceased's siblings and their children, children are also given the responsibility of caring for the person before he or she dies. "Why should his family take care of him [a hypothetical older man] if they won't inherit?" a minister in Kwawu asked rhetorically in a conversation in English with me (fieldnotes, July 25, 2014). My sense is that children are also taking more and more of the responsibility for funerals, although the extended family continues to play major roles. Christianity, particularly in its Pentecostal variations in Ghana, has further emphasized that Christians should focus their resources and attention on their spouse and children because the extended family is seen as a potential source of demonic influence (Meyer 1999). Another sign of the weakening of the extended family is that parents increasingly aim to raise their own children, rather than fostering them out to their siblings, and they devote their resources to their own children, giving less to their siblings' children, who then feel, in turn, less obligated to care for their parents' siblings in the future (Coe 2013b; for an older study, see Oppong 1974).

The orthodoxy of "family" care is thus a conglomeration of different ideas, generated through a variety of performances like the play and actions and statements within households, churches, and state policy documents. The orthodoxy presented in the Ageing Policy, which highlights the extended family, overlaps enough with local norms about adult children and the growing prominence of the nuclear family, thus cementing the orthodoxy across a range of social fields. The shape and boundary of this orthodoxy can never fully be seen because each statement, performance, or action emphasizes slightly different elements, revising the orthodoxy. As a result, imperceptibly, the orthodoxy of "family" care has changed over time, with responsibility shifting, slowly and inconsistently, from extended kin to adult children.

As noted by many studies, but particularly by Aboderin (2006), although children are expected to provide care in exchange for the gift of life from their parents, they rationalize providing elder care only in exchange for assistance in their own childhoods, using the proverb about teeth (discussed in the introduction) as justification. Care depends on reciprocities and obligations that have been incurred previously or are expected in the future, which Parker Shipton terms entrustments: "Entrustment implies an obligation, but not necessarily an obligation to repay like with like, as a loan might imply. Whether an entrustment or transfer is returnable in kind or in radically different form—be it economic, political, symbolic, or some mixture of these—is a matter of cultural context and strategy" (2007, 11). If school fees were not paid, particularly by their fathers, then children may decide to eschew providing care when that father ages. Mothers are much more likely than fathers to receive care from their adult children because men are constructed in the popular imagination as having many children with many women and not caring for all of them well, while women are considered impoverished but sacrificing themselves for their children's well-being (Coe 2011; Van der Geest 1997). Sjaak van der Geest (2002a) quotes one older man in the town of Tafo in Kwawu saying, "It depends on the sort of life that the sick person led before he got sick. A person who looked after his children very well will never experience such a thing [neglect]. The children will do everything they can to make you comfortable before you die. But if you did not look after them, how will they take care of you when you are sick?" (15–16).

Children are also more likely to be members of their mother's family than their father's family in the areas of the Eastern Region where this research is based. As investments in children, particularly educationally, increased and became normalized over the course of the twentieth century, the entrustments between the generations shifted, with children expecting more from their parents.

The orthodoxy on care by the family, in its invention and construction of the "traditional family," neglects two other aspects of elder care practices in Ghana. First, such a narrative obscures the work of non-kin in providing elder care in southern Ghana historically and in the present. In southern Ghana, such persons have included domestic slaves, househelp, and fostered children and adolescents, who are sometimes kin and sometimes not. In southern Ghana, in the 1860s, domestic slaves—who might also be daughters or wives—were available to supplement or substitute for the care work of free or non-slave wives and daughters who were not kin (*abusua*) to adult men. In the 1990s, a younger generation of kin women were most likely to be recruited to provide the daily labor of helping an older generation of women within the kin group. By the early twenty-first century, as the pool of care providers narrowed to the adult daughters of older persons, they felt the pinch of elder care, particularly those who were migrant in the cities and abroad. Migrant daughters found substitutes among paid female caregivers and fostered adolescents, whether extended kin or non-kin, as I discuss in the next chapter. The opposition of "tradition" to "modern" has also obscured the historical role of non-kin in the West. Although histories of elder care in Western Europe and the United States similarly highlight the work of kin in the past, in contrast to contemporary institutional facilities, family care was often supplemented with domestic servants—often non-kin adolescents who lived temporarily with a household until they got married (Narotzky 1997); and in the United States, slaves from the transatlantic trade and immigrants from Europe (Dudden 1983; Glenn 2010). The study of non-kin relationships and transactions reveals the limits of what kin can provide (Vaughan 1983). To expand Stack and Burton's formulation, non-kin are involved in kin-work, that is, in the labor of sustaining families over time and across the generations, including in elder care.

Second, the invention of the traditional family overlooks the conflicts over obligations between possible caregivers, in which some members of the kin group are recruited into care provision and others into care management. While "family" as a collective term might seem to indicate sameness, in fact there are different kinds of family members, with the major differentiations of kin role made through the social categories of age, gender, and status position (Brightman 2013). Many West African households are heterogeneous, containing members of different educational levels, social status by virtue of age and gender, and social class positioning (Alber 2019). This is particularly true of wealthier households, which attract dependents, domestic servants, and foster children and adolescents, some of whom are kin and some of whom are not (Ardayfio-Schandorf and

Amissah 1996). For example, in Mrs. Ollennu's statement above, the family is constructed as a single unit, denying the inequalities and differences within the kin group, although she also acknowledges that the older person will be dependent on particular sections within it: "whatever family is available."

In southern Ghana, adult women, female adolescents, and children of all genders have tended to provide personal care, which has usually involved living with or near older persons—the role of the care provider. Care providers' status vulnerability makes them more easily recruited to such a role. Men, on the other hand, are expected to support their sisters and parents financially, and to help persuade their sisters and daughters to take up their obligations—the care manager role. This care manager role reveals their power, as patrons within their families. As Felicity Aulino has noted in Thailand, "Forms of care emerge in and sustain oppression" (2019, 17). Gender intersects with socioeconomic status, in that women are likely to be poorer than their male counterparts, and poorer women are recruited as care providers.

Ethnographic studies of elder care suggest that care is generated through "negotiated commitments" between different kin members (Finch and Mason 1993). Elizabeth Cooper (2012) describes how families in western Kenya "fix trust in uncertain times" by meeting together, either regularly or after a crisis like a death. During these meetings, families will determine who will take care of their orphans and create a sense of family unity. Methods of getting others to live up to kin-scripts include shaming those who can provide orphan support but choose not to. Furthermore, Maria Cattell (1999) notes how older people in western Kenya lament the lack of good care, not because they do not receive it but to ensure that those around them live up to their commitments. Similarly, the fellowship's drama that opened this chapter may serve as a public reminder, a kind of scolding, rather than as a reflection of reality in which some children abandon their elders, illustrating how aging persons are involved in pressuring others for care (see also Lang 2019 for Kerala, India). As Sjaak van der Geest (2002b) has argued, in Kwawu, Ghana, elder care is improvised and never fully settled. Thus, kin-scripts put pressure on particular people to provide care, but obligations and commitments are always negotiated and can change through those negotiations.

What is significant is that non-kin care and the division of kin-work among kin are not framed as being the opposite of kin care, as a heterodoxy, and thus disparaged as antithetical to Ghanaian tradition—in the way institutional facilities are. Instead, these practices function as alterodox inscriptions. "Family" care can therefore mean a variety of different arrangements that have shifted over time, without much recognition of that fact. Such shifts in care practices and substitutions of people in care roles were subtle, with the substitutions not necessarily noted or commented on, given the flexibility of Akan family life (Clark 1994). Through the substitution of non-kin for kin in certain roles, and the provision of elder care in different ways by different kinds of family, these practices are viewed as compatible with—to the extent of even supporting—kin care. Thus, alterodox inscriptions help people live up to the ideal of the orthodoxy of kin care.

Echoing Evelyn Nakano Glenn (1983), this chapter emphasizes that what is viewed as "tradition" or "the traditional family" is itself the product of ongoing social change. Elder care practices are shaped by changing expectations as people respond to new political and economic conditions, including changes in fertility and demographics; methods of exploitation and domination within households and society at large, whether slavery or social class; the labor demands on women; increased expectations of schooling for children and adolescents, which reduces the fosterage of any but the poor; and urban-rural disparities in commercial and educational opportunities, which prompt the migration of young and middle-aged adults. This perspective complicates the romantic narrative that there was once "a golden age" of "the extended family" that is now in decline, which has been so dominant in the scholarship on aging in Ghana and the West (Abel 2000; Aboderin 2004, 2006; Apt 1996; Williams 1973). Instead, this history shifts our lens toward understanding how people in every era manage—or fail to manage—the kin-work of recruiting care for themselves and others and providing care to those in need, in the circumstances in which they find themselves. They use their entrustments to negotiate the conscription of themselves and others to care—or not care—for older persons in their families, which involves the regeneration of inequalities both within and beyond the kin group.

Domestic Slaves' Involvement in Elder Care in the 1860s

As Megan Vaughan (1983) notes, "Direct historical sources for the 'history of the family' are sparse for most areas and most periods of African history. Whether we are dealing with the writings of colonial anthropologists, or with oral sources, we are faced with the problem of how to interpret both continuity and change" (276). In particular, she notes the difficulties of recognizing changes in practices—such as labor cooperation or food sharing—when people themselves do not self-consciously interpret those as changes. There is "a lack of 'fit' between socio-economic realities and their cultural expression" (278). She rightly diagnoses the problems I faced in assessing the degree of social change in elder care in southern Ghana.

For the 1860s, I rely primarily on the records of the Basel Mission, from the Ga, Akuapem, and Akyem Abuakwa presbyteries, the areas of my ethnographic research. Active in southern Ghana, the Basel Mission later became the Presbyterian Church of Ghana. Its extensive records include reports of Basel missionaries, mainly from southern Germany, and of ministers, catechists, and Christians from the Gold Coast. Another important source is a notebook written by Jonathan Bekoe Palmer, a Christian from Akropong in the Akuapem area, who records in detail disputes with which the missionaries were involved in Akropong and Akyem between 1860 and 1867. During this period, the Basel Mission was deeply enmeshed in dealing with slavery and debt pawning because converts and schoolchildren were being pawned or sold and because the mission obtained labor and schoolchildren by paying off a person's debts. Furthermore, beginning in 1862, African Christians were under pressure to give up their domestic slaves.

The records are not particularly focused on aging, in part because most of the converts were young people, but there is some information on older Christians. This lacuna is in contrast to Wesleyan Methodist and London Missionary Society missionaries among the Xhosa in South Africa during the same period, who emphasized the degradation and misery of aging among the Xhosa through the figure of the "Abandoned Mother," in part to legitimize the missions' civilizing project in southern Africa (Sagner 2001).

Within the romantic narrative of the decline of the status of older adults, many studies of aging in Ghana note the historical prominence of older people. Yet Twi proverbs collected by Basel missionaries and African Christians during the 1870s indicate contradictions in the status of older adults (Christaller [1879] 1990). On the one hand, those that mention both children and aging definitely indicate that the older and more senior person deserves respect, in contrast to the child and more junior. For example,

Abofra, woyaw panyin a, wonkyɛ ade (Child, if you insult an elder, you won't prosper) (no. 585)

Onua-panyin yɛ owura (The senior sibling is the one in charge) (no. 2501)

Other collected proverbs are more ambiguous, particularly regarding older women, and about the limits of entrustments:

Aberewa ano yɛ den a, ogye ne ban (If the old woman is quarrelsome, she makes her own fence [rather than receiving help from others]) (no. 103)

Aberewa a onni se no, n'atadwe gu ne kotokum (Even if an old woman has no teeth, her tiger nuts remain in her bag [that is, she does not share her tiger nuts even though her lack of teeth means she cannot chew them]) (no. 100)

Thus, the proverbs collected during this period suggest that not all older people were respected as elders and that older people were sanctioned for not sharing their resources, complaining too loudly, or generating conflict.

In terms of the care provided older adults, the Basel Mission records provide several tantalizing pieces of information that suggest that domestic slaves played an important, if perhaps supplementary, role in elder care in the past. Slaves were quite common in Akuapem. Proverbs collected by Hans Nicolaus Riis (1854) in

Akuapem reveal quite a few concerned with slavery and freedom as well as with poverty and wealth, suggesting the prevalence of social and economic inequality. Michelle Gilbert reports, "In mid nineteenth century Akuapem, it is estimated that probably one half of the population of Akropong were slaves and captives from the Ewe wars" (1995, 378n15). The colonial court records show that after the Ashanti invasion of the area now known as the Volta Region in 1870, many refugees from that area fled into Akuapem or were reduced to slavery in Akuapem during the 1870s. Slaves were captured in war or as refugees but also individually. In Akuapem and neighboring Akyem and Krobo, they were primarily used in long-distance trading, the transportation by headloading of agricultural products such as palm oil, and cash-crop farming (Addo-Fening 1980; Haenger 2000). Other areas may have experienced a loss of young people due to slave raids (Perbi 2004), but the areas associated with the Basel Mission were primarily slave-receiving areas and received young people, particularly young women, as slaves.

Slaves enlarged households, with the size of households a determinant of social status and power (Addo-Fening 1980). In 1861, the missionary Mader described households in Akuapem as composed of fifty to a hundred people made up of a family head, the wives and children of the current and previous family heads, and inherited and more recently purchased slaves and their children (Haenger 2000).

Slavery and kinship existed on a continuum (Miers and Kopytoff 1977), in which slaves could achieve a quasi-kin status, including the ability to inherit, although they were not equal members of the family. Slaves and masters used kin terms to refer to one another. Slaves and family members ate and worked together, but slaves, more than family members, were used for the most onerous and dirty work, like processing palm oil (Abun-Nasr 2003; Perbi 2004). Kin groups acted as corporate bodies that had rights in and responsibilities to family members, whom they could transfer to another family house or person in return for goods or money—in other words, they could be sold or pawned. Although slaves inherited by the kin group were not so easily sold as individually owned slaves, they could be pawned or sold in case of *abusua* debts, protecting kin with higher status from a similar fate. Thus, there was a pecking order for alienation from the kin group, in which in the absence of slaves, junior members—other, less equal kin—could be sold or pawned by the kin group.

In a matrilineal society, men could not command the labor of their wives and children, who belonged to a different kin group (Allman and Tashjian 2000). For men, the value of slave wives and children from slave wives (who inherited their slave status from their mothers in a matrilineal society) was that they could be more easily used in the household work of production and reproduction because they had no kin group to protect them. Slaves' lack of kin made them more vulnerable and therefore controllable. Disjoined from the kin group into which they were born (Patterson 1982), they became subject to the kin group to which they belonged by sale.

In 1862, after heated discussions, the Basel Mission decided that any slave-holder who wished to be baptized must first free his slaves and that current members of a parish should release their slaves within two years (Haenger 2000, 22). The Basel missionaries were somewhat inconsistent in implementing this regulation, making exceptions in individual cases and allowing slaveholders to make their slaves pay off their sale price through wage labor. Furthermore, the missionaries themselves, in freeing Christian slaves owned by non-Christians, expected them to work off their purchase price for a period of time at the mission, and as a result, others around the mission may have considered the missionaries to be engaged in slaveholding themselves. It is from records of these kinds of dilemmas that we learn of cases in which slaves provided elder care. Although such cases may overemphasize the role of slaves, they do suggest that, in the past, adult children were not the only ones involved in providing care to frail older people, particularly to older men, who were not their kin. Furthermore, such narratives suggest that elder care was a fraught, negotiated process; older adults were in danger of being abandoned; and older adults worked actively to prevent neglect.

I became interested in the 1860s because of one particular record, in which the missionary David Eisenschmid in Akyem Abuakwa reported in 1866 on an old man who had been attending Christian services for several years but had not requested baptism (Eisenschmid 1866). When asked for his reasons for delay, the old man said that he was loath to give up his two slaves because he was worried about who would care for him in his old age. He himself was a house slave, or inherited slave; in other words, his mother or grandmother was a bought slave who had had children with a kin member. In a matrilineal society, her descendants would also be considered slaves. However, reported Eisenschmid, the old man had hit on a solution to his dilemma: to marry a young woman who was a slave! That way, he could return his original two slaves to his master. Unfortunately, because the old man is not named, I cannot track him in further records to see whether his strategy was successful. It is also not clear to me whether he was more vulnerable in old age precisely because he was an inherited slave.

Other documents show that wealthier and free older men in Akropong also could struggle to secure care. Elizabeth Gyabisa, a childless Christian slave, fifty years old, was taking care of an older and sick relapsed Christian patriarch, Abraham Kwaku Sae, after his two wives left him for younger men (Haenger 2000, 44). This example suggests that a slave was more biddable than a wife.

One possible outcome for Christian men without young and loyal wives and who did not own slaves was manifest in the example of an Abokobi Christian elder, whom the missionaries thought about the age of seventy. In 1866, a Basel missionary noted, "Old Abraham Tete, community elder in Abokobi, a man with grey hair who has been a Christian for years, is all alone with his old wife and is not in a position to keep a servant according to the conditions of our regulations [that is, paying the servant a wage]. Consequently, besides everything else he must carry his daily water requirements an hour's distance. One time he went missing and someone found him en route lying exhausted next to his water pot" (Haenger 2000, 108). That he had to do his own household chores was clearly beneath his dignity as a Christian male elder and more than he could handle physically, prompting the Basel missionaries to advocate for an exemption in his case to allow him to keep some "servants," a euphemism for slaves.

There are certainly cases of daughters as young women providing care to their older or invalid mothers. A young woman attending a school in Abokobi left for a period of time to attend to her sick mother (Locher 1863). Heinrich Yaw, a young Christian carpenter from Akropong, earned money by sawing wood for the Mission to buy back his sister Afua "so that his sick old mother would have her support" (Haenger 2000, 43). Through his wages at the Mission, Heinrich Yaw was successful in redeeming his sister from slavery and bringing her back to Akropong to care for his mother.

Another Christian whom the missionaries sought to protect and whose story involves elder care was Rosine Opo (or Po). Her conflict-ridden story is well documented in Basel Mission records (Haenger 2000; Sill 2010). In one incident in 1867, when she was probably in her mid-thirties, she was put in the stocks by her family (Palmer 1860–1867, 402–12). The immediate cause was that, instead of looking after her sick father, she went to live with another man, a Christian, whom she considered her new husband. In the airing of the conflict before a visiting government official, a kin member told Rosine Opo, "We told you, stay with your father and give him water in the morning to wash, and cook something for him to eat." The family heir, Kwame Asiedu, stated similarly, "I let them put her in stocks if she doesn't stay in Aboasa [a neighborhood of Akropong] and look after her father." She was not simply a daughter to her father, but also an inherited slave because her mother was a slave. Furthermore, the *abusua* had incurred many debts because of Rosine Opo's conflicts with her ex-husband, to the extent that her own children had been pawned. For all these reasons, the *abusua* felt that they could control her residence and labor, to force her to care for her sick father. They were quite annoyed with her: the family heir threatened to kill her as a sacrifice to accompany her father when he died, as happened to the slaves of important men. When she complained about this threat, another male member of the *abusua* told her to be quiet because she had no brother (like Heinrich Yaw) to support her. A third accused her of potentially causing her father's death because of the court cases she had brought to the *abusua* through her previous marriage. Male members of the *abusua* thus emerged as care managers, trying to secure her care labor for her father. Her case, as well as that of Afua, Heinrich Yaw's sister, suggests that daughters who were indebted to their families could be more easily recruited to provide care—although not in this case! Rosine Opo was kept in the stocks for eight days in July 1867 before the missionaries secured her release (Haenger 2000, 38). Missionary presence created a route for one slave daughter to refuse kin-scription to care for her father, and for another to be kin-scripted by her brother, with help from his wages at the Mission, to help her enslaved mother.

Despite the proscriptions against Christians owning slaves, Christians continued to keep and buy slaves to provide care in cases of sickness and disability, suggesting that they would do the same for aging relatives. In a 1894 report on slavery among Christians, the missionary Johannes Schopf documents that in Tsui, a hamlet near Accra, Johannes, a Christian with leprosy, with neither wife nor children, and with a lame adult brother living nearby, bought a boy "whom he treated like his own child" to "fetch water or firewood for him or buy food for him in the market" (Haenger 2000, 179). A catechist within the Ga Presbytery bought a slave girl when he was in a remote station because he had an ill wife and small children. He bought the girl to help fetch water. He said, "I was driven to it by need"—a need no doubt exacerbated by his work for the mission, which posted him among strangers, making it difficult to receive assistance from kin. In a third case, a Christian bought a girl to help his "sickening, argumentative, and mentally somewhat disturbed wife" (Haenger 2000, 179). In her study of slavery in Accra, Ghanaian historian Deborah Atobrah similarly argues that Ga women used slaves, pawns, and foster children to help with household tasks. One of her informants, a seventy-seven-year-old woman in Central Accra, talked in 2008 about how a slave girl assisted her blind grandmother, probably in the 1940s or 1950s (2012/2013, 92). Another Ghanaian historian, Akosua Perbi (2004, 110), has noted that one of her informants in Dormaa in the Bono Region told her that slaves did the work one became too weak to do in old age, probably discussing the same period of the 1940s or 1950s.

The cases discussed here suggest that, in the 1860s and probably in the decades thereafter, domestic slaves were recruited by men, both family heads and brothers, to provide elder care in the absence of other possible caregivers with greater status and a protective kin group, such as their free wives and daughters. Inherited slaves who were also daughters were particularly coerced, as we see in the case of Rosine Opo, but such elder care was always negotiated and might be deflected through reliance on other patrons, like the missionaries. With the demise of slavery and pawning over the course of the twentieth century in southern Ghana, new caregivers had to be recruited. Allman and Tashjian (2000) note that as men could no longer use slave and pawned labor for cash-crop farming in the 1940s and 1950s, they turned to their free wives and children, transforming bride price into a debt by which women became obligated to them. They substituted adjacent relations when they lost the ability to purchase and control their domestic slaves. In the case of elder care, women continued to be more ready to provide help to their maternal kin—their mother and their mother's sisters. Like the older man discussed by Eisenschmid, men could pursue the strategy of securing care in old age by marrying younger women.

Elder Care in the Second Half of the Twentieth Century

Other than what I have noted above, I have very little information from the archives on older people's lives from the 1860s to the 1980s, during a period of widespread political, economic, and social changes, including migration to agricultural areas for cocoa farming and to urban areas to take advantage of the new commercial opportunities. Life expectancy rose from 28 years in 1921 to 42.5 years between 1948 and 1960 (Caldwell 1967). The twentieth century saw an increase in literacy, particularly in the years after independence in 1957, with more and more children attending school. Development in both colonial and postcolonial periods exacerbated regional inequalities, with southern Ghana becoming more prosperous and receiving more infrastructure than the North and with urban areas privileged by national programs, prompting widespread urban migration. An educated elite and middle class became more prominent. In many ways, although Nkrumah mobilized "tradition"—connected to the elders—to legitimize his rule, he was associated with youth because of his imprisonment of older political leaders and his more radical vision of "Self-governance Now." During the Nkrumah years before and after independence, government energies were focused on the needs of the young as central to national development, through the rapid expansion of primary education. His youth organizations like the Young Pioneers created intergenerational tensions, as the rumor was that children were told to inform on their parents for political comments, during a frightening period when political dissidents were imprisoned (Coe 2005). One example of aging during the postindependence period comes from Ayi Kwei Armah's novel *Fragments* (1971). In a multigenerational household in Accra, an older woman, the *Nana* or grandmother, figures prominently as the voice of morality concerned with future and past generations, and the ritual knowledge to sustain them. Despite her knowledge and moral certainty, Armah depicts her as ignored and marginalized by the other members of the household. The grandmother serves in the novel as a potent symbol of the moral decay of postindependence Ghana.

Subsequent democratic and military governments did not have many generational associations, until Flight Lieutenant Jerry John Rawlings took power through a military coup in 1978 and then again in 1982. A young man himself, and seizing the leftist mantle of Nkrumah, Rawlings was associated with mobilizing the youth against older people. The rumor is that he said that all those over the age of fifty should be killed, to make way for new ideas, although I can find no citation to corroborate what many Ghanaians said to me. Illustrating Ghanaians' propensity to find ironic humor in politics, as well as their excellent political memories, Ghanaians in the 1990s and 2000s joked about this statement when Rawlings grew old himself and recognized older people in a state ceremony on Republic Day, beginning in 1997, the same year Rawlings turned fifty.

Studies of older people from the late 1980s onward were carried out by Nana Araba Apt (1996) in a survey of 1,000 older people followed by in-depth interviews with 35 of them in 1988 and 1989 in urban and rural areas of the Central Region; by Barbara Stucki (1995) in 1990–91 through 153 interviews with those age fifty and older in a rural area of the Ashanti Region; and by Sjaak van der Geest (1997–2004b) through interviews with 35 older people in the town of Tafo, Kwawu, in the Eastern Region from 1994 to 2000. Ghanaian sociologist C. K. Brown (1999) conducted a national survey of almost 1,500 older adults in 1991. In general, these studies highlight the anxiety of older adults about their future well-being. Their status as respected elder was not secure. As Stucki (1995) and Van der Geest (1997, 2002b, 2002c, 2003) particularly emphasize, becoming a respected elder means accomplishing the tasks garnering respect—that is, having children and grandchildren, taking care of dependents, and building a house. An older person has to have "something to give" in order to secure help (Aboderin 2004), which privileged the more wealthy and more healthy and younger older adults who could maintain control over their properties (see also Häberlein 2018 for northern Togo). It was easier for men to gain the status of respected elder because of the increased opportunities available to marry many wives and to work in more profitable occupations, but many failed to do so or were anxious about achieving this status.

Adult children seem to be the major sources of support for older people in these studies, even though their remittances could be insufficient and inconsistent. Brown (1999) found that 25.5 percent of older adults were aided in the performance of household chores by daughters. Surveys of older households in the 1960s and 1970s show that very few older people received remittances from their children or other people (cited in Apt 1996, 42–43). Apt (1996) and Brown (1999), in contrast, found that 79 percent and 55 percent, respectively, received remittances from their children. In Apt's survey, 46 percent also received remittances from other relatives, but in much smaller amounts, and nieces and nephews were also important caregivers on a daily basis. Another study of Accra in 2002 (Addo 2003) similarly reported a reliance on adult children for support among Ga older adults, particularly in relation to medical costs. As a result of the dependence of older adults on children and grandchildren, these studies show that childless adults, mainly older women, were particularly vulnerable to not receiving care (Aboderin 2004; Dsane 2013). With respondents able to choose multiple options, Brown (1999) found that four-fifths of those he surveyed felt that older adults should rely on their children to support them in their old age; only a third (36.8 percent) thought the family (that is, the *abusua*) should be the main provider, positing the difficulties families might face in helping. Interestingly, 20 percent chose an option posed by the survey that the care of the elderly was the responsibility of the whole society, implicitly challenging the Ageing Policy's focus on kin elder care.

In the 1990s, the most common pattern for older adults was to live in multi-generational households with children and grandchildren. Only a few lived without any relatives: Apt (1996) found that only 12.2 percent of her respondents lived without any relations, with 9.8 percent living with domestic servants only, including in rural areas. Stucki (1995) similarly notes that 30 percent of women and 20 percent of men in her study of a rural area of the Ashanti Region were living in four- or five-generation households. At the same time, 62.8 percent of older adults in the Central Region had most of their children living away from them, either elsewhere in Ghana or outside the country (Apt 1996).

What is quite clear across these studies is the continuity across the second half of the twentieth century in grandmothers' role in child care, particularly of young children. It illustrates how elder care is bound up in other intergenerational relations, including the care of children. Sometimes grandmother care occurs in the context of multigenerational households. However, ethnographic accounts across southern Ghana note the significance of grandmother fostering in rural hometowns in the 1970s to allow the adult generation of parents to migrate, as noted by Philip F. W. Bartle (n.d.) in Obo (in Kwawu) in the 1970s, Margaret Hardiman (2003) in Konkonnuru (in Akuapem) in 1971, Lynne Brydon (1979) in Amedzofe (in the Volta Region), and D. K. Fiawoo (1978) in Kaneshie, a neighborhood of Accra, and Mampong in the Ashanti Region (for a summary see Coe 2013b, chap. 3). Sixty-seven percent of rural older women and 79 percent of urban older women surveyed in the Central Region in 1988–89 were involved in child care, and almost all rural youth had lived in a household with a grandparent or was currently living there (Apt 1996). Although grandmothers emphasized their role in helping children, children also served as helpers to maintain older people's independent households (Brydon 1979). In my own research in Akropong, a seventy-five-year-old woman reported that her grandmother had asked her to stay with her as a child, probably in the 1940s, because her grandmother did not have anyone to send on errands.[8] Furthermore, fostering a grandchild helped secure the remittances, visits, and eternal gratitude of the parent of that child.

These studies suggest that neglect is not a recent phenomenon among aging people in Ghana. Barbara Stucki (1995) reports on a national survey of eleven urban areas conducted from 1948 to 1954 that found that many of the destitute beggars were older people abandoned by their families. In addition, 5.8 percent of older adults surveyed in the Central Region said that they were extremely lonely, and 35 percent were sometimes lonely (Apt 1996). In a 1983 survey of aged people in Accra, 40 percent cared for by kin said that they were "not satisfied with their lot" and 33 percent said that they did not get enough to eat (reported in Stucki 1995, 31).

One sign of challenges in aged care comes from Brown (1999), who notes that caregivers of older people were generally not happy with their work. In his national survey of 1352 caregivers, two-thirds (62.3 percent) considered the care of the older person a burden, mainly financially and in terms of their own health and anxiety about the older person's health. Almost all (87.3 percent) caregivers were looking after someone else, namely their own children, in addition to an older person, and Brown contemplated the various stresses that increased the caregivers' burdens as well as the support systems that would allow them to care with greater contentment.

The social changes most convincingly argued in these studies come from Isabella Aboderin's study (2004, 2006) based on fifty-one interviews with an older person in Accra and subsequently one of their children in the middle-aged generation and one of their grandchildren. She argues that the two major changes based on these generational interviews were the withdrawal of support from the extended family (*abusua*) with a greater burden put on children and the increased contingency of the children's care on their experiences of parental care. The older generation in her study, looking back on their childhoods and adulthoods in the late 1930s to the 1960s, reported retrospectively that the extended family would help adult children take care of older people, even childless ones. Partly, this was the result of economic prosperity, in which household expenses were cheap in comparison to incomes. Furthermore, she argues that children increasingly cared for older adults only if they had contributed to their welfare as children, by educating them. The most common cases of nonsupport, albeit rare, were of older men who had "reneged on their parental duties and whose children, in turn, 'retaliated' by not supporting them, or they were older women who were accused of witchcraft and consequently were refused support" (2006, S131). In contrast, she argues, the older generation discussed supporting their own parents out of duty because of the gift of birth, not because of the support in childhood: "Today, adult children make support increasingly dependent on their judgment of their parents' past conduct" (2006, S134). The threat of sanction from the wider family no longer had force because younger cohorts did not receive much support from the extended family. Aboderin attributes this change to the economic context, in which many young people were not launched into economic independence and social adulthood, making it impossible for them to support dependents (see also Roth 2007, 2008 on urban Burkino Faso). In addition, Aboderin notes the significance of the priorities of the needs of the young over those of the old: "The underlying principle, it seems, is that the old have no 'right' to absorb the resources that the young need for their life" (S135). Ghanaian anthropologist Kodjo Amedjorteh Senah, in a study of a Ga village on the outskirts of Accra in 1991–1993, similarly finds that "Bortianor is full of aged men and women who are literally neglected both by their siblings and the extended family" because they did not take good care of their children (1997, 201).

Thus, the extensive scholarship from the 1990s, occasionally looking backward in time, indicates the ambiguous status of older adults, particularly of older women and those who are not successful in childbearing, child raising, or wealth creation. It suggests, somewhat nostalgically, that care for older adults shifted from the extended family (*abusua*), who provided care generously during times of economic prosperity, to adult children, who were more parsimonious and contingent in their care because of more difficult economic times. Many older adults lived in multigenerational households but were affected by the migration of their adult children, who sometimes left behind their children in the care of a grandmother, cementing intergenerational ties and securing some care, in terms of both remittances and daily household support for the older person in the hometown.

The Migrant Daughter Who Returns to the Hometown to Care

My own ethnographic research on elder care comes from life-history interviews of ninety-three foster parents I conducted in Akropong in 2008 to understand child fosterage in the context of migration. Some foster parents were teachers and retired pastors; some were sellers of charcoal and prepared food. Some could pay for their child's secondary school education, at the time a major expense, while others were barely scraping by. Most of my interviewees were Akan in ethnic origin, either from Akropong or from another town in the Eastern Region, but one was Ewe, one was Ga, and one was Frafra from northern Ghana. Akuapem people are best considered to practice double-descent, partially acknowledging both maternal and paternal sides of the family (Brokensha 1972). What I discovered in the course of these interviews was how child care and elder care were intimately connected. Older women returned to their hometowns to care for both their grandchildren and an older generation. I use this material, originally collected to document the history of child care (Coe 2013b), for its insights into elder care in the late twentieth century.

In the kin-scripts of the late twentieth century in southern Ghana, the eldest daughter was the ideal, normative care provider of an older person: that is, expected to live with him or her and help with daily chores and personal care as needed.[9] Jessaca Leinaweaver (2010) talks about the same process in Peru as filling "the care slot." Since the 1950s and 1960s, women in southern Ghana have migrated in their late teens and early twenties from their hometowns to the urban areas to work as traders (Brydon 1979; Middleton 1979). This has meant that since the 1960s, some aging parents have been left behind in rural households and have had "sporadic" contact with urban migrants (Apt 1996, 38). The expectation of filling the care slot as the previous generation of women in their kin group aged meant that female urban migrants returned home in middle age. Among the women I interviewed, they returned to live in their hometowns between the ages of forty and sixty in the 1980s or 1990s after a change in their or another's life circumstances. One woman returned to Akropong after her husband's death, which devastated her financially; another woman when the company for which

FIG. 1.1 A compound family house in Akropong.

she worked folded; and a third when she retired from a job in the formal sector. Although ideally this woman was the eldest daughter, a broader definition of kin seemed to apply in terms of actual care practices, in which a woman from the younger generation within the kin group would care for an older woman or set of kinswomen considered sisters. More recently, supporting Aboderin's contention based on her Accra data from the same decade (2004, 2006), the orthodoxy seems to have shifted, narrowing down to a smaller number of potential care providers.

The hometown functions as a social safety net and is particularly important for women, who tend to be poorer than men. One can live more cheaply in one's hometown because one can stay in the family house, built by a father or family head, for which one does not pay rent (fig. 1.1). Other relatives live nearby, and they may be able to share labor and resources and provide companionship, although they may also be a source of conflict. In her hometown, a woman may also have access to family land, where she can tend a small food farm that reduces her need for cash. Such a return often coincides with the end of a marriage through death or separation, as most husbands of these women do not follow them to their hometown. Thus, the vulnerable—who require such a safety net— are the ones called upon to care for the young and old. Furthermore, because the hometown is not as economically vibrant as the larger towns and cities, moving back home to provide care makes one poor and dependent on one's social network for financial resources. Unlike the migrant men in the Ashanti Region noted by Stucki (1995) who were anxious about planning their successful return, the women I met returned out of necessity.

In their stories of return migration, women's personal circumstances and the decline of an older person coincided, which suggests they, of all their siblings and among the children of sisters, came to live with the older generation in the family because they were available to do so and in need of the safety net of the home-town. Although returning to the hometown entailed a loss of financial resources, filling the care slot helped female family members justify financial support from their brothers, the children of the elderly relatives for whom they cared, and their own grown children whose children were staying with them. Of course, a survey conducted in the hometown meant I did not encounter those women who refused or avoided such obligations.

Abena Oforiwa illustrates some of the general features of this care practice that corresponded to the general orthodoxy of kin care.[10] She lived in a family house in her hometown with her maternal cousin, Akosua Yirenkyiwa, whom she considered her sister, along with eight grandchildren, many of whom were toddlers although the oldest was fourteen. In the late afternoon, I often encountered the older children returning from the family plot, laden with firewood and produce. Forty-eight years old in 2008, Abena had gone to work in a sugar factory in a nearby town in her youth, but returned to her hometown around the age of thirty when the sugar factory closed. Her mother had been living in the family house and died, leaving her cousin, an elderly woman, alone. Abena explained how she inherited her mother's position:

> When my mother died, it meant no one lived here. My sister [Akosua Yirenkyiwa, now living with her] was in Accra. I was here for a little time—I lived in Akropong but I didn't live in this house. But my mother died and no one, all the children, all our children had given birth so no one wanted to live at home. It isn't good when there is no one in the [family] house, so I came to live here. And at that time, our one cousin lived here, and she was sick and no one lived here, so she couldn't get up to go out, and no one was at home, so it wasn't good at all. And I came to live here to look after her. That's the only thing that brought me here. . . . So I came to live here, and my daughter wanted to go work; she migrated so I had to look after . . . I had to look after her children for her back home.[11]

Akosua Yirenkyiwa, sitting nearby, commented on her sister's narrative: "You who are the eldest female will come home, and the [adult] children will go work hard to look for something to make their living."[12] The older woman in the next generation is recruited to return home, allowing others—the young and the male—to focus on economic gain to provide financial support for the hometown household. This pattern in which female migrants retire from trading to take up the care of others—both grandchildren and older adults—has been noted in studies of urban migration from 1968 to 1970: a quarter of female migrants surveyed in Ashaiman and Tema noted that their return to the hometown was a decision dependent on others (Peil 1981, 73). Van der Geest (2002b), from fieldwork between 1994 and 2000, also mentions the case of a daughter returning from Kumasi eleven years before to her hometown Tafo in Kwawu to care for her aged parents. Van der Geest notes, although she considered it a sacrifice, she did it because she remembered her mother caring for the daughter's own children when they were in school.

Men also expected to return home from migration as they aged, but this was connected not to caring for others but instead to caring for the properties of members of the *abusua* who had died (Miescher 2005). Describing a situation of cyclical migration for men and women, in the 1970s in the town of Obo in Kwawu, Bartle (n.d.) describes how men returned to the hometown and accepted responsibilities for managing the *abusua*, the matrilineage or extended family, which involved settling disputes and organizing funerals. In Akropong, too, in 2019, I noticed my older male friends living in their hometown assuming often time-consuming and emotionally difficult tasks of managing property and resolving disputes on behalf of the *abusua*.

Women are recruited as care providers in part because the economic sectors in which they work make them poorer than men, on average, and liable to experience economic ups and downs in their work as traders or entrepreneurs (Clark 2010; Heintz 2005). This makes them both more prone to be asked to help when there is a need for kin-work and more willing to accept such a request. Women's structural inequality makes them dependent on their brothers and grown children for support; they are more willing to assume the care slot in their family because of their need for the assistance of others. Abena Oforiwa said that her older brother had recruited her to move to the family house: "My elder brother, the one I come after in birth order [thus, from the same mother], said that no one was at home and the cousin also was alone at home, so if anything happened [to her cousin, such as an accident or an illness], no one lived here. So I should come with my children so that she would be happy. This is why I came to live here."[13] Although not mentioned, such persuasion was no doubt accompanied by the older brother's promise to help with her household expenses. Taking care of grandchildren also helps ensure those children's parents seeking their fortunes elsewhere and relieved of child care will send remittances.

Not all women were as content as Abena Oforiwa to care for their elderly relatives, because of the loss of personal income that it entails. A forty-three-year-old woman, Yaa Ofosua, had traveled as a young woman: she had first apprenticed as a seamstress in the commercial town of Suhum, in the Eastern Region. There, she married and worked as a trader. Later, her husband died, and she became involved with another man in a more short-lived relationship. After that relationship ended, she returned home to take care of her mother, whom she described as having difficulty moving around and unable to prepare food or fetch water for herself.

Yaa Ofosua was less happy than Abena Oforiwa about returning home to care for her mother, and she complained about how difficult it was to make a living in Akropong. She made clothing alterations occasionally and received firewood and other foodstuffs from working as a laborer for other farmers. She also worked on her own small plot. Her mother ran a little bar in the house, and her brother sent money once in a while, but not enough to satisfy her. She scrimped and saved to pay her seven-year-old son's school fees. Yaa Ofosua wanted another one of her ten siblings to take her place in looking after her mother, so that she could return to work in a more commercial town or city. In the presence of her mother, she stated baldly, "I would like to tell my siblings that I am exhausted of looking after my mother; I would like to go look for work in Suhum or Tema or Kumasi [all commercial towns or cities] and if I could find someone who could take me on [in a seamstress shop] or if I found work, I could bring money back to my mother, and she could look after my child or something like that. Or if I go with my child, I could bring something to my mother. And that would mean that my siblings would come; they are many."[14] Yaa Ofosua was not willing to continue filling the care slot but instead positioned herself as a migrant who could work and a mother who could leave behind her child in the hometown. Such public statements stated so forcefully might well put pressure on her siblings, either to send more money to their mother so that Yaa Ofosua did not have to suffer in such poverty or to replace her so that she could earn money to send home. She did not challenge the orthodoxy of kin care but instead proposed shifting her position within it, from care provider to care manager.

For some women, the return home seems more voluntary, where the timing of personal circumstances coincides with an older person's need for care, as for Abena Oforiwa; for others, like Yaa Ofosua, the return home is perceived as an economic hardship and a burden. The return migrant's interpretation of her situation may fluctuate over time and be partially dependent on the degree of financial support she receives from her brothers, her children, and other migrant relatives. Women are called upon to be flexible in their physical location because of their economic dependency and because they, along with children, are associated with the daily and practical tasks of providing care: cooking, cleaning, laundering, and marketing. The male eldercare role involves managing care, by sending remittances, visiting occasionally, and organizing funerals (Van der Geest 2002b).

Some gender care roles are fluid, as Oyěwùmi (1997) suggests is the case among the Yorùbá in Nigeria. Women can take on the role of care manager, without any repercussions on their gender identity. Claudia Roth (2008) reports a similar phenomenon in Burkina Faso, in which only sons were duty bound to provide material gifts of cloth and money to their parents. Now daughters are doing the same out of choice (53). However, the care provider role in Ghana is highly gendered: men would be stigmatized for taking it on. Although children, including boys, do domestic work and provide elder care, adolescent boys often begin to perform domestic chores incompetently because it is incompatible with their sense of themselves as young men (see also Van der Geest 2002b). The gendered nature of providing care is illustrated by the life history of one woman in her seventies in Akropong, now looking after three grandchildren. She explained that she had taken the place of her father and his brothers in caring for her grandmother when she was a child in the 1940s: "On my father's side, they were all men, so they didn't have anyone, they didn't have a woman to stay with their mother, so they brought me to live with her."[15] Essentially, a daughter of one of the brothers substituted for a nonexistent sister to fill the care slot.

Because economic opportunities have been increasingly located in southern cities from the 1940s onward, an example of Ghana's geographically uneven development, young people have been attracted to urban areas to make a living. As a result, the rural towns and villages are now associated with older adults, becoming what in the United States would be called "naturally occurring retirement communities." In the hometowns, older adults are joined by grandchildren and other impoverished kin who both appreciate the social safety net of the hometown and lament its lack of economic opportunities, while those working in the cities, for the same reasons, hesitate to return "home," even as they rely on it for child care and their own anticipated aged futures. Over time, from a wider kin group, like the children of sisters, the onus to care narrowed to adult children, specifically the biological children of the older person. The smaller pool of potential recruits to care provision created more intense pressure on adult children, who were more eager to be care managers than care providers because of their reluctance to return to the hometown. I detail their alterodox coping practices in the next chapter.

Conclusion

When I talked to Ghanaians about my research on aging, many of my male interlocutors would respond that traditionally family members would take care of their elderly relations. Their responses supported the orthodoxy presented by the aged fellowship group's drama in which adult children were held particularly responsible for elder care. Family care, writ broadly, was also the orthodoxy supported by the state, which had formalized and codified the common sense of my interlocutors with the assistance of advocacy groups and academic scholars. Those who venerate kin care overlook the complex negotiations among kin to care for the older generations, including the recruitment of more vulnerable kin, such as slave women in the past, to reside with an older person and be involved in daily care provision.

The play also suggested that the orthodoxy was not working as well as it should, leaving one upstanding couple to be cared for, but another, equally pious and dedicated to their children's well-being, to be neglected and accused of witchcraft. The orthodoxy of kin care, out of sync with the reality of contingent care by impoverished or migrant adult children, generates concerns about neglect as well as alternative practices to deal with potential neglect. The pool of potential care providers and care managers has narrowed from the wider kin group, including the daughters of sisters and grandchildren, to adult children who stand to inherit and in whom parents are increasingly concentrating their resources, rather than spreading that labor obligation more widely across children in the *abusua*. In urban Burkina Faso, by contrast, necessity has prompted an expansion of caregiving responsibilities rather than a contraction: the expectation was that the oldest son would care for the parents, but because of economic hardship, the range of caregivers has widened to include the whole sibling group of the same mother (Roth 2014). In Ghana, adult children now face more pressure to care for their biological parents, and some either are not inclined to or cannot meet their obligations incurred by the care bestowed on them in childhood or middle age, through older adults' care of grandchildren. Some adult children do not feel that they have received adequate care, particularly from biological fathers, and thus spurn their recruitment to care, or take it on reluctantly. Older adults most at risk seemed to fall into two categories: childless women and men with difficult relationships with their children, including a failed marriage with the children's mother.

Women, particularly older women, seemed less enamored with the orthodoxy. They were willing to explore new practices, perhaps because they themselves had been recruited to care for an older man or woman in their middle age or because they had sympathy for an overextended daughter. They therefore did not view kin care through rose-colored glasses. They approached the problem of their potential care pragmatically, rather than thinking about what *ought* to be the case. Some men also sought greater independence from unreliable children and preached self-reliance through a variety of means or advocated for other institutions like the state or the church to take their children's place in providing care. Older men seemed more dependent on marriage to a younger woman and the labor of that wife and young children living in the household to secure care, rather than from adult women from their kin group.[16] The next chapter turns to the variety of ways older people and those around them were meeting their needs for care. These were not framed as heterodox to the orthodoxy of kin care and thus escaped the censure expressed about Western residential facilities. Instead, these new practices and discourses emerged as alterodoxies, care practices that differed from the orthodoxy of kin care but were seen to be neither competing with it nor threatening it.

This history situates contemporary practice within a longer context, exploding any pretense about differences between "traditional" and "modern" families. It shows that care practices are sensitive to changing economic and social circumstances, including the labor demands on women, increased educational expectations, and the allure of urban areas in providing economic and educational opportunities. As these shift over time, there is pressure on care practices to also shift. New kinds of people are recruited to care, attesting to the dynamism of elder care arrangements in Ghana and making visible the negotiations around the labor of regenerating families. Who is recruited to care provision and management matters. It is an indicator of existing status, in which care managers have status for recruiting the kin-work of others, and care providers are eligible to be asked or pressured because of their social and economic vulnerability. Furthermore, taking on the care provision role makes it difficult to earn a living because of one's residence in the economically stagnant hometown. These roles both signal and reinforce inequalities within the kin group and household—whether slave or free, male or female—as well as in the society at large.

Part I

Changes in Aging in the Rural Towns of the Eastern Region

● ●

2

Heterodox Ideas of Elder Care

• •

From Nursing Homes to Savings

As discussed in the previous chapter, the government of Ghana, with the support of NGOs involved in generating state policy, supports a social norm of kin providing elder care, in part to avoid what would probably become a major financial expenditure, as it is in Western state budgets. Thus, the orthodox discourse concerns children living up to their responsibilities. From the perspective of older Presbyterians in the towns of the Eastern Region I talked to, this solution to the problem of elder care is not reliable, and perhaps not viable.

As a result, older people in Ghana are coming up with their own solutions. In the discussions I had with aging Ghanaians, the Presbyterian Church of Ghana provided a forum for, but was not the instigator of, heterodox discourses. Religious institutions have historically been significant sources of social welfare in Ghana and other African countries as well as in the United States and Europe, and they can be important actors in civil society when state resources for care decline or have never existed (e.g., Muehlebach 2012; Scherz 2014). At the same time, religious institutions may be as reluctant as the state to care for aging adults (discussed in chapter 4). This chapter draws mainly from my conversations with older people involved in the Presbyterian Church in three areas of the Eastern Region in southern Ghana: Akuapem, Akyem, and Kwawu. These areas have a long history of Presbyterian activity, and the Presbyterian Church is dominant in these rural towns (Gilbert 1995; Middleton 1979; Mohr 2013). On Sundays in all three areas, the congregations are mainly filled by older women, who are sometimes living with and looking after their grandchildren or great-grandchildren because the middle-aged generation is working in the major cities in Ghana or abroad. Younger men and women are more attracted to Pentecostalism or other new churches with dynamic ministers and founders. In addition to my long-term ethnographic research in Akuapem, I spent a week each in Kwawu and Akyem in July 2014 and, with the help of the district minister, attended hour-long programs of several fellowship groups with fifty to seventy-five people in attendance: seven meetings in Akyem and eight in Kwawu (map 2). Most of the participants were over the age of seventy, the definition of the aged (as they called themselves) within these churches, though some who had reached retirement age (sixty years) within the civil service also considered themselves aged. Conversations were in Akyem or Asante Twi.

In Akyem, because fellowship groups for older adults were just forming, they offered no structured program of activities, and so my visits turned into group conversations about the difficulties of aging and what solutions they would like to see for those troubles. They complained of various bodily pains, spoke proudly of children who were abroad or living in another part of Ghana, and talked about loneliness and living alone. Participants were oriented toward presenting a certain perspective on aging to me and to one another, in a context in which they knew one another and had spoken about aging with one another previously. The discussions thus reflected public discourse about aging that circulated within the Presbyterian congregations in Akyem and, like other group discussions, were sites for "the collaborative construction of meaning" (Hollander 2004, 632). These group discussions were audio-recorded. One congregation, New Tafo, had a vibrant aged fellowship group that met regularly in 2014 to do aerobic and stretching exercises, sing hymns, and play games. I returned in August 2019 to make a short documentary film about the fellowship group, deepening my ethnographic understanding.[1] In Kwawu, where the aged fellowship groups met once a week, I was less often a participant in than an observer of their ongoing programs, which involved singing and dancing, board games, religious sermons, health information, and competitions and debates. In Akropong, Akuapem, I draw on longer-term relationships with a number of older people, whom I visited regularly.

In my conversations with older people in the Presbyterian congregations of Kwawu, Akyem, and Akropong, they expressed openness to the heterodox possibility of residential facilities, a surprise given the extensive criticism of them by government officials, academics, and NGO staff. Although residential facilities were associated with foreign countries, older people transformed them in their imagination to be like residential secondary schools in Ghana and to meet their needs for companionship, food, easy access to medical care, and dignity. Furthermore, they did not distinguish strongly between senior residential

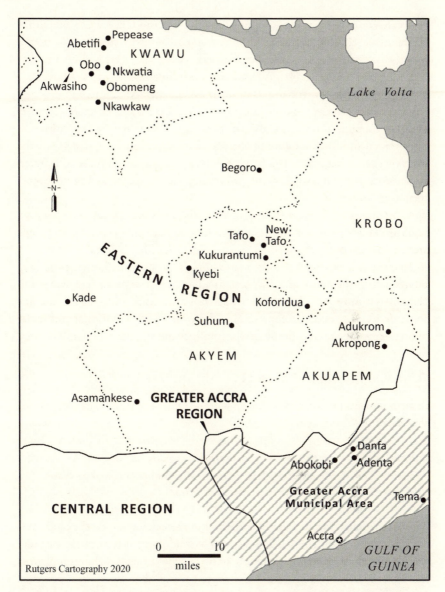

MAP 2 The towns and areas of the Eastern Region and Greater Accra Region. Created by Michael Siegel, Rutgers Cartography.

facilities and senior day centers since both were institutional settings, despite the fact that HelpAge Ghana has supported senior day centers, but not nursing homes. The foreignness of institutional residences and the fact that they were not available in their communities was what allowed them to be imagined in this way, rather than as sites of neglect, loneliness, and indignity, as they tend to be viewed in the United States. Nursing homes were able to be appropriated in this way because of the discursive orthodox comparisons that were made between Western modes of helping senior citizens and Ghanaian ways within the family, even though these orthodox comparisons evaluated nursing homes negatively. Thus, the negative comparison between the West and Ghana produced by the state and HelpAge Ghana made nursing homes available as a heterodox solution, in the minds of older Ghanaians looking to address their concerns about neglect and loneliness when kin care was their main recourse. However, in many ways senior residential facilities were discussed speculatively. They served simply as a figure in the social imagination. As I discuss in the next chapter, what was actually emerging in practice was the use of fostered adolescents and domestic servants to provide elder care, replacing or supplementing kin care.

In Ghana at the present time, care for the aging is very much in flux, with a wealth of emergent possibilities and no dominant patterns of care. Older people are anxious about the fragility of kin care and, given what is at stake, are willing to imagine and explore heterodoxies, even those from abroad, such as nursing homes, which the dominant discourse in Ghana posits is deeply antithetical to "Ghanaian tradition." Whatever happens in the future, older people are key actors in shaping elder care in Ghana, as they use their emotional and social responses to aging to imagine unseen possibilities and remake more familiar ones.

Fears and Realities of Neglect

In a group conversation, three women had the following exchange that spoke to their anxieties about aging:

WOMAN 1 If you don't have a child, no one is there to care for you.
WOMAN 2 Even if you have a child, sometimes your child doesn't look after you.
WOMAN 3 Even your own child won't look after you.[2]

All three women, in their sixties, were looking after someone in the older generation, relatively unhappily. Two women were looking after their fathers; one woman was looking after her mother's sister who had dementia. They complained that other kin had traveled, leaving them to cope on their own. Although they were fulfilling the ideal of kin care, they were thinking of their children and their own siblings with these statements. Each cascading statement posited a more negative scenario, suggesting that these women could not, in fact, depend on their children for care. Their statements did not clarify whether they were thinking about care management—through remittances—or care provision, and possibly they were concerned with both.

Anxieties about care provision were framed by older adults through the language of "living alone." An older woman said, "At this time of life, you have given birth to many children, but they have all left you to go work somewhere and you are alone at home."[3] An older man in the same group echoed her words: "You are there alone, like another person already said. All your children have left you, and your grandchildren also. Only at the end of the year [when people come to the hometown for festivities] will you see your child or grandchild."[4] A woman said, "As for me, in our elderly home, all our children and grandchildren have traveled. So we are often alone in the house and feel very lonely."[5] Another woman in the same group put it poetically, "All our children have scattered; everyone is looking for work."[6] They also complained about being left alone during the day by working adults and school-going children. As Catherine Allerton (2007) notes, who is considered to be alone is socially constructed, and older people in these rural towns depicted themselves as living alone.

In fact, when I visited older adults in these towns, very few lived strictly alone, that is, in one-person households, corroborating national statistics. In a national survey of 5,157 households with adults older than fifty in Ghana, only 1.0 percent lived in single-person households (Biritwum et al. 2013), although an earlier survey in the Central Region noted a higher percentage (Apt 1996, 41). Two-generation households represented 44 percent of households with older adults, and three-generation households another 28.5 percent (Biritwum et al 2013). Most older people in Akuapem, Akyem, and Kwawu lived in compound households with other relatives and grandchildren. Sjaak van der Geest (2002b), in his fieldwork in Tafo in Kwawu from 1994 to 2002, noted, "Many of the elderly have people around them throughout the day. When they sit in front of their room they can watch what is going on in the compound: mothers bathing their babies, children sweeping, people returning from farming and spreading ground-nuts over the yard to be dried in the sun, women washing clothes, others pre-paring meals, children playing, etc." (17). Two-thirds of the schoolchildren aged twelve to eighteen in Tafo lived with an older person (Van der Geest 2003). In the national survey, skip-generation households, in which grandparents lived with grandchildren, were less than 1 percent of all households (Biritwum et al 2013), but they seemed to predominate in rural towns, with many older adults taking care of grandchildren while their own children had traveled and benefit-ting from the household labor such grandchildren can provide (see also Apt 1995; Grieco, Apt, and Turner 1996; Turner and Kwakye 1996).

A seventy-two-year-old man reported taking care of four grandchildren with his wife, while his five children lived elsewhere; the problem he mentioned was that the grandchildren's fathers did not send enough money to help the rural household, bringing only a bag of rice now and then (group discussion, Begoro, Akyem, July 9, 2014). A seventy-two-year-old woman reported that she "lived alone" with a grandchild and farmed, as many older adults did if they could, to reduce their reliance on market-bought provisions and cash. Her husband left her two years ago, and her children are in urban areas in Ghana: Tarkwa, Kumasi, Obuasi, and Accra (group discussion, Kyebi, Akeym, July 8, 2014). One man reported that he was divorced but continued to live with his wife and she man-aged the household. Grandchildren who attend nursery school also live with them. Their children visited, bringing Milo (a chocolate drink) and tea, considered imported and expensive items worthy as gifts (group discussion, Begoro, July 9, 2014). (Other examples of grandmother fostering from Akuapem were discussed in chapter 1.) Households composed of aging adults with children and households headed by older persons were associated with higher rates of poverty in Ghana in 1998, unlike households with no older persons or those that included middle-aged adults along with older persons and minors (Kakwani and Subbarao 2007). Taking care of grandchildren can ensure that migrant children visit regularly and bring remittances or provisions when they do, although some children do not meet these expectations. Older adults discussed how difficult it was for their children to send remittances. Grandmother fostering is a strategy by which older women garner and legitimate support from their adult children, and many adult children mentioned to me that their mother's fostering of their children warranted reciprocal care when she aged.

Children's and grandchildren's absence—whether temporarily during the day through work and school or more permanent migration made older adults feel lonely. A woman complained that in her grandmother's time the town had been full, but now everyone had moved to the larger towns and cities. Although she had looked after her grandmother in her own middle age, no one is now returning the favor to her (group discussion, Asamankese, Akyem, July 12, 2014). In my research, an older woman in Akropong lived with her daughter-in-law and four grandchildren yet was alone during the day, when they went to work and school. As a result, she expressed interest in attending a senior day center (fieldnotes, June 23, 2013). She also admitted to her peers at a quarterly aged fellowship gathering organized by Christchurch that she cries sometimes because she misses her five children who all live abroad (fieldnotes, June 21, 2013).

Older women told me that it is becoming more difficult to convince an adult child to send a grandchild to live with an older person because of the longer period of schooling that is considered a young person's right. Because many people aspiring to the middle class consider schools in the rural towns in southern Ghana to provide low-quality education, those living in urban environments with better and more private schools view sending a child to live with a grandmother in the hometown to be a sacrifice of that child's educational future. From research in the Asante region in 1990–1991, Barbara Stucki (1995) found that although older women felt entitled to the help of a grandchild, young adults were reluctant to send their children to a rural area because of the quality of the schools. An older woman said that the reason that her grandchildren were not living with her is because her children said that the schools in her town of Begoro were not good, and so her grandchildren lived with their parents: "As for my grandchildren, everyone [of my own children] is looking after his/her own children, and the schools are not good here, so everyone is living with their own child. So I have no one. No one has brought me his/her child."[7] An older man, also in Begoro, suggested that his children preferred to support their own children, to his detriment: "My children have given birth to their own children and traveled to other places. It is hard for them to take money from their own children and send it to me, unless I force it a little so that I can get food to eat."[8] The preference for living with one's own children, a sign of the nuclearization of the family, means that the only grandchildren likely to come live with a grandmother are the children of impoverished or desperate parents, who then cannot help their caregiving mother or father very much with remittances and support. A still-employed friend of mine in her sixties, with whom I stayed in Akropong in 2019, lived with two grandchildren, ages eight and eleven, whom she appreciated for their help around the household in fetching water, running errands, and sweeping. However, she told me that the only reason they stayed with her was because their father was poor and welcomed having the expense of feeding them lifted off his shoulders. The grandchildren of her more successful children lived with their parents in urban areas, and those children would never have sent their children to live with her (fieldnotes, August 4, 2019). Comparing Stucki's research with my own, what has changed in the past twenty-five years is that older women no longer feel entitled to ask their grandchildren to live with them.

I encountered one man in Kyebi who in fact seemed to fit my definition of living alone: a stranger to the town, he had married a Kyebi woman who had recently died. They had sold some land to surface gold miners (*galamsey*), active in the area, to fund the building of the simple two-room house in which he was living, just behind his wife's family house. His wife's sister, who stayed nearby, brought him food daily. After the one-year celebration of his wife's death, he was planning to return to his farm at Asamankese, also in Akyem, which his son with a mental illness tended (fieldnotes, July 10, 2014). It was because he was a recent widower that he lived alone, and his daughter was encouraging him to marry again. Thus, although he seemed to live by himself, he in fact had support from his adult children and his wife's family. His living alone was a temporary phenomenon associated with his period of mourning.

"Neglect" (said in English) was a significant concern in these towns and among the Presbyterian congregations which wanted to do something for older congregants. An Akyem pastor, for example, talked about visiting those who were shut into their rooms and could not go out. "Many do not have anyone to look after them. If they want even water to drink, they have to call and call to get it. The same is true for food. I visited one person who said even food was difficult."[9] One afternoon, a minister in Kyebi (Akyem) took me to visit three older women whom he considered neglected, one of whom had been given rice without any stew by her relatives. He told me that her family was just waiting for her to die (fieldnotes, July 11, 2014).

Other than these reports by ministers, I found it hard to find a case of outright neglect. A presbyter in Akropong told me that according to her own observation during Communion for invalids in their homes, most congregants are well taken care of; with only a few does she sense that things are not right (field-notes, June 11, 2013). A minister in Akropong recalled what he called an "extreme case," a person to whom he gave Communion at home (fieldnotes, August 5, 2019). This "extreme case" was a woman who did not have a child of her own but was taken care of by her sister's child. He "felt uneasy" listening to the way the caregiver talked to the woman. There was "no personal touch." The woman had overgrown nails, so the presbyter advised the caregiver to cut her nails. When I asked him if there were many cases like this or just a few, he responded that it is just a few who do not get care. However, he emphasized that even those with care do not obtain care that is "satisfactory" or ideal. I found his assessment com-pelling. Thus, in a way, everyone suffers some neglect.

The closest I came to seeing neglect in Akropong were two women who could no longer walk; one had children and the other did not. Both lived with kin. The first was Charlotte Odamea, aged eighty, whom I first visited with the church nurse and then several times thereafter in Akropong in August and Septem-ber 2019. The church nurse had been asked to visit Odamea by a neighbor, who was concerned about Odamea's care. Odamea had fallen four years before and never walked again. She was in great pain because of her swollen legs. Despite living with several grandchildren and great-grandchildren, including three girls aged eight to fourteen who helped their mothers with household labor, the room smelled terrible with the scent of urine and Odamea often sat alone in the squalid room. She was not being bathed regularly, which is central to a dignified person-hood in southern Ghana (Van der Geest 2002b). She was given food, as indi-cated by the dirty bowls left in her room and a cup with what looked like the remnants of Milo. They also must have helped with toileting, as there was no evidence to the contrary. Odamea slept in her chair, as she said her relatives had difficulty moving her from bed to chair and back again.

The grandchildren, mainly young women, were busy with their own labor-intensive, income-generating activities, like selling charcoal and making street food (*waakye* and *burkina*).[10] Making street food ensured that the household had access to food, which they shared with Odamea, but it was labor-intensive and did not generate much income. Although some of Odamea's children had died, three were still alive, two in Accra and one abroad. Her children visited, but did not bring much money, as the world is difficult ("*wiase yɛ den*"), explained Odamea. As usual, it seemed as if the mother Odamea accepted her children's inability to provide more care.

One of the questions I was unable to answer from my visits was why the grand-children who lived in her household ignored Odamea's needs, besides providing her with food and helping her with toileting. Perhaps it was because of their own poverty or because the grandchildren seemed to consider the children's genera-tion (their uncles) to be responsible for providing Odamea with medical care. Perhaps they considered their grandmother a witch, as some old women in other towns in the Eastern Region complained and as the play discussed in chapter 1 suggested was common. As one seventy-nine-year-old woman in Begoro said, "Even if we have children and grandchildren, they think we are witches."[11] A former minister in Akropong said there were a few cases of abandonment he heard of, but he had never encountered one directly. The ones he heard of happened with women, who were said to have an evil spirit. If the woman has children who are not progressing in life, then it was suspected that the old woman was using "wicked spirits." He concluded, "Abandonment is there, but the percentage is not high" (interview, September 13, 2019). I did not learn enough of the family history in Odamea's case to find out whether this sentiment played a role.

Why too did Odamea not receive medical care after her fall, preventing her from walking for the past four years? The decision to go to a clinic or hospital is complicated by numerous factors, including perceptions of the severity of the illness and the distribution of resources within households (Wouterse and Tankari 2015). Transportation to clinics is expensive, particularly when a taxi must be hired to drive a disabled person door to door. Medical care in Ghana is expensive, and there is reluctance to spend money on it when someone who is ill may die anyway (Van der Geest 2004a). In a study in the Accra suburb of Bortianor from 1991 to 1993, the Ghanaian anthropologist Kodjo Amedjorteh Senah (1997) discusses households' availability of funds as determining health-seeking behavior, within a context where health care is commodified and primarily means pharmaceuticals. Scarce money is more likely to be spent on children than the old, and Senah documents some older adults who refused medical treatment as a result. Toward the end of my stay, one of the sons who lived in Accra took Odamea to the hospital, where she was given an anti-inflammatory medication. Unfortunately, it had still not relieved her pain several days later, suggesting that the trip to the hospital had indeed been useless.

This was the most painful case of neglect that I witnessed, and yet it was also clear that Odamea was not abandoned outright: she lived with her grandchildren and great-grandchildren who provided her with food, but they did not bathe her, help her shift positions, or interact with her in a friendly manner. In addition, her children occasionally visited and helped inconsistently with medical care.

The second case involved Joanna. The church nurse in Akropong took me to Joanna, a seventy-three-year-old woman who could no longer walk or talk because of a stroke (see fig. 2.1 for an example of the church nurse's home visits). In June 2013, Joanna lived in a compound house with three middle-aged women: a sister by the same mother and two cousins on her paternal side. The church nurse checked Joanna's blood pressure and finding it was high, encouraged these three women to obtain some more of Joanna's blood pressure medication. They said that another sister, a retired nurse, brought medication from Accra when she visits and so they would just wait for her next visit. Joanna had previously stayed with this same sister in Accra. Joanna's care had shifted to the next oldest

FIG. 2.1 The Christchurch nurse checking a congregant's blood pressure during a home visit, June 2013.

sibling, who had returned to Akropong from her farm in Suhum at the age of fifty-one. Joanna's other siblings remitted some money to her.

The church nurse was also troubled that Joanna usually crawled to the toilet facilities across the compound. She berated them to give Joanna a chamber pot in her room and help her empty it. Surprisingly, the sister living in the house refused bluntly to do so. A discussion of Joanna's lack of children ensued. Joanna had no children of her own, but she had raised her husband's children. These step-children, now adults, visited with a small amount of remittances every three to four months. As one of the cousins said, "Pardon me for saying it, but she didn't give birth, so they bring money out of love, not force."[12] Force or duty, in this context, was considered stronger than love: the child's public reputation was at stake, and others felt empowered to remind a biological child of the obligation to care because of the gift of life from the parent, even though not all adult children were persuaded by such entreaties. After we left, the church nurse said that Joanna's care was the responsibility of the sister on the maternal side, both because Akropong families are matrilineal and because of the closeness of the relation, and if Joanna's sister would not care, then the cousins, more distant as both paternal relatives and as children of siblings, certainly would not, as they would consider it the sister's duty. One of the cousins also took care of her own mother, who lived elsewhere in Akropong. The church nurse thought that the reason they did not take Joanna to the hospital was because of transportation costs, given that they lived far down the hill from the main road and Joanna could not walk.

A year later, we visited Joanna again and found her locked in her room, while her sister had temporarily left on an errand (fieldnotes, July 18, 2014). When Joanna's sister returned, the church nurse found Joanna's blood pressure to be very high and again encouraged her sister to obtain blood pressure medication, but she responded without much interest in the topic. The church nurse told her how to apply for a free wheelchair from the church, but this also did not elicit much interest. Perhaps her kin saw Joanna as less than fully human because of her inability to walk, as Stucki (1995) reported for an old woman who crawled about in a village in the Asante Region. Possibly, Joanna's childlessness may have rendered her to be a less-than-successful adult who did not deserve respect and scarce resources from kin.

These two situations, even if they are rare, suggest that neglect even by close family is possible. Concerns about neglect by kin are what push people to explore heterodox and alterodox solutions. It is for this reason that institutional facilities seemed attractive to older Presbyterians in Kwawu and Akyem in 2014, as they co-constructed a narrative about them in group discussions.

The Attractions of Senior Institutional Facilities: A Heterodox Idea

What made nursing homes attractive in theory to the older people I talked to in Akyem? First, nursing homes were seen as places of sociability, where older people could gather to talk to one another. As noted above, older people in towns in southern Ghana often complained about living alone. Loneliness was considered a major problem for older adults, causing illness, depression, and ultimately death. A man said, "Excuse me for saying this, but I know that sadness kills people. At this time, our children have grown up and left us at home, so sometimes we are not happy and we are in financial distress."[13] Another man in the same place offered, "As somebody already said, it seems to me that staying in one place is bitter, and a person's spirit declines. Maybe someone's classmates have died, all of his contemporaries."[14] Being alone at home is associated with worrying over one's current finances and previous losses. A woman said, "Thinking [worrying] makes one sick."[15] Older people I knew well spent considerable time planning their funerals down to last detail of the songs, the cloth, and the funeral program, and thinking about what would happen to their property—whether a building or farms far away—after their death. Sociability, amusements, and moving around are the cures for this worried and worrisome kind of thinking, in distracting older adults from their problems. The New Tafo aged fellowship group, during my documentary filmmaking in August 2019, particularly highlighted the loneliness and sadness for which the fellowship group activities served as a distraction.

Second, nursing homes are associated with a cooked meal. Food is taken as the sine qua non of good care more broadly in Ghana, as is true in neighboring Togo also (Häberlein 2018). Its discussion in my interviews and the public meetings I attended signaled that many older people were seen as going hungry, a sign that they were badly cared for (see also de Jong et al. 2005). A man said, "All the time, hunger is there and it makes you worry, and this makes you very sick."[16] A woman described another man who lived alone without anyone looking after him, and therefore had difficulty getting food (group discussion, Kade, Akyem, July 12, 2014). The nurse and nurse's assistant running the aged program at Christchurch in Akropong said they had met some older adults who did not receive good care. What they meant was that they were not given a well-balanced diet, such as eating porridge without bread, or *kenkey* with hot pepper but no fish (fieldnotes, June 10, 2013).[17] Abandoned and neglected older people were viewed as eating plain cooked rice, without stew or gravy. Sjaak van der Geest (2002b) notes a similar concern with food from his research in Tafo (Kwawu) from 1994 to 2000; food was provided haphazardly by relatives and older people might have to wait long periods for food to be prepared because of the mobility and work of their relatives. Food is a symbol of good care and attention in general, and a way to index other forms of care, like cleanliness and medical attention.

Some older adults talked about losing interest in food because of loneliness. One seventy-six-year-old woman, a recent widow, lived with a grandchild who is a baker. When the daughter leaves the house to sell her pastries and loaves around town, "I am alone in the house. So as for food, I don't feel like eating because I am alone and so this is my small sadness."[18] A man said, "Sometimes, at the time when they should bring you food, they have gone to work or to farm and haven't come home quickly, so when they come they cook food and I won't eat it [because it is too late in the day to eat]."[19] The rejection or loss of interest in food puts pressure on the caregiver, who will face public criticism for the older adult's physical weakness as a result of poor eating.

Third, nursing homes are associated with free medical attention with a nurse on site, although the imagined medical care was often preventative, like checking blood pressure or blood sugar levels, rather than more intensive nursing care or technology-reliant tests (e.g., X-rays). This type of preventative medicine was provided in the aged programs of the Presbyterian Church, which serves as a model for a senior residential facility. Older adults can spend much of their time and energy seeking health care, waiting in decrepit waiting rooms in hospitals and clinics where they are treated harshly and disrespectfully by arrogant medical authorities, in their opinion. Access to health care is a long-standing problem: in a master's thesis (Ani 2002) from before the implementation of the national health insurance program, a change in policy making those over the age of seventy exempt from health fees did not affect the health-seeking behavior of older adults, except those over eighty. Abena Asamoabea Ani (2002) posits that one reason is because drugs were excluded from the exemption. The national health insurance scheme (NHIS), instituted in 2007, has an annual premium; as a result, it has not helped the poor, as they have trouble paying even this small premium (Kotoh and Van der Geest 2016). Currently 500,000 Ghanaians over the age of seventy have been exempted from the premium (Takyi-Boadu 2018).[20] However, the cost and ease of transportation to medical facilities remain obstacles to older adults' medical treatment. In 2018, the government promised to soon introduce a "Freedom Pass" that would give older adults priority access to transport and health (Takyi-Boadu 2018), although I heard no more about this plan since.

Furthermore, not all medications and lab tests are covered by the national health insurance program. A woman in Begoro said, "If you go to the hospital, they say buy medicine. What money will we use to buy medicine? We don't have it."[21] Another woman in Begoro said, "Maybe you have one cedi, and medicine costs ten cedis [about $3 at the time]. What will you do to get the remaining nine cedis to make ten cedis? If you don't get it, you stay at home. It means that if you go to the hospital, it is useless."[22] A woman in Begoro also talked about a time when she was sick with typhoid. None of her children was with her because they lived in Accra and Kumasi. Although she went to the hospital, she did not have money to buy medication, so she went home without any medicine. She looked after herself during that time of sickness. Although her children send her money, it is never enough (group discussion, July 9, 2014). One doctor in Koforidua, admittedly in a private hospital with more expensive care and which did not accept the national health insurance, told me that he sees very few aged people among his patients because they cannot afford to buy medicine (fieldnotes, August 24, 2019). These comments were supported by national surveys. A national survey of five thousand households with older adults found that the average out-of-pocket household spending on medical care was 6.4 percent of total household monthly expenditure and 14.7 percent of discretionary spending (Biritwum et al. 2013). Poor households reduced their health spending and did not receive care when they needed it (Biritwum et al. 2013). As a manager for the Osu senior day center run by HelpAge expressed succinctly, "Free NHIS has not solved the issues" of health care for aging adults (fieldnotes, June 18, 2014).

As a result of these complaints about hospitals, some people in conversations at Kade and Begoro proposed that senior citizens should be treated first in hospitals or that a special hospital for the aged should be opened. A retired teacher in Begoro said, "Here, if you go to the hospital, they tell you your problem is old age so they only give you paracetamol [a pain reliever] and you go home."[23] He recommended a hospital be opened just for older adults. A man in Kade made the suggestion in this way: "Something else is that our hospital makes you wait, so that you don't want to go there. Because you will take a long time, so that by the time you come home, you are tired. So it means that many times when you are sick, you stay at home. . . . I believe that many do this, and die as a result. So

I would ask the government to give preference to older people. So that when we reach there, we are immediately seen."[24] A woman, also in Kade, said, "We need money; we need a lot of money in our old age. If you worked for the government and retired, and are at home, once you reach the age of seventy and above, your life is pitiful indeed. You are weak all the time. If you lie down, you can't get up, unless someone comes to ask, 'Grandmother, how are you?' So we are pitiful; we need medicine to become stronger. Even if you can't go to the hospital, if you have money, you can buy medicine from home and little by little it will help you."[25] Indeed, as the example of Charlotte Odamea above shows, visiting the hospital, despite its considerable effort and expense, does not necessarily result in relief of pain or other symptoms.

These concerns about hospital care result in older people's avoidance of hospitals and clinics; instead, they rely on a variety of cheaper and more convenient herbal medicines at home, which do not require transportation. Many older adults whom I visited in Akropong had a special practice or medicine they praised and relied on, and which they shared eagerly with others. Mr. Opoku practiced "oil pulling" in which he swirled ordinary vegetable oil around in his mouth and spit it out, which he said protected him against diabetes and cancer (fieldnotes, May 31, 2018). Another man in his nineties recommended an herbal medicine called "Black Seed" and gave me a bottle to share with the other older people he knew I was visiting (fieldnotes, June 22, 2013).

In addition to the concerns about health care, institutional spaces were familiar. Educated older men made the analogy to schools. Many secondary schools in Ghana are boarding facilities, and while they are associated with physical discomfort, strict teachers, and heavily scheduled days, they also generate deep, lifelong friendships because of the intensity of sharing daily life over several years. Social networks formed in boarding schools enable alumni to navigate bureaucratic and business environments in adulthood. One man spoke about nursing homes in this way: "If we had a place like abroad when you grow old and no one lives with you, you could go live there, like a school where they sent you, where there are doctors, and they cook you food; everything! You will meet your classmate, and it makes you happy, and it will make you live long. That kind of place is not in Ghana or our region, so that is our problem."[26] Thus, previous experiences with institutions like schools, particularly for educated men, meant that they saw nursing homes as having the potential for intense sociality and friendship within a peer group.

Finally, these spaces were taken as a symbol that a society cared for its senior citizens. The foreignness of the institution was taken to critique the Ghanaian state as deficient on the world stage. The presence of nursing homes as an institution for older adults in Western countries was interpreted as a sign that these societies recognize and have not forgotten their aging citizens. One nursing agency owner in Accra commented on a trip to Denmark, where she observed senior citizens living together in a residential facility: "Society was giving back to the elderly people because of the sacrifices they had made for the nation" (field-notes, July 18, 2018). Older people in Akyem interpreted residential facilities similarly. For example, one man said, "This government [here in Ghana] has the idea that older people do not matter. No one helps you."[27] A man shared, "Pardon me for saying this, but the government doesn't see our pain [or, is not compassionate toward us]."[28] A retired social worker said, "In Ghana we don't have a system for helping older people. If someone ages, we leave them there."[29] A woman asked me "to build a building for them to meet in. Or for older women who can't do anything; we could live in it."[30] In my conversations, just as Egyptians formed a critique of the state around their failing kidneys and experience of dialysis centers (Hamdy 2008), senior residential facilities functioned as a tool of political critique and advocacy to highlight older people's plight in Ghana. Older persons were concerned about their low status in society that they felt contributed to their neglect and abandonment by their children, by their church to which they had contributed over the years, and by the state. A woman said, "The church doesn't think of us; even when we always come, they don't think of us. The ministers themselves, whose salaries we pay, don't think of us."[31] Men seemed particularly critical of the state. Advocating for institutional facilities was a way to make that complaint stronger by showing that other societies respected their senior citizens by building them facilities in which to live and rest. Senior residential facilities were seen as their right given their previous contributions to society. If children were not going to step up, then perhaps the state and the church would. Thus, residential facilities in Ghana became a symbol of dignity and respect, which they felt they lacked in society at large. In contrast, in the West the nursing home is presented as a "symbol of cultural failure and a fate worse than death" in popular culture representations because of the loss of autonomy and independence it signifies (Chivers 2015, 134).

Thus, when asked what they would like to have happen, in public forums organized by the church, such as the ones I attended in Akyem, senior residential facilities were one of the solutions articulated. Sjaak van der Geest (2016) similarly noted an openness to senior care homes in his discussions with older people in Kwawu, where he has long done research. In contrast, middle-aged Ghanaians expressed much less interest in these initiatives, although some who were concerned about their aging relatives mentioned them. For example, the Kwawu Presbytery minister discussed his own family concerns that led to his interest in nursing homes. His sister had been transferred by her work to Wenchi (in the Bono Region), resulting in a loss of support for his mother who now lives with his nephew and his wife, with two adolescents, in Kumasi. Although she is healthy at the age of eighty-three, she is getting weaker. If they could find a residential facility for her, he said that they would use it. In fact, he was thinking of opening one in his station in Kwawu (fieldnotes, July 25, 2014). However, the most common response from middle-aged respondents to my research was similar to that made by a middle-aged caterer in Akropong. She told me that the family system takes care of the elderly, so there is no problem. Families do not want to move older adults from their homes, so a daughter will move in to care for the older adult (fieldnotes, June 4, 2013).

In general, in these discussions about senior facilities, there was some lack of distinction between nursing homes, where they would live, and senior day centers, where they might go for the day for food, companionship, and medical attention while younger members of their households were away at work or school. Interestingly, older adults were not concerned about institutional facilities as a response to physical frailty, disability, or a serious illness, but rather as a response to social abandonment and neglect by their families and the state. Similar to aged persons in Burkina Faso (Roth 2014), insecurity in aging by these older Presbyterians in Ghana was perceived as a social problem, not a physical one. Perhaps it is too emotionally difficult to imagine a future of debility, like that experienced by Odamea or Joanna. Their openness to institutional forms of care, which did not exist in the communities around them, highlights their concerns about abandonment, their positive experiences of institutional residence in the past, and their general knowledge that senior homes exist elsewhere rather than a specific and informed knowledge of what they are like in practice. Thus, they adapted senior residential facilities in their imaginations to look like secondary schools and to meet their needs for food, sociability, routine medical care, and recognition.

Because of the concerns for getting money for health care as they aged, another, less prominent idea that emerged from these discussions was a focus on providing for oneself through savings or insurance, as a supplement to what children could provide. A woman articulated this perspective the most forcefully:

> When we were strong, we should have made an investment to look after ourselves. But instead we used our money to live our life. We forgot we would grow old and we would reach a time when our bodies would shake [with tremors] and we can't work. So we should look after ourselves so that we can depend on that later. . . . And there is no small child to live with an older person to look after him, so you should look after yourselves well and put something aside, so you can depend on that in your old age. Depending on your grandchild or child is a burden.[32]

Another man made a similar argument that one should plan for "retirement" by building a house so that one did not have to depend on children who had scattered across the country and could not necessarily help an older person (group discussion, Asamankese, Akyem, July 12, 2014). A minister in the same congregation was organizing workshops on retirement planning (fieldnotes, July 12, 2014). Savings has historically not made much sense in Ghana because of high inflation, whereas an investment in building a house is more stable. Pensions in Ghana, pegged to a previous salary that has been made into a pittance through inflation over decades, are often small and inadequate. Furthermore, 80 percent of workers work in the informal sector and generally do not contribute to pensions (Dovie 2018). A range of financial products, including life insurance, are increasingly being marketed in many African countries like South Africa and Eswatini, indicating the financialization of the Global South and the reworking of kinship relations through insurance (Bähre 2012; Golomski 2015; Kar 2018). A master's-level study in Ghana in 1998 found that 26 percent of pensioners (that is, retired civil servants) had undertaken investments or savings alongside their pensions (Nelson-Cofie 1998). Although insurance was initially marketed only to the wealthy and to middle-class civil servants in sub-Saharan Africa, it has become increasingly available to the poor. Yet retirement planning through commercial financial products remains a minority experience in Ghana, most prominent among the educated, urban middle class. Most commonly, retirement planning is actualized in Ghana by building a house (Van der Geest 1998).

Alongside the discourses of critique of the next generation presented in the previous chapter, there was a willingness to experiment and engage imaginatively with different possible futures, including ones that were perceived as foreign or even antithetical to Ghanaian ways of life. Nursing homes loomed large in the imagination but were relatively unknown in the rural towns of Ghana. Financial forms of social security were also being discussed. Used mainly by former civil servants, these were increasingly marketed to more ordinary Ghanaians.

Conclusion

Given government policy and NGO advocacy against nursing homes, it is surprising that older Ghanaians find them attractive. The social imagination can play an important role in generating social change in aging and care practices. Even when the images of residential facilities seemed quite fantastical and unreal, they can prompt new initiatives that create quite different realities, and they mobilize a critique of the state and the church. To my knowledge, there are currently three senior residential facilities operating in Ghana: two in the capital Accra and one on its far outskirts. They are small by American standards; the largest has twenty-seven residents. They generally do not provide medical care on site, and older adults there also express dissatisfaction with the food as well as with the sleeping and bathing routines. Despite the small number of institutional facilities that are operating in Ghana and their difficulties with financial viability, they are floated as an imagined or potential solution among those concerned about older adults. For example, some owners of home nursing agencies, along with the manager of the St. Vincent de Paul Center in Accra-Tema and the district minister of the Kwahu Presbytery of the Presbyterian Church of Ghana, expressed their eagerness to build residential facilities. (I will discuss the residential facilities in Accra further in chapter 5.)

The nursing homes operating in Ghana are not known to the older people I spoke to in Akyem, nor have these older adults visited them. Instead, they imagine nursing homes operating in other countries, namely in Europe and North America. They do not seem to be influenced by Ghanaian migrants in the United Kingdom and United States who work in these kinds of facilities abroad and whose representations of these care environments tend to be quite critical and even horrific (Coe 2017). Thus, Presbyterian congregants' knowledge of nursing homes arises within the context of highly general discourses in Ghana in which, loosely, "We take care of our own older people, unlike you [foreigners] who put your older adults in a nursing home." Nursing homes were discursively set up by the government and advocacy groups as the heterodox position to the orthodoxy of kin care, without concrete representations of what they are actually like. In the absence of direct experience, this heterodox position is therefore available for aging persons to reimagine.

The resources for care-inscriptions include representations from societies constructed as Other and different, as illustrated in the interest in senior institutional facilities. Knowledge of other societies' aging trajectories can be used to harden national boundaries and cultural identities (Amselle 2002). Even when negatively evaluated through contrasting dichotomies, as in "we do things this way and they do it that way" or "this is traditional and that is modern," such dichotomies can introduce heterodoxies that can become incorporated as possible solutions when "the way that we do things" or an orthodoxy no longer seems to be viable or reliable. Globalization allows ideas and institutions to travel and become modular. NGOs like HelpAge that have promoted this dichotomy have encouraged these ideals to travel, and not only in one direction (Grimm 2016). Discussing how cultural and technological models travel, Behrends, Park, and Rottenburg (2014) focus on the importance of the token, which represents a particular social order and set of arrangements. For a particular model to travel, the token has to be adapted to mean something significant in the new context because it lacks the institutions and social networks that support that model in the original context. "While the token enters into a new setting with a different ontological and epistemic background, a different institutional set-up and technological infrastructure, it needs to adapt to these new circumstances in order to connect to them. So the first thing that changes is the traveling token" (Behrends, Park, and Rottenburg 2014, 3). Nursing homes thus function as a traveling token of senior care. Similarly, Manu Goswami (2002) critiques Benedict Anderson's concept of nationalism—as a traveling token—being imitated around the world. Similar to Behrends, Park, and Rottenburg (2014), she considers that "the transposition of strategies, cultural schemas, and social resources through their initial contexts of production to new and diverse arenas occurs through the creative capacities of social actors and entails a dynamic process of the reconfiguration of social structures" (2002, 784–5). Sarah Lamb illustrates this transposition in her research on aging in India. The idea of institutional facilities for aging adults traveled to India, despite representing "alien, Western-inspired institutions" (2016, 183). These facilities have been adapted to local contexts, becoming equivalent to ashrams, where older adults can withdraw from the bustling world to focus on their spiritual development, or to joint family households, with a middle-aged couple taking into their home a small number of older adults for extra income and calling them grandparents as if they were family members. However, over time, institutional facilities in India have become larger and serve the elite (Mayer 2017).

In southern Ghana, older Presbyterians' interest in care institutions is predicated on the fact that they have not directly experienced such institutions but have only heard that they are common in the West. Senior residential facilities can function in this way only because they *are* strange and not experienced or known. They are still only at the discursive level, without a framework that naturalizes them. They are only a token of a model of care, which is transformed in older Ghanaians' imagination to address their particular needs. Thus, they imagine these institutions as promoting their goals for a comfortable and happy old age, in which food, medical care, friendship, and public recognition are highly significant.

Older Ghanaians express interest in institutions that they see as common in the West as a sign that the state, the church, or outside benefactors might make up for their children's failures in caring for them. In other words, they use the foreign figure of a senior care home to advocate for their well-being within the local social and political context. They seem particularly interested in the symbolism of residential institutions, as a sign of a community's care for older persons and of their importance, and not as a practical solution to disability in the failure of kin care. By using residential institutions to lament their current condition, they propose a particular ideal community, which takes care of those who have contributed to it in the past and thus might replace kin. The use of senior residential facilities to think through the problems of aging means that older persons situate themselves—and Ghana—within a "global horizon" of value and orientation, and not simply within a social field of kin (Graw and Schielke 2012). Within this wider horizon of the social field of nations, Ghana is positioned as failing; other nations are used by older Presbyterians to criticize the inadequate efforts of the Ghanaian government to care for them. In practice, however, older adults in Ghana do not exercise much political influence in Ghana, unlike their counterparts in the United States who have a powerful lobbying group in the AARP and mobilize around the protection of Social Security.

The age inscriptions being generated in Ghana—including the transformation of a heterodoxy into a possible solution—signal the agency of older persons, which is often neglected and overlooked (Cole 2013). Encountering new problems as they age, older Ghanaians reimagine what a period of aging might be like. For some, it might become a return to the Eden encountered in adolescence in a boarding secondary school. For aging Ghanaians, the heterodox becomes an important hook on which they can hang their dreams of a happy old age. It is unclear where such dreams will take them or Ghana as a whole.

3

Alterodox Practices
of Elder Care

• •

Domestic Service
and Neighborliness

Not all alternative discourses and practices, or inscriptions, are heterodox, seen as a direct opposition to the orthodoxy. Instead, some of these discourses and practices are simply alternatives to the orthodoxy, or *alterodoxies*. Options can be discussed, but not practiced; new practices can emerge, but not be discussed or debated. In addition to the heterodox discourses of the previous chapter are a range of alterodox practices that were not discussed but were becoming more common in the rural towns of the Eastern Region. The most prominent was the adaptation of existing practices of domestic service and child fosterage for the purposes of elder care, in which adult children pay for care and supervise it (as care managers), perhaps from a distance, but do not provide it directly themselves. Instead, poorer, more rural, and more distant relatives or unrelated middle-aged women provide care to older people who usually remain in their own households in the hometowns. This strategy exploited existing inequalities and generated new inequalities between differently positioned persons within households; elder care contributed to new manifestations of social class. Although some young people moved on from domestic service, others were becoming permanently stuck in it. Although most visible in the cities, where domestic service has been more established and greater discrepancies in social and economic status exist, it is present in the rural towns of the Eastern Region also.

Paid care relied on the financial support of adult migrant children, who could send remittances to pay for such care, and thus was not available for those adult children who could not afford to send much in the way of remittances to their mother or father. It allowed children of older people to maintain their sense of self-worth in that they could say they were caring for their parents by helping them financially; their parents also felt able to discuss their children's support proudly. It also meant that the grandchildren of these older persons did not have to sacrifice their schooling, seen as critical for their own futures, because they could remain with their parents in the urban areas. Thus, this alterodox practice was not only seen as compatible to kin care, but actually supported the orthodoxy of kin care because adult children were viewed as caring for their parents by paying for their care by others.

In addition, other alterodox practices were emerging: older women moved to live with their migrant daughters, rather than migrant daughters returning to the hometown to live with them. Neighbors filled in gaps in daughterly care. These alterodox practices are more amenable than institutional facilities to social norms that children provide care to reciprocate the care given to them as children. It seems likely that alterodox practices will become more widespread than the heterodox of residential facilities discussed in the previous chapter: one age inscription may become a social norm and another may wither away or be used only as a mechanism to critique the state for its neglect of older adults.

Elder Care through Child Fosterage

Although institutional facilities and other ideas like investing in retirement were discussed speculatively and as a form of critique in my fieldwork, what busy adult children seemed to be actually doing, but not talking about, was using fostered adolescents or domestic servants. Those daughters who are reluctant to return to the hometown and who have the economic or social means to recruit someone else to fill the care slot found a substitute for themselves. Fostering has long been common in southern Ghana, particularly among children over the age of ten for the purpose of their education, training, and discipline. Children were often sent to live with an educated professional—a nurse or teacher—who lived in an urban environment. This was viewed as benefitting them as well as the household to which they contributed their labor (Coe 2013b).

Fostering out one's own children is becoming increasingly antithetical to the middle class and to those who aspire to be middle class in Ghana, although they are amenable to having a child fostered into their own households for assistance with chores (Coe 2013b). As Erdmute Alber (2011) found in Benin, the rural-urban exchange of children has become unidirectional. Whereas previously children moved in both directions, urban middle-class people tend to no longer give their children to kin, although they continue to accept the children of poorer kin into their households. The movement is as much about differences in social class as geographic: children move from poorer to richer households, which are normally located in cities.

Generally female, fostered adolescents are kin who have been taken into the household and are providing domestic service in exchange for some promised support in the future such as apprenticeship into a trade like sewing and hairdressing or current support for school fees (Goody 1982; Sanjek 1990). Fosterage relationships are becoming more commercialized, particularly in urban areas. From the 1960s onward in Accra, non-kin or more distant kin have replaced nieces and nephews as foster children and have been treated more like domestic servants, sleeping and eating separately from children of the household, and are more liable to be exploited or abused than kin foster children (Ardayfio-Schandorf and Amissah 1996; Oppong 1974; for a discussion of a similar process in Benin and Cameroon, respectively, see Alber 2013 and Argenti 2010). Furthermore, with the expansion of free education in Ghana, first to the end of basic education (nine years of schooling) in 1996 (with actual enforcement in 2005) and then to the end of secondary school (twelve years of schooling) in 2017, it has become more expected for all children to continue their schooling, making fewer children available to foster. During the 2000s, the age of most domestic servants rose to late adolescence (fifteen-plus years, after the completion of basic education) and young adulthood. These older domestic servants expect more, particularly in requesting monthly pay rather than a bulk reward like a sewing machine at the end of their service. I met a number of young women from Akropong who had worked as domestic servants for distant kin and non-kin in Accra and Cape Coast while they were in their late teens and early twenties. Although officially schooling is free, the incidental costs of schooling and child raising continue to make the out-fosterage of children somewhat attractive for poor parents.

The practice of fosterage is thus a fully developed norm, with participants aware of the "rules of the game," such as knowing to pay adolescents' school fees in exchange for their labor. What makes it an alterodox age inscription is its adaptation to elder care. Fostering is not articulated as a narrative about how to help older adults, but it is enacted in practice as a way to provide care for them. Because adult daughters living in the cities have competing responsibilities, and because they have access to cash, they may delegate the work of daily elder care to paid labor, whether an adult woman or an adolescent girl. Thus, the focus on the responsibility of adult children to send remittances, as illustrated by the play in chapter 1, obscures the daily care labor of extended kin, fostered adolescents, and domestic servants. Adult children support such care financially by paying the wages, incidental school costs, or apprenticeship of the fostered child or domestic servant. They also manage medical crises, but generally the day-to-day care is in the hands of the girl or woman living in or near the household with the older person. In China, a similar dynamic of using domestic servants is emerging, despite an ideal of kin care by adult children (Wang and Wu 2016; World Health Organization 2015).

I encountered the household of Mama Adelaide during a survey I conducted of child fosterage in Akropong in 2008. Mama Adelaide was a seventy-eight-year-old woman who could not walk easily. She was living with Esther, the fifteen-year-old great-granddaughter of Mama Adelaide's maternal uncle (*wɔfa*). In exchange for her domestic care, Esther's junior secondary school costs were paid by Mama Adelaide's four adult children who all resided in Accra with their own children. Mama Adelaide's children worked in a range of occupations, with varying status, educational levels, and income: one son owned a beer hall, the second installed car alarms, and the two daughters worked as a nurse and a trader, respectively. Esther had come to live with Mama Adelaide from a village near Suhum, where her father grew cocoa and she had gone to primary school. In Akropong, in Mama Adelaide's household, after school each day, Esther went to the market and cooked the main meal. During my interview with Mama Adelaide one morning during the school holidays, Esther was washing clothes in the courtyard.

When Mama Adelaide had been in her fifties, she had returned to Akropong to look after her mother's sister, a former seamstress and matrilineal kin, for eight years, before the older woman died at the age of eighty-two. She thus conformed to the social norms of kin care discussed in chapter 1. The reasons that brought Mama Adelaide back to her hometown did not have the same significance for her migrant daughters or sisters' children, given the changing intergenerational entrustments. While living in Akropong, Mama Adelaide had farmed a small plot of land, but a year ago she had become too weak to do so. At that point, her children realized that she needed help and recruited Esther. Mama Adelaide framed this decision as her children's, indicating her pride in the fact that they took responsibility for her care.

I was not able to speak to Mama Adelaide's children about why they did not come to live with their mother or send one of their own children to live with her in Akropong. However, other older women in Akropong told me that they did not expect their children or their grandchildren to come to live with them to help run the household and provide daily care. For example, one vigorous woman in her sixties who made money trading in yams (and a paternal cousin of Joanna discussed in chapter 2) anticipated that her children in Accra would not return home to take care of her but instead would pay for another woman to help her, a situation to which she seemed resigned. Her yam marketing involved hiring a truck with other women and going to farms in northern Ghana to buy yams to sell in the town, so perhaps, given the strength and energy this activity entailed, thoughts of future frailty seemed a bit hypothetical (fieldnotes, June 20, 2013). This concern is long-standing: many older women in a cocoa-growing area of the Asante region in 1990–1991 also were anxious that any children would live with them in their old age because of the prevalence of education and urban migration (Stucki 1995).

Another older woman, seventy-three years old and a retired teacher in Begoro, Akyem, had retired from work early to care for her sick husband, who had subsequently passed away. She also did not expect her adult children, who had all traveled, to come home to take care of her. Instead, they had found a non-kin child (*obi ba*) from a village (*akuraa bi*) to stay with her, while the adolescent boy went to day secondary school in Begoro, for which she paid his tuition, a substantial sum at the time in 2014. She anticipated that when the boy received the results from the secondary school exam, he would leave her, and she and her children would have to find another boy to stay with her. He primarily helped her with domestic chores and with a small farm behind her house (group discussion, July 9, 2014).

Although they are in a minority, boys do serve as foster children. Mr. Opoku, a widower and friend of mine, a retired principal now in his late eighties and generally in good health, lived in a decaying house on the outskirts of Akropong with an adolescent boy named Kwame. Kwame heated Mr. Opoku's food, which was sometimes brought by well-wishers and friends, but did not cook anything besides instant ramen noodles. Kwame fetched and heated water for Mr. Opoku to bathe, and ran errands for him. Although Kwame did these tasks as asked, he did them with bad grace, perhaps because they went against the role and status of the adult man that he was aspiring to become. Mr. Opoku did not receive much kin care because he had had no children with his wife and had not taken care of his only child, with another woman outside of his marriage. He had also not fostered any of his own kin's children, despite being a teacher and principal, a preferred foster parent. Instead, his wife's siblings' children had been fostered in his household. He also refused to remarry, out of his devotion to his widow. As a result, Mr. Opoku could obtain care only through love, not obligation, like Joanna in chapter 2, and love was less desirable because it was less reliable. Although Mr. Opoku's foster daughters were concerned about his well-being, they were busy with their careers and children in Accra and abroad and were closer to their deceased mother's family, including their wealthy maternal uncle, than to Mr. Opoku and his family. Instead of directing his complaints toward them, Mr. Opoku complained about Ghana, saying that his country did not treat the elderly well. To all who listened, he said they should have social workers as they do in Britain to visit older people and see how they are doing (fieldnotes, August 31, 2019). From his position as a retired civil servant, with a previously high position, he felt entitled to critique the government, using other countries' imagined elder care practices as the whip to do so, like older adults discussing residential facilities in chapter 2.

In addition to being the sole caregiver of an older person, foster children also supplement the care of adult daughters. I regularly visited a blind woman named Mercy Amankwah in Akropong. From 2013 to 2019, when she was eighty-three to eighty-nine years old, she lived with her son; a younger brother (both men were in their sixties); a daughter; a grandson of the brother, age eleven; and a fostered adolescent girl, age eighteen. A former nurse, Aunty Mercy had taken care of all six of her siblings in their childhood and youth. Her younger brother said that she had fostered him when he was fourteen or fifteen, taking him into her house and paying for his schooling; therefore, he wanted to take care of her now. Aunty Mercy had returned to Akropong from Accra some years ago to care for her own older sister, who died after a short illness. In Accra, she had lived with cousins in the floor above her, but they went out during the day, leaving her alone. So she said she was happier in Akropong than in Accra. By all means, one has to come home, she said, showing support for the expected migration pattern of older women discussed in chapter 1 (fieldnotes, June 24, 2013). The fostered adolescent Gina had first been fostered by Aunty Mercy's sister in Accra until Gina was six years old, when the sister died, and Gina came to live in Akropong. All members of the household participated in Aunty Mercy's care to some extent in 2019, when she could no longer walk. Gina bathed her in the morning; her grandson checked her blood pressure daily; her daughter did the laundry; and her brother helped sort out her life insurance papers, which entailed trips to Accra. Gina also helped the daughter run a small provision shop in front of the house and attended a day secondary school in town. Kin care from siblings, children, and grandchildren thus dominated in Aunty Mercy's care, but Gina did the most difficult work of bathing her in the morning, when Aunty Mercy, usually gentle and sweet, complained angrily that she was an old woman and that Gina did not pamper (krɔkrɔ) her enough (fieldnotes, August 9, 2019). Aunty Mercy was well taken care of by this combination of persons, although she occasionally quarreled with her daughter and her brother refused to take her to the hospital for physical therapy for her arm because of the trouble of transporting her there three days a week. Living in her hometown, Aunty Mercy received visitors among relatives on weekends when there are funerals in town (as I witnessed in 2013) and from neighboring children, age two and five (as I witnessed in 2019).

Another adaptation of fosterage was exhibited by a recently retired nurse who had built an impressive house in her hometown of Adukrom, the next large town up the road from Akropong. She lived with her husband, a private school teacher; one of her siblings' children (a man in his thirties); and her aging mother. The nurse's own children and grandchildren were all abroad in South Africa and the United States. When the nurse moved her mother, now ninety-seven years old, from Koforidua to live with her six years before, she had taken in a young woman named Susana who lived near Kumasi to help take care of her mother. Susana at twenty-eight years old was short and thin, looking like a teenager ten or fifteen years younger, as if she had been malnourished as a child. Susana called the retired nurse her mother, as the nurse was a distant relative of her father, but the nurse denied any kin relationship. The nurse's mother, for whom Susana cared, lived in a bedroom on the first floor, somewhat isolated from the rest of the household members, who lived on the second floor of the house. The nurse's mother could not walk because of a fracture she had suffered, and she was frail and thin. She also had dementia, the nurse told me matter-of-factly, commenting that her mother did not know if it was day or night. When the nurse had been studying in the United States, her mother had taken care of her three children, although the nurse had been dissatisfied with the level of care given to them. The nurse's husband told me that his mother-in-law was difficult to care for, shouting at her caregivers, and he wondered if Susana was losing patience with her.

Many fostered adolescents are compensated for their services by their employer paying for an apprenticeship, most typically dressmaking or hairdressing. In this case, the retired nurse sent Susana to a nursing assistant school in Adenta, on the outskirts of Accra, run by her friend (see chapter 6), as a kind of apprenticeship, which is where I met Susana in May 2015. I later visited the family in Adukrom in July 2015 and December 2016. The nurse explained that she wanted Susana to learn how to take good care of her mother. From Susana's perspective, home care served as vocational training to compensate her for her services as a foster child. While Susana was in school during the day, another relative of the nurse, a middle-aged woman, helped out, but it was a hardship for everyone, reported the nurse's husband. The nurse's husband worried that Susana was delaying her own proper life course progression while she was helping them and that she might soon want to marry, as her sisters in Kumasi were doing. Thus, he was afraid that she was becoming permanently trapped in a position associated with adolescence.

Domestic service is usually seen as a stage in the life course appropriate for childhood and adolescence. Doing such work is part of what propels young people into successful adulthood, not only by inculcating diligence and persistence, but also by resulting in the gratitude of older adults who can reward such hard work. However, as I discuss in the next section, women at different stages of the life course are now entering domestic service, and for a few, it may become a career, signaling a hardening of class divisions in contemporary Ghana. In some ways, too, as they have aged, domestic servants have gained greater rights and negotiating power in the past few decades, although they are usually positioned as socially "junior" in age, no matter their biological age, to household members. For multiple reasons, foster children are becoming replaced by adult caregivers and paid a monthly wage.

The Hired Caregiver

When I was first introduced to Mary Kwatia, age fifty-five, in Akropong, she told me that she took care of her seventy-seven-year-old mother and two-year-old granddaughter, fitting the portrait of an adult daughter kin-scripted to fill the care slot, as discussed in chapter 1. Although her mother walked with a back bent deeply by scoliosis, she seemed capable of taking care of herself, as I saw her lighting a charcoal fire and fetching small buckets of water. Like Yaa Ofosua from chapter 1, Kwatia was quite unhappy with the situation, complaining that neither her brothers nor her adult children sent her enough money, and saying she would like to go to Kumasi, a large city, to start a business. When I wondered aloud how Kwatia actually survived on the remittances she said she was receiving, she told me that she had also worked as a caregiver for older people for the past seven years. She was currently taking care of a neighbor, a former trader who had had a stroke and lived with her mentally incapacitated middle-aged daughter and adult grandson. The trader's other two children, a daughter who taught in a private school in Accra and a son in Koforidua, sent money to pay Kwatia to bathe and feed both their mother and their disabled sister. Thus, Kwatia fulfilled the orthodoxy of kin care. She provided daily care to her mother and grandchild, but because of the paucity of remittances from her kin and the difficulties trading in her income-impoverished hometown, she supported herself through paid caregiving for a neighboring family, an alterodox practice.

In a context in which daughters have historically been responsible for the daily care provision of aging relatives, and sons for financially supporting their sisters and mothers, daughters of older people are hiring more vulnerable women to provide care in their place; they can be good daughters by being care managers, rather than care providers. A retired primary school headmistress, disabled by unmanaged diabetes, told me that all her friends in Akropong were hiring women to care for them (fieldnotes, January 2017). A member of the Presbyterian Church's aged committee in Akropong said similarly that she knew an older person in Akropong who was bedridden and whose relatives were all in Kumasi. The relatives can pay for someone to sleep in the room, or to come in the morning to do the household chores and then leave in the evening (interview, June 6, 2013). An older man in his nineties had been taken care of by a paid caregiver, a young woman, but she left abruptly once his daughter (in her sixties, and the least successful among her siblings) arrived to help out. In order to remain with her father in Akropong, the daughter had to leave behind, in Accra, the three-year-old grandchild she was carrying for, whose mother lived in the United Kingdom (fieldnotes, June 10, 2013).

In August 2019, I talked to four women in Akropong, ranging in age from their forties to their sixties, who seem to have fallen into a career of paid caregiving. Some supplemented the care of daughters and other extended kin, who also lived in Akropong, but others were the primary caregivers of their older wards, whose adult children lived and worked in other cities or towns. None were constructed as kin members, although some wished that they were treated less like employees. Some care workers mentioned the stigma of doing domestic work, and they all mentioned its difficulty. They felt that the work constructed them as social inferiors, as domestic servants, not only within the households in which they worked, but also within the community at large, because of the nature of the work and their status as adult women, and they actively resisted such downgrading. Furthermore, they did not feel that they were adequately compensated for the work, whether in terms of pay or respect.

One paid caregiver had been working alongside her patient's daughter for four years, and there was a lot of trust between them. The daughter slept with her mother, who had many nights of sleeplessness, leading the daughter to lose sleep also. The paid caregiver usually cooked and cleaned for the older woman during the day, but sometimes she minded the daughter's shop on the main road. Despite what seemed like a happy situation for all, the paid caregiver was unhappy with the job, feeling that it paid too little; she was waiting for another job to come her way, although she was not actively looking.

Another paid caregiver was Mary Kwatia, mentioned above. Kwatia was a neighbor to a bedridden older woman, a former trader, whose children lived and worked in Accra and Koforidua. Kwatia fed, bathed, and dressed the older woman when she came by twice a day. When she did so, as I observed, she spoke sharply to her, pulled her arms when she dressed her, and did not attend carefully to her bedsores. She complained to me about her treatment from the patient's daughter Abena. She said that because Abena was paying her wages, Abena never said thank you or gave her gifts. Kwatia remembered taking care of another man previously, and his son brought her cloth, a watch, a bag of jewelry, and other things, as appreciation for helping his father. The week before, when Abena was staying in the house because her mother was in and out of the hospital, Abena complained that Kwatia treated the mother roughly. Kwatia felt that this rebuke was uncalled for, when she was doing work that Abena as the daughter could not do. As a sign of Abena's dependence on her, she said, once Kwatia traveled to Kumasi, and after two days Abena was begging her to come back. Although the work is very difficult, she does not feel appreciated (fieldnotes, September 5, 2019). When I spoke to Abena, I learned that this was the fourth caregiver that the family had hired, and Kwatia had been with them a year. Abena had felt that her redirection of Kwatia had made her more gentle with her mother and she was generally satisfied with her. Abena felt very grateful to her mother because she had fostered her eighteen-month-old grandchild for two or three years, which allowed Abena to finish teacher-training college and thus allowed her to become a professional and more well-paid teacher. Abena was raising her three adolescent children in Accra as a single mother and was clearly stretched thin between her different roles as mother; teacher in a private, reputable school that did not give her much time off; and caregiver to her mother during this period of crisis, when her mother had just left the hospital.

A third caregiver, Esi, aged fifty-two, had taken care of a bedridden man from Akropong living in Kumasi for two years. She then returned to Akropong to take care of her sick husband, who died in the past year. At the time I spoke to her, Esi was taking care of a very old, bedridden, and obese woman, who lived with a distant kin member in her sixties or seventies but whose care was supplemented by a roster of paid caregivers because it was so difficult to lift and turn her. Esi had pride in her work, saying it is God's work (*Onyame adwuma*). She told me that you cannot do this work if you do not have patience and love for people. Otherwise, you will feel anger in your heart. She dismissed any sense of stigma in care work saying that all work is work and that she does not care what people think, only what God thinks (fieldnotes, September 4, 2019). She thus dismissed the society at large as irrelevant, focusing on her relationship with God, which is similar to some responses by underpaid and underappreciated care workers in the United States to elder care work (Ibarra 2010).

The fourth paid caregiver, Gifty, age forty-eight, took over from an older woman's daughter when the care of the woman became too difficult. The mother had been brought to live with her daughter and her husband who lived in Akropong, but both worked, as a teacher and for the church, respectively, and so they left the mother alone in the house during the day. The mother had dementia and was apt to wander and give away all her money, and so they locked her up in the house. When Gifty took over from the daughter, the mother moved back to her own house, where she preferred to be. Gifty lived nearby. Gifty gave her food and bathed her twice a day, leaving her locked in the house otherwise. Gifty considered the mother an in-law, although the woman's children did not mention that affinal relation to me. Gifty had taken care of a lot of different people, as a nanny in a suburb of Accra for seven or eight years, and then a string of older women in Akropong. After the woman with dementia died, Gifty took care of a blind woman whose children had all died. She made ends meet in other ways too, by being an evangelist and having a small farm. Currently, when people ask her to do elder care work, she refuses because she said that people in town do not respect her if she does care work. However, she needs money to pay for her child's university tuition, and so she is thinking of looking for care work in Accra, where no one knows her. Domestic service held such a stigma for her that the alterodoxy of paid care was more easily pursued in anonymous urban areas. The care workers' concerns about respect speak to the tensions between different social classes emerging through alterodox practices of paid care.

More anecdotally, some evidence from the Akyem rural towns I visited in 2014 suggested that hiring a caregiver was a practice that was familiar, although it was not the most common form of care. An older woman in Begoro, who had difficulty walking, had hired a young woman from the Krobo region to help, paying her a wage every month. She said she could not lift a bucket of water to carry for her bath and needed her cane to go to the toilet. She said she had children and grandchildren but none of them lived in Begoro (group discussion, July 9, 2014). An older woman in Kade said that if you raised your children well, they would hire a caregiver for you:

> It seems to me that happiness in your old age comes from your life as a young person. You need to raise your children to serve God, so that they have compassion and love for people. If it happens like that, and your children reach

a certain place [of economic stability and social status], they can help, because they have that feeling. Even if you don't have someone to care for you (*hwεfoɔ*), they can find someone to live with you. They will pay their wage, for their food, their everything so that they take good care of you. Happiness comes from when you were strong and the path you took to raise your children.[1]

The care-script has been modified to allow daughters to be good daughters by being care managers, rather than daily care providers. Other, more impoverished women can be brought in in their stead. Adult women doing care work worry about their status within the household or society at large, or reframe social status as irrelevant, in which only God's judgment of one's personhood matters. Newer class divisions are connected to these status tensions between caregivers and their patient's kin. A more permanent social class inequality is made visible in care-making arrangements, in which an adult serves another adult who is not her kin but an employer.

Moving in with One's Daughter

Besides moving back to the hometowns, another possibility for daughters is to move their mothers to live with them, possibly with the assistance of foster children or paid help, as we saw in the household of the retired nurse who sent Susana to nursing assistance school. This solution poses a new set of problems. One is that all parties have to manage relations between in-laws, that is, between mother-in-law and son-in-law, in what may be construed as his house in which the mother-in-law is a guest. In a study of civil servants' domestic arrangements from the 1960s, Christine Oppong (1974) notes the sense of restraint and avoidance that pertains to interactions between a man and his in-laws (82). Second, the older person can become more lonely because he or she is in a new place without the dense social relations built up over time that accrue in the hometown. Finally, by staying in the place where she works, the daughter remains busy, with multiple responsibilities, so that she cannot devote herself to a parent's care.

I met Margaret Appenteng when she was eighty-nine years old in 2013 in Akropong. From an illustrious family, with a prominent early African Christian as an ancestor, she was a former secondary school principal, unusual for a woman of her generation. She was staying in a family house, cared for during the day by a paid caregiver, a middle-aged woman who lived nearby, while her three adult children lived in Accra and another town in the Eastern Region. Aunty Margaret herself had returned to her hometown to take care of her father, "sacrificing" herself (as she said) and leaving her husband and children behind, although her children were already grown at that time (fieldnotes, June 7, 2013). Humorous and talkative, she enjoyed my company and received many visitors, both neighbors and relatives visiting from other towns. The wife of her tenant, who wished to remain in her landlady's good graces, swept the whole courtyard, checked in with her daily, and sometimes did some washing for her.

Later, she had to change caregivers, as she complained that the woman who had taken care of her had been doing "foolish things" and so she had hired a young woman with a child who lasted just three days because she liked to watch television (in Aunty Margaret's bedroom) at night. Because of the unsatisfactory situation with caregivers, Aunty Margaret was moved from Akropong to stay with her daughters. She first went to stay with her oldest daughter, a divorced bank manager, in a small house in Accra. At that point, Aunty Margaret had just lost a brother and her only son and was feeling bereft. It is the sad fact that those who live long suffer the many deaths of loved ones, including their own children. Her grandchildren were in their late teens and early twenties and were busy with their own educations and careers during the day. Because of loneliness and boredom, she told me she would like to be in Akropong. She said that her children had their burdens, and she had hers; she did not want to place a burden on them. She laughed that she was "going on strike," like many of the workers in Ghana were doing at the time (fieldnotes, May 25, 2015).

By 2016, she had moved from the house of the older daughter in Accra to live with her younger daughter Kate in a village in the Eastern Region near Nkawkaw. She had been tricked away from her older daughter's house and told she was returning to Akropong, but instead she was taken to Kate's place of residence, where Kate's husband worked as a pastor. Kate commuted seventeen kilometers (ten miles) daily down a bone-shaking unpaved road to work in the regional education office in Nkawkaw, and she was also studying for her master's degree, so she was often away from the household. Aunty Margaret had taken care of Kate's children when they were small. Aunty Margaret told me on the phone that "in the village" (as she termed it) she did not go anywhere. She bathed in the morning and had breakfast and went back to bed. She spent her time looking at her clothes, remembering her life (phone conversation, July 15, 2018). She also noted that she was missing the many funerals of her neighbors and friends in Akropong, where she would have liked to have given her condolences (phone conversation, July 5, 2018).

I visited Aunty Margaret in this village for three days in July 2018, when she was ninety-four years old, staying in her room on a separate bed. In addition to her son-in-law the pastor, who often traveled internationally, and her hardworking daughter Kate, Aunty Margaret lived with one of her great-grandchildren, an eight-year-old boy, as well as a nineteen-year-old househelp Akosua who had been hired two years ago to help Kate care for Aunty Margaret. By my observations, Aunty Margaret was actually quite independent. She could get up by herself, with some effort. When she moved, she staggered quite a bit, using the door frame and other items like low tables and the sink to steady herself. Her back was bent with profound scoliosis, upsetting her balance when she walked. In the night, she used a chamber pot, and she emptied it herself in the morning into the toilet. She also had another pot into which she spit when she cleaned her teeth in the morning. She bathed herself. All her clothing and personal items were in bags around the bed, in easy reach. She needed Akosua's help only with water. Without running water in the house, Aunty Margaret needed Akosua to fetch water for the barrels that stood in the bathroom. Akosua also heated water for Aunty Margaret's bath and brought her the hot water. After bathing, Aunty Margaret returned to her bed by herself to powder and spread shea butter on herself. As she dried herself, Aunty Margaret recounted her bodily injuries to me. She remembered a time when her arms got burned from a lantern she forgot to extinguish when one of her grandchildren was staying with her. She pointed to a scar on her leg from when she was three years old. She was mainly on her own during the day, surrounded by her memories and her own thoughts. During my visit, no one called her on the phone or visited. She seemed much more isolated living there than she had in her hometown five years earlier.

The significant tension in the house was between the househelp Akosua and Aunty Margaret; perhaps conflicts with other parties were displaced onto the least powerful member of the household: the househelp. Aunty Margaret complained that Akosua did things for Kate and her son-in-law, but not for her. Aunty Margaret reminded Akosua that Akosua came to the house because of her. Akosua was doing all the difficult work around the house: the cooking, the washing, and the fetching of water from a pump up the hill (the latter task accompanied by the great-grandson). Aunty Margaret complained that Akosua liked the kitchen too much, rather than coming to her room to serve her. Akosua did not listen to her, complained Aunty Margaret. She said that Akosua pretended not to hear, although at least during my visit, Akosua always responded, perhaps because of my presence. In what seemed like a particularly unfair accusation, she blamed Akosua for her difficulties walking because Akosua had once left Aunty Margaret standing and waiting for some time.

Two incidents during my stay illustrated this tension. Aunty Margaret was very worried about the time of my departure, as I was leaving early in the morning the next day to make the long trip back to Accra. She told Akosua she had to get up early, and she worried that Akosua and her great-grandson liked to sleep late on a Sunday when they did not have to go to school. She wanted Akosua to be sure to tell Kate, but Akosua did not tell Kate that Aunty Margaret wanted to talk to her. As a result, Aunty Margaret queried Akosua again at a more disruptive time, when Kate had already gone to bed. Akosua had to call Kate from the bedroom. Kate came to her mother's bedroom and kindly reassured her mother that it would be well, but Aunty Margaret was still anxious about it. The other family members, including Akosua and the great-grandson, seemed to be amused at her worry.

In the other incident, when Aunty Margaret and I were sitting outside, chatting, the clothes from the big weekly Saturday washing were drying on the clothesline. The clouds gathered, and rain threatened. Aunty Margaret repeatedly told Akosua to remove the washing from the line. Akosua said that the clothes were still wet, and when I, goaded by Aunty Margaret's anxiety, checked, I found Akosua was correct. I could see how annoying Aunty Margaret was about the laundry, continuing to speak very sharply about it both to Akosua and more generally. It was because the clothes were in front of where we were sitting that she kept worrying about them. Despite her concern, it did not rain that day. When the clothes were collected at dusk, they were still damp because of the day's cloud cover, and they lay in a heap on the sofa in the living room in the evening. Aunty Margaret berated Akosua again and again to spread out the clothes on the furniture so they could dry inside. But I think Kate had told Akosua something different. During Saturday night, in particular, Akosua seemed very tired and unresponsive to Aunty Margaret's imperiousness.

Akosua may have served as a scapegoat for conflicts with Kate and her son-in-law, which Aunty Margaret sought to avoid, given her status as a guest in her son-in-law's house. Aunty Margaret praised her son-in-law highly for taking care of her so well, but his main role seemed to be to stay out of the way and tolerate her presence, rather than provide any direct care. Aunty Margaret continued to want to live in Akropong. She told Kate in front of me that she would like to go home to Akropong, and Kate responded that such a move would shame them because it would suggest that Kate's care was not good enough. In another shame-inducing complaint, Aunty Margaret also lamented to Kate, in my presence, about the lack of meat and fish in the food.

Other women I met in the Presbyterian congregations of southern Ghana had joined their working daughters for permanent or temporary stays. A seventy-five-year-old widow lived with her child who was a teacher in Kyebi (Akyem), while her other six children lived in Accra. Both she and her daughter were strangers to the town. Her daughter was married to a catechist who worked in Kyebi (group discussion, July 8, 2014). Another ninety-three-year-old woman, from Kyebi, described visiting her daughter in Asante Akyem when she was sick and enjoying the company of her grandchildren; her other child lived in South Africa. She appreciated the care of her daughter, saying she would have died otherwise. But now that she is better, she is back in her hometown (group discussion, July 8, 2014). An older woman in Akropong had joined her child in Accra for a year and half but then returned to Akropong because she found Accra too hot and she did not want to be a "burden" on her child's family. In contrast, one of her friends, after the death of her husband, had been taken by her child to Tema, where she remained (fieldnotes, June 3, 2013). Older women thus seemed to accommodate moving in with a daughter, although they did not always enjoy it.

Joining one's daughter allows an older person to be with grandchildren or great-grandchildren in an intergenerational household. However, it puts pressure on the adult daughter's busy household, sometimes prompting an addition of a fostered adolescent girl to provide household labor. A woman who ran a small senior residential facility in Accra told me about taking care of her own parents and commented that elder care "can break marriages" because if you invite your mother into your home, your husband may not like it (fieldnotes, June 10, 2014). The older person may perceive herself to be a burden on her child's household and be lonely without the company of her friends and other relations in her hometown. Church members and Women's Fellowship members in the daughter's town of residence may not know the older woman and therefore not visit her, leading to greater isolation. Aunty Margaret displaced most tensions with her daughter onto the more vulnerable adolescent househelp and exempted the daughter's husband altogether because he was perceived as being extra patient for allowing her to stay with him at all. Thus, another alterodox practice was the migration of the mother, rather than the return of the migrant daughter to the hometown. This was one way that working daughters could live up to the orthodoxy of kin care.

Neighbors

I noticed that neighbors were also very important in supplementing daughterly and paid care, even though they were rarely mentioned as significant in conversations about elder care. When Mama Adelaide collapsed one day in the kitchen, where Esther was cooking, Esther screamed, and neighbors, both non-kin who lived in the same compound as tenants and kin who lived in a neighboring house, rushed in. I happened to be visiting at the time of this crisis. The neighbors tried valiantly to rouse Mama Adelaide, pouring water on her, and then, having made the decision to take her to the nearest hospital, changed her wet house clothes into the more appropriate public outfit of kaba, slit, and headwrap. Esther was sent to fetch a taxi, and a male non-kin tenant who was a civil servant and a female older kin member went to the hospital with Mama Adelaide, where she sadly died. The daughter in Accra was called by the tenant. Because of Esther's adolescence, a visit to the hospital was considered too much for her to handle, and, weeping and upset, she stayed behind with the tenant's wife and toddler children (fieldnotes, September 21, 2008). Similarly, a daughter in Accra described how her mother used to live with a little boy in a village in the Western Region. Her mother had a stroke while the foster child was in school, and he returned to find her mother stricken. Too young to take her to the hospital, he called the daughter living in Accra, six or seven hours' drive away. She organized some neighbors to take her mother to the hospital, while she and her husband drove to the village, later bringing her mother back to live with them to Accra. However, when the daughter started a master's program, she could no longer care for her and placed her in a nursing home, where I met her mother (fieldnotes, August 10, 2018). As these two incidents illustrate, neighbors and tenants help fill in the gaps in paid care and kin care. As Kwatia's and Gifty's experiences in Akropong suggest, neighbors are also the first adults to be recruited as paid caregivers.

Likewise, in Abetifi, after church on Sunday morning, Pa Yirenkyi, the friend with whom I was staying, visited an older woman Boahemaa who had fallen down (fieldnotes, July 20, 2014). Pa Yirenkyi said he was like Boahemaa's brother because they were from the same town, Akropong, both living as strangers in a town in Kwawu. After the church service, we walked down the hill to the house where Boahemaa lived, and we found her lying on her back on a plastic sheet and several cloth sheets on the cold cement floor of the public area (the hall) of the house. Water to drink was within arm's reach, on the floor. There was no entertainment for her, and she was facing away from the door. Short and thin, perhaps in her seventies, Boahemaa seemed depressed, but perhaps her quietness was the result of the great pain she was in. She was not inclined to say much. She had broken her hip two weeks ago, the third time she had fallen in the past few years. She seemed to be wearing disposable diapers. Her relatives had taken her to the hospital twice before they obtained a clear enough X-ray for the doctor to read. Boahemaa was also visited by a traditional doctor three days a week. If the traditional doctor had seen the X-ray sooner, he would have begun treating her sooner and perhaps she would be walking now, said Boahemaa's relative, an older woman who lived with her and was very welcoming and voluble with us, perhaps to make up for Boahemaa's silence. Pa Yirenkyi asked this relative about Boahemaa's children, as if expecting them to take care of her. Although she had given birth to four children, two had died, and the relative did not know where the others were. She complained that Boahemaa always liked to go outside, to stand in front of the house and see what was happening on the street and greet passers-by, although she encouraged her not to do so, worried that Boahemaa would fall. Boahemaa's relative thus performed for us a model of good kin care, since, as Boahemaa's caregiver, she could be blamed for Boahemaa's latest fall. After praying for Boahemaa and giving a small token of money, we got up to leave. The relative, seeing us out, praised two neighbors who also helped with care. One neighbor grew up with Boahemaa's daughter and had played in the house. When the daughter died, the neighbor took Boahemaa as her mother. The neighbor also had an Akropong connection because her son-in-law was from Akropong and so Pa Yirenkyi knew her. Another neighbor lived across the road and came forward when the kin caregiver called her to introduce her. Mute, she could not speak, but seemed to understand our greetings and thanks or at least made noises as if she did. "Neighborliness," said Pa Yirenkyi approvingly as we walked back to his residence on the school grounds.

Neighbors and tenants, like paid caregivers, are underrepresented in the dominant discourse on kin care and yet in practice can provide care at critical times in the gaps left by kin care because they live near an older person. Sjaak van der Geest (2002b) notes that one old man with poor eyesight in Tafo (Kwawu) during his fieldwork from 1994 to 2000 was led to the toilet by his tenant when his wife was otherwise busy. In a national survey of five thousand households with adults older than fifty, 15 percent reported receiving physical or personal help from the community, whereas only 11 percent reported receiving it from family or kin (Biritwum et al. 2013). Neighbors and tenants, resident in the hometown, provide important forms of elder care, including in emergencies, when children were absent, sometimes temporarily in their stead and sometimes more permanently.

Conclusions: Age Inscriptions Articulated, Age Inscriptions Practiced

Simultaneous with the strong critique of adult children discussed in chapter 1 are various heterodox and alterodox age inscriptions. Those whose children were living up to their obligations were content with the current orthodoxy. It was those who perceived the reliance on adult children's support to be precarious who explored alterodox practices. These alterodox age inscriptions urged acceptance of children's financial and emotional limitations and expressed openness to alternative arrangements, including hiring a domestic servant to care for an aging person and moving older adults to live in a daughter's home. This chapter has examined the quiet changes in practice that are occurring without much attention.

Unlike the heterodox discourse about senior residential facilities, alterodox age inscriptions come from within, through adaptations of familiar practices like child fostering, or substitutions or supplements of adjacent relations to enable adult daughters to live up to the orthodoxy of kin care. These age inscriptions are less articulated and formulated than standardized discourses about the significance of children's care in old age, although they are shaped by this dominant discourse. In fact, such alterodox practices are seen as compatible with an adult child living up to his or her responsibilities, who can send remittances that allow someone else to provide personal care or move an aging parent to live with them outside the hometown. Unaccompanied by a clear, articulated discourse, they are age inscriptions without the strength of a social norm.

In thinking about aging and social change, we need to account for the ways that practices and discourses do not always fit together. The state's relative silence about and lack of attention to aging creates a weak hegemonic discourse about aging. As a result, older people in Ghana and those who care for them have the space and are forced to construct alterodox and heterodox practices and discourses, however tentative and disconnected, from which new norms may be generated. Despite their variability, these discourses and practices arise from a common ground: an anxiety that the contemporary situation places older adults at risk of neglect. Older adults perceive current government policy as disregarding them and blame their plight on a lack of state care. In the absence of a strong state policy about what to do, they and their children are free—or pushed—to imagine and construct their own solutions to the difficulties they face. They draw on the cultural and social resources available to them. As kin groups and individuals personally encounter new life problems like aging, they create unintentional consequences, like exacerbating social class divisions and status tensions within households.

4

"Loneliness Kills"

• •

Stimulating Sociality among
Older Churchgoers

Churches have historically been, and still are, a major provider of social services in Ghana. They used to run the educational system, which was slowly taken over by the government of Ghana over the first half of the twentieth century (McWilliam and Kwamena-Poh 1975), and they continue to be key in private-public partnerships through which the state governs (MacLean 2002). Churches are important sites for creating fictive kinship and social capital (Adogame 2014; Meyer 1999; Mohr 2013). The effect of private forms of charity has been noted in other scholarship on the development of social policy: in Britain, before 1914, philanthropy contributed to the whirl of ideas that influenced the role of the state and the policies that it developed (Laybourn 1995, 153). When the state retreats, religious institutions sometimes take over the role of social welfare (Muehlebach 2012). Thus, for those thinking about alternatives beyond kin care, it is natural to expect churches to play a major role. Advocates for older persons have directed some of their energies within religious institutions, particularly the Catholic Church, the Presbyterian Church of Ghana, and the Evangelical Presbyterian Church of Ghana—all mainline churches, which, more so than the newer Pentecostal churches, serve older populations and have a history of social mission by running schools and hospitals in Ghana.

Ideas circulate within a congregation, between congregations, across denominations, and beyond religious institutions to wider social circles. Through these organized groups, alterodox practices have the possibility of becoming institutionalized because institutions naturalize certain practices, make distinctions and classifications, and bestow sameness (Douglas 1986). Thus, religious institutions are important sites for both maintaining orthodoxies and for making new orthodoxies out of alterodoxies and heterodoxies, with tension generated as orthodoxies shift.

This chapter focuses on how certain solutions for the aged in Ghana seem to have stabilized and cohered through the activities of religious institutions. The proposed solutions generated through these institutions are senior day centers and fellowship groups for the aged. Both types of gatherings are primarily aimed at producing sociality and fellowship. The problem of older people has been defined through these solutions as the loneliness of relatively well and mobile older adults, who can walk or obtain transport to a center or gathering, rather than those who are bedridden or have dementia. A secondary goal of these gatherings is providing information regarding nutrition, insurance, or other aging issues, as well as preventative medical attention, like ear and eye examinations, blood sugar tests, or blood pressure tests. Although Pakistan and Singapore have opened senior day centers for those with dementia, to give families relief during the day (World Health Organization 2015), fellowship participants in Ghana are the relatively healthy and young among the aging population, who are the most likely to be active in the communities, control resources that they can distribute, and be respected. Social gatherings also seem natural because other social organizations in Ghanaian society similarly formalize active older people's participation, particularly among the elite and middle class, through alumni associations (old boys' and girls' clubs), church fellowship groups, and councils of elders.[1]

The earliest religious initiatives to focus on the needs of older adults came from the Catholic Church and took the form of a senior day center in the capital Accra. In cooperation with HelpAge, an international NGO concerned with aging, a Catholic priest, Father Andrew Campbell, helped set up several senior day centers in Accra in 1992 and 1993 (Ayete-Nyampong 2008; Dodoo et al. 1999). These urban centers provided a hot meal, activities like games and songs, a nurse on site to conduct medical checks, and occasional excursions for participants, funded by the Catholic Church. At its height, the oldest day center, at Derby Avenue in the heart of commercial Accra, fed thirty people a day (conversation, Aunty Mary, August 13, 2018). The rationale for a senior day center, according to Father Campbell, Irish-born but long resident in Accra, was:

> In my pastoral work, what I see, you know, Africa is always known for its, sort of, families, you know, the grandmother, the grandfather, the children, you know, and the grandchildren, and they all stayed together, they all helped one another. The grandmother would be there; the children who had gone to school would come back; the mother would be at work; and the grandmother

would take it [that is, take care of the household in the absence of other household members]. But that is breaking down. And in the various parishes I've been to, I've noticed that these people are left on their own, which is sad. It's really sad. In Derby Avenue, many of them were just living on their own. Nobody to help them. You know? And we used to bring them every day to the center, cook them a meal, and then we would [give] medical care. A doctor would come in to make sure their medical care was taken care of. So um we took care. . . . It was a place to come to, where you could meet your friends and chat and chat. At times we would take them on an excursion, take them off somewhere so they had something to look forward to. So that was, sort of, that's the reason we moved forward because I saw many of my parishioners living on their own in their houses. This is in the center of the city, you know, living on their own. Maybe they have come from upcountry [the rural areas] and settled in Accra, and they've gotten old, and the children have gone away from them and they are left on their own. This [the senior day center] is a place of contact, where they can sort of sit and chat, and feel loved and cared for. In your old age, you need that. (taped interview, June 27, 2014)

His resistance to nursing homes, which led instead to day centers as a solution, was shaped by his visits to his aunt in a residential facility in Ireland, but it was very much in line with the feelings of Ghanaian activists involved in HelpAge, like Mrs. Ollennu and Dr. Asare.

Of the centers established by HelpAge, all but one in the Osu neighborhood are now defunct because of difficulties participants had getting to the facilities, including the expense of transportation. The Osu HelpAge center is in a dense urban environment and thus is accessible to many neighboring households. The Catholic Church continued to support another senior day center in the neighboring port city of Tema, called the St. Vincent de Paul Center, which attracted five or six older adults daily between 2013 and 2017. At the St. Vincent de Paul Center, participants held a small worship service, made handicrafts, and ate a hot meal, arriving in the morning and leaving in the early afternoon. The center also held monthly health screenings, which were attended by a wider group of about twenty people. Given the slow decline of the St. Vincent de Paul Center, the current manager, a nun, wanted to turn the center into a nursing home and a school to train care workers.

Despite their unsustainability, the senior day centers garnered media attention during the time they were in operation. A short film about HelpAge was shown on Ghanaian television, and the organization was savvy about attracting media attention (interview, Dr. Asare, June 28, 2013). Because of the media attention, HelpAge's senior day center served as an inspiration for the construction of the senior day center by the Presbyterian Church in Akropong, discussed in the introduction. However, instead of senior day centers, what was most successfully enacted within the Presbyterian Church of Ghana and the Evangelical

Presbyterian Church of Ghana, dominant in the rural areas of the Eastern and Volta Regions, respectively, were regular gatherings for older adults aimed at increasing sociality. Perhaps one reason for the success of fellowship groups for older adults is that churches already organize generational groups. For example, most congregations within the Presbyterian Church of Ghana organize a Young People's Guild for young people, a Men's Fellowship for adult men, and a Women's Fellowship for adult women, which are very lively and vibrant social bodies within most congregations and serve as major forums for social, financial, and emotional support. The fellowship groups for older adults added a fourth associational category of "the aged" to this array of generationally organized bodies.

There are several reasons why the Presbyterian Church of Ghana and the Evangelical Presbyterian Church of Ghana have been involved in aging initiatives. The rural areas where they are located have a higher proportion of older persons than in Ghana as a whole, mainly because of younger people's migration to the cities. Rapidly growing urban areas across West Africa are associated with a younger demographic, as young adults migrate to the urban areas (Peil 1981). Of adults over sixty in Ghana, 59 percent live in rural areas (Biritwum et al. 2013; Tonah 2009). According to the 2010 national population census, those over the age of sixty-five constitute 4.6 percent of Ghana's population, or about one million people out of a total population of 24.7 million (Ghana Statistical Service 2012). Fifty-seven percent of these are women. In comparison to the North, with much poorer health outcomes, many areas of the Eastern and Volta Region are characterized by better access to health care, with concomitant higher life expectancies. The Volta Region has the highest proportion of older persons in Ghana (6.4 percent of its population is over the age of sixty-five), followed by the Eastern Region (5.7 percent). These proportions are even higher in the areas I studied: in the district where Akropong is located, 8.18 percent are over the age of sixty-five; in the districts of the Kwawu towns I visited, the proportion was 7.35 and 8.14 percent, respectively. In the three districts in Akyem that I visited, the proportion was lower, at 5.51, 6.7, and 4.85 percent, respectively, but still represented a higher proportion of older adults than in Ghana as a whole. In general, most of Ghana's older population live in rural areas, rendering them more easily overlooked by the state, harder to reach by state services, and more invisible to the media focused on the capital.

The ministers in the congregations in the rural towns of southern Ghana became aware of the problems of older adults because they visit the sick and disabled at home to give Invalid Communion every month. Although Communion can be given quite quickly, some ministers liked to sit and chat with those they were visiting, leading to enhanced understanding of their congregants' experiences and lives. Through these home visits, they learned of cases of neglect and became open to proposing heterodox or alterodox solutions for older adults. For instance, a minister in Kwawu told me that he visited a man whose wife and daughter had died, thus leaving him without caregivers. The stench in the room was terrible. For those like this neglected man, he thought a nursing home might be useful (fieldnotes, July 25, 2014).

Although ministers in these churches learned of the needs of their frail congregants through Communion in their homes, the solutions that they organized were for those who were relatively well, mobile, and lonely, rather than for those in need of personal care like bathing and feeding. As Jaco Hoffman and Katrien Pype (2016) argue, care for the aged occurs in social spaces shaped by power and differing interests. The churches in the rural areas were driven by the needs of one set of people to do something for the aged, but they hit on a solution for a healthier, wealthier, and more powerful group of aged within their congregations. In the next section, I describe the activities of four aged fellowship groups to highlight the similarities and variations in this form of social gathering, before turning to the reasons why the Akropong senior day center was built, but a day program never organized.

Aged Fellowship Groups

As noted, the fellowship groups for older adults tended to have several common features. First, they were focused on the mobile and healthy older population. The Presbyterian Church of Ghana defined "the aged" as those over the age of seventy, because otherwise they would have had too many participants. However, Bethel Presbyterian Church in New Tafo (Akyem) received permission from the Head Office to reduce the age of membership to sixty-five years because they found that the members of the aged fellowship group, if they were over the age of seventy, became too frail to participate in the social gatherings of the group. They also needed healthy and active organizers under the age of seventy to organize excursions and other activities, which involved traveling to places and communicating with host organizations as groundwork (interview with leadership team member, August 13, 2019). Participants in aged fellowship groups needed to transport themselves to the church—whether by walking, taking a taxi, or driving their own car—as the church did not have funds to provide transportation. In Pepease (Kwawu), the aged fellowship president told me that many people would like to come to the aged fellowship meetings but their bodies were soft and weak ("wɔn honam yɛ mmerɛw") and so they could not walk to the church (fieldnotes, July 23, 2014).

As with other church activities, the aged fellowship groups provided opportunities for female leadership. Although ministers and other official church leaders in these churches are overwhelmingly male, the congregants are overwhelmingly female. Likewise, the majority of participants in the fellowship meetings were women. The membership of the committees that organized the aged fellowship group often included both men and women, allowing for some leadership roles to be played by older women. The key organizer driving the establishment of the aged program in Akropong was a female retired nurse. A woman founded the very active aged fellowship group in New Tafo. In Kwawu, the district co-organizers were a retired kindergarten teacher (a woman) and a retired minister (a man). Much of the work of organizing aged initiatives in the church was done by older female lay leaders who were from and resident in the town, and they found their interests sometimes conflicting with those of male ministers, who rotate between congregations every few years. Because the aged fellowship groups were often organized by older people themselves, albeit it the youngest and most active, the groups also created the opportunity for older people to have a more prominent role within the church.

The central features of these gatherings displayed some variety. In some groups, the main focus was on games and having fun, such as playing *oware* and board games like Ludo (Parcheesi) and Snakes and Ladders; doing physical exercises, dancing, and playing *ampe*, a physical game involving jumping usually played by girls; and telling jokes, riddles, and Ananse folk stories.[2] In others, there was an emphasis on health and the provision of expert information, through health screenings or a talk given by a nurse or social worker. In yet others, there were opportunities for income generation, which were important for older adults who wanted to continue to earn money, given sporadic and uncertain remittances from relatives and the small pensions for the very few (mainly men) who received them. Each group had a slightly different emphasis, as I describe below in the different fellowship groups I came to know.

Shepherd's Center in the Volta Region

Rev. Seth Agidi had become interested in the needs of the aging from visiting older adults at home during Invalid Communion in the hilly town of Peki in the Volta Region. During his PhD study at Eden Theological Seminary in St. Louis, Missouri—which is affiliated with the Evangelical Presbyterian (EP) Church—he did his dissertation on aging where he outlined the Shepherd's Center concept (interview, July 30, 2014). When he returned to Ghana, he put the ideas developed in his dissertation into action, organizing groups, beginning in Peki in 2002. He institutionalized it as an NGO outside the EP Church because the then-moderator of the church was not interested. Shepherd's Center coordinated 101 aged fellowship groups, mainly in the Volta Region of Ghana but also including three in Togo, where the EP Church was also active. Some of the groups had a center (a building) but most did not. As he explained to me, these fellowship groups were run *by* older adults *for* older adults, and so they went through periods of intensity, when the organizer was healthy and vibrant, and periods of inactivity, when there was a transition between organizers. Rev. Agidi later became the moderator of the EP Church (2015–2021). Thus, while the group was not part of the EP Church, it was closely affiliated with it.

I visited three Shepherd's Center aged fellowship groups in July 2014, accompanied by Rev. Agidi. At one, called the RTC Ho chapter, started two years

FIG. 4.1 Making banana porridge, Sava Ho Shepherd's Center, July 31, 2014.

before, the twenty-six participants ate a breakfast of porridge and beans, were tested for hypertension and diabetes, and sang songs with accompanying exercises and dances (fig. 4.1). They met twice a month, under the leadership of a retired (male) minister. The Sava chapter in Ho, in contrast, met under a tree and the organizer, a queen mother, taught the others how to make a nutritious banana porridge with spices and beans, for their own use at home or to sell for income in "doorstep trading" which allows older women to continue to contribute economically without the strenuous labor of going to sell in the market (Apt 1996; Turner and Kwakye 1996). At other meetings, the queen mother told me, they have screenings for hypertension and diabetes, or discuss income-generating activities, like making liquid soap or fruit juice, or growing mushrooms. They, like the RTC Ho chapter, also sang while dancing, while they waited for the porridge to cook. They met weekly and had thirty-five active members, who wore Shepherd Center T-shirts. At the end of the meeting, everyone enjoyed a bowl of the banana porridge they had cooked.

We also visited the oldest Shepherd's Center, which had its own building just opposite the EP Church in Peki-Blengo. Twenty-nine people were in attendance that morning. They meet weekly, on Friday mornings, and during their meetings they always eat something, even if it is something simple like rice water or gari with beans. Usually, they gather to make handicrafts like brooms and jewelry. They also do physical activities, tell stories, organize health screenings, and sing songs. Once a month, they visit members who could not attend. During Christmas time, they celebrate with those who are bedridden. In case of a death of one of their members, they travel together to give the person a fitting burial. On members' birthdays, they celebrate with them in their house. Thus, although their activities were focused on the mobile, they were able to attend to some of the needs of the more sick and disabled, particularly if they had formerly been active members.

The chapters of Shepherd's Center that I visited seemed vibrant and lively, engaging the participants. I visited them only once.[3] I knew far more about the Christchurch aged fellowship gatherings, which were far less frequent, and less under the control of older persons themselves, which I discuss in the next section.

Christchurch Presbyterian Church in Akropong (Eastern Region)

In Akropong, the stimulus for the aged program, which began in May 2006, arose similarly from giving Communion to the ill and disabled in their homes. Rev. Kwapong, the Christchurch minister in 2003, noticed that the presbyters were spending all their time giving Invalid Communion to about two or three hundred people in their homes every month (interview, June 21, 2013). To reduce the workload of the presbyters, he and his leadership team decided to gather this group of persons together for Communion periodically, and they slowly expanded to giving food and medical advice during these gatherings.

These events turned into gatherings four times a year for those over the age of seventy-five. In events from 2007 to 2017, between 53 and 132 people attended, as noted in the records kept by the church nurse. The attendees for the gatherings were overwhelmingly women, with men less than 15 percent of the participants. At one gathering I had the opportunity to attend in June 2013, the church van went to pick up those who were disabled or had trouble with transportation. When participants arrived at the social hall behind the church, they sat down in chairs organized in rows in order of arrival, so that their blood pressure could be checked. This arrangement reduced opportunities for socializing because they were not sitting with their friends. The retired public health nurse who organized the event also kept berating them to be quiet so that the nurses from the hospital could do their work. They received Communion from the minister, singing hymns that seemed to give them pleasure. After everyone's blood pressure had been checked, snacks and used clothing were distributed. The church nurse spoke loudly and clearly about diet, exercise, and rest. They then had a discussion of how to deal with their children. Although several participants enjoyed it, Margaret Appenteng (from chapter 3), then living in Akropong, attended the June 2013 event and complained that they sat like schoolchildren (fieldnotes, June 22, 2013). Indeed, the older adults seemed to sit around for a very long time waiting for the various activities, and much of the activity was quite passive, listening to the speakers and waiting to be checked, unlike the Shepherd's Center gatherings, where there was more singing and dancing. Mercy Amankwah (from chapter 3), who also attended, enjoyed it but was anxious that she had to go to the restroom twice during the event, because she needed someone to accompany her each time because of her blindness (fieldnotes, June 24, 2013). The program lasted from ten in the morning until three in the afternoon.

One of the organizers told me that they vary the programs: sometimes an ear, nose, and eye specialist visits; sometimes a doctor tells them about nutrition, because food throughout the life course is really important (interview, July 17, 2014). Usually the Christchurch senior program tested for hypertension and diabetes, until they ran out of the testing equipment for diabetes. In 2012, Christchurch budgeted 4,000 Ghana cedis ($2,128) on four such events during the year, out of a total church budget of 285,000 Ghana cedis ($151,596), or 1.4 percent of the total budget (interview with Christchurch accountant, June 21, 2013).

I was told by many that the end-of-year celebration was a high point of the gatherings and something special, although unfortunately I never had the opportunity to attend one. I saw many pictures and videos of it, however. The end-of-year celebration features a dance competition, and the number of participants was far higher, between 113 and 177, according to the records kept by the church nurse.

Through the initiative of the organizer, a recently retired nurse, Christchurch convinced the Ministry of Health to designate a nurse who worked at a local clinic to help the church two days a week. State resources were thus used to support one church's aging congregants, rather than all older adults in the district. The church nurse worked diligently, visiting six to ten congregants at home each day between 2007 and 2013. She did not provide personal care but instead instructed those in the household about care and took the congregant's blood pressure and blood sugar levels. She would chat and pray with the older people (interview, June 10, 2013). She also gave public talks, for instance about malaria, diet, and menopause (records, 2007). When she retired and returned to her hometown elsewhere in the Eastern Region, her work was continued by her assistant, who did not have nursing training and was far less involved with visiting congregants. Although Christchurch tried to obtain another government nurse, the organizer's connections to the regional Ministry of Health and local hospitals had weakened since her retirement from nursing, a common problem for aging professionals. Instead, the organizer said that the local clinic had now hired several community health nurses, who were designated to do home visits. I thought perhaps that the church's initiative of a nurse doing home visits to older adults had been adopted by the government, with the benefit of serving the wider community, including those who did not attend or were not in good standing with Christchurch. However, when I accompanied two community health nurses in their visits around Akropong in August 2019, I learned that they were completely focused on infant and maternal health. They did not visit any older residents, except those living in households with infants (and many healthy, older women were deeply involved in these infants' care). I was impressed that the community health nurses were doing home visits, and they seemed passionate about maternal and child health, but they certainly did not consider older adults within their purview.

In comparison to the other groups I visited, health was more of a focus at Christchurch, because of the interest and professional background of the organizer. The focus on health was also prompted by the children of Akropong residents who were abroad. The son of an Akropong resident started sending blood sugar testing equipment to Christchurch in 2008 (phone interview, July 30, 2013). A retired hospital administrator in Brooklyn, his interest had been prompted by the death of two of his brothers from diabetes, which has a prevalence rate of about 7 percent in Ghana (Ayernor 2012; de-Graft Aikins 2007). The emphasis on health at Akropong led to more didactic presentations by health professionals and a more passive role for the older participants than I saw at Shepherd's Center. Among all the groups, Christchurch also had the least frequent fellowship group gatherings, organizing them once every three months rather than weekly or biweekly.

Akropong is known within the Presbyterian Church of Ghana for having an aged fellowship program and has been visited by other congregations interested in adopting its practices. For example, during a meeting to discuss her plans for operating a fee-free senior day center in Accra, an Anglican minister in Accra showed me her photos from Christchurch's Christmas celebrations from December 2012 which she had attended (fieldnotes, June 29, 2013). Because of Akropong's geographic nearness to Accra, it receives more media attention and is more visible through the social networks of those studying and advocating for the aged than the other fellowship gatherings discussed in this chapter.

Bethel Presbyterian Church, New Tafo (Akyem)

New Tafo has a vibrant aged fellowship group which was started in 2011 by a congregant (Mrs. Adwoa Agyekum), now deceased, who visited her sister in Tema and saw a similar fellowship group in her sister's church. I visited the group in 2014 and again for a week in 2019, for the purposes of making a short film about their activities.[4] Thirty to forty people meet twice a month, to sing songs, do physical exercises accompanied by Presbyterian hymns, play board games like Ludo and *oware*, and generally meet to have fun (fig. 4.2). Participants also went on excursions to various places, like the Presbyterian Women's Center at Abokobi or to the Bunso Arboretum, and visited sick and debilitated members at home. The organizer's husband commented that their activities "make us more

FIG. 4.2 Exercising while singing Presbyterian hymns, New Tafo, July 11, 2014.

vibrant than other churches that just sit there quietly,"[5] like when older adults listen to a speaker and receive food and drink passively, as at Akropong. A female participant said that at the fellowship group "we enliven ourselves."[6] Happiness was frequently mentioned by participants and organizers in their interviews. Interviewees commented on how much fun they had in the group, allowing them to escape their worried thinking at home.

New Tafo's practices have spread, and they have also made efforts to learn from others. A minister I met in Kade in 2014 had been previously posted to New Tafo, and he brought the idea to his new post when he was transferred. However, in contrast to the older people organizing themselves in New Tafo, he put a young man in charge of organizing the group, leading them in aerobics and bringing nurses to check their blood pressure, missing the importance of older adult leadership (group discussion, July 12, 2014). In 2015, the New Tafo group came on an excursion to Akropong to learn about Akropong's aged program, although they organize their fellowship group meetings quite differently. They have also received visitors from other groups in the Presbyterian Church of Ghana.

Kwawu

Fifteen Presbyterians churches in Kwawu had an aged fellowship group that met weekly in 2014. I visited eight of them briefly: Mpraeso, Akwasiho, Abetifi

Ramseyer and Abetifi Ebenezer, Nkwatia, Pepease, Obo, and Obomeng. As in New Tafo and Shepherd's Center, there was an executive committee of older people in each congregation organizing the aged fellowship group. Most of the churches in Kwawu had had an aged fellowship group since 2010, although Akwasiho was the first, with its group forming in 2007. The district organizers who supported the congregational aged fellowship groups in Kwawu had distinct personalities and backgrounds. One was a retired daycare teacher, a woman in her sixties who told me that she used the same techniques with older adults that she had in her work with young children. She told me that she sometimes forgets that she is working with the elderly, rather than children. She was full of energy and joy, engaging participants in physical and participatory activities like storytelling, discussions, and competitions. The second district organizer was a more dour retired minister, who was focused on bringing older adults to Christ before they died. He complained to me in private that some old people did not die as Christians because they cursed their relatives, God, and the state for not taking care of them. He told me, "Loneliness is killing the elderly," stating what I heard over and over again in my visits with Presbyterian congregations (fieldnotes, July 20, 2014). He often mentioned death in his talks at group meetings. He told the Obo aged fellowship group when I visited that its main goal was for everyone to be happy, so that they forget about their problems at home. He said that the church wants to prevent older men and women dying in sadness (fieldnotes, July 23, 2014). He spoke quite insistently about death in his interactions with the aged fellowship groups, a message that was well received.

In the groups I visited in Kwawu, women far outnumbered the men. The women sat in the front and tended to participate more, while the men tended to sit in the back, mirroring their participation in regular church activities. Twenty to sixty people showed up at each of the eight fellowship group meetings I attended. They played board games, told jokes, or sang. At one meeting (Nkwatia), older adults drew small pieces of paper from a basket in which they were asked to publicly perform different activities: recite a Bible verse, tell an Ananse story, sing a Presbyterian hymn, or tell a joke. They made themselves and one another laugh. In another congregation (Obomeng), a social worker gave advice to a group sitting quietly. I was told that Abetifi Ebenezer sometimes has a health talk, tells riddles, or goes through the interpretation of a Presbyterian hymn line by line. On the day I was there, a man in training to be a minister explained the Ten Commandments.

Like New Tafo, the aged fellowship groups in Kwawu seemed focused on participatory activities, through the impetus of one of the organizers, but they occasionally had didactic or religious-related lectures or discussions. Health was much less of a focus than at Akropong. There is variation in these social groups, therefore, in the focus, organization, and frequency of these gatherings, but also some similarities in providing older women a forum for participation and leadership.

The New Social Category of "the Aged"

Yɛyɛ mmasiriwa	We are old people
Ɛyɛ Onyame adom enti na yɛte ase oow,	It is by God's grace that we are alive
Ɛyɛ Onyame adom enti na yɛte ase oow,	It is by God's grace that we are alive
Yɛndɔ, yɛmpam, nanso yɛdidii daa,	We don't weed, we don't sew, but nonetheless we always eat
Yɛndɔ, yɛmpam, nanso yɛdidii daa,	We don't weed, we don't sew, but nonetheless we always eat
Ɛyɛ Onyame ara oow, yɛanyini.	It is because of God that we have grown old.
Yɛanyin, yɛanyin oow,	We have grown old, we have grown old.
Yɛnyɛ mmɔfra bio mu oow,	We are no longer children.
Yɛyɛ mmasiriwa.	We are aged people.

—Song sung by Akwasiho aged fellowship group (Kwawu), July 21, 2014

Through the aged fellowship groups, a new category of person has emerged: in Twi, "*mmarisiwa*"; in English, "the aged"; and in a Twification of English: "aged-*fo*." *Mmarisiwa*, which originally just meant an adult or grown-up, was particularly used in Kwawu. Its meaning has shifted to delineate older adults in general. "*Mmarisiwa*" had different meanings than "*Ɔpanyin*" (elder) or "*Nana*" (a term of respect for grandparents and chiefs), in that it encompassed all people who had attained a certain age, not just those who had brought forth new generations or were wealthy. Its claims for respect depended on long life, not personal achievements.

As noted by scholars of youth in Africa, "Generational categories . . . are not neutral or natural but rather part of the struggle for influence and authority within almost every society" (Christiansen, Utas, and Vigh 2006, 11). The creation of the new social category of *mmarisiwa* or the aged was connected to a political struggle within the church, and more broadly within society at large, to signal that a group of people existed who deserved resources, respect, and recognition. They should be taken seriously (Bolten 2020; Enloe 2013). *Mmarisiwa*, as a new term, identified who they were to themselves as well as to those outside the group. The T-shirts, slogans, and anthems were material elements critical to branding the social group, creating cohesion within it and generating recognition beyond it.

All the fellowship groups, as expressed in the slogans and anthems generated for the groups, worked hard to give the aged positive associations. Uniforms, such as T-shirts, also reflected this sentiment. For example, I was told that one of the lines in the Ewe-language anthem of the Ho RTC chapter of Shepherd's Center was "growing old is a very good thing, so we should be proud of it"; the lyrics

FIG. 4.3 "Celebrating the Aged," T-shirt of the New Tafo fellowship group, July 11, 2014.

had been composed by the group (fieldnotes, July 31, 2014). At the Sava chapter, they sang, "We must be happy we are old" (fieldnotes, July 31, 2014). In Kwawu, the group's greeting was "Mmarisiwa," to which the response was *"Onyame na Ayɛ"* (God has made it so). New Tafo's T-shirt read "Celebrating the Aged," and their greeting was *"Onyin kye"* (Long life), to which the response was *"Adom ne nhyira"* (God's grace and blessing) (fig. 4.3).

The perspective that aging was God's gift served two purposes. One was to thwart older participants' complaints about the aging process: to live long was better than dying early. Many older people seemed to associate aging with sickness and physical weakness (or softness: *bɛtɛɛ*). As a seventy-two-year-old man complained, "Generally, you hear that after the age of fifty or sixty, aging is only trouble."[7] Women in particular seemed concerned with the loss of strength that allowed them to farm or do household tasks (see also Van der Geest 2001). A seventy-three-year-old woman said, "When I was young, I was strong. I could go anywhere, I could go to farm and return to go to school; I could do anything. When I reached the age of sixty, I became feeble, my knee, my back, my whole body. In the morning, you would say it was like I worked all night. If I go to work, I don't make any headway, and I am weak (*bɛtɛɛ*)."[8] A retired teacher in his seventies said that even if you had always been in good health, you would suffer from one illness or another once you reached seventy.[9] Because many older people wanted to remain economically active (Apt 1996), at the very least by growing food crops, they were concerned about the health and strength of their bodies.

While in Japan loss was considered an opportunity for creativity (Danely 2014), it was mourned by Ghanaian older people. Older people were full of complaints about the trials and tribulations of aging, and the positive sentiment expressed in the groups was oriented toward changing those laments into expressions of gratitude and joy to God for being alive at all.

The second was to thwart younger people's witchcraft accusations, suggesting that the reason why an older person had lived longer than his or her generational cohort or even the generation of his or her children was because he or she was a witch who had destroyed others in order to achieve a long life (see also Van der Geest 2004a). As a woman said, "If you send someone on an errand two or three times, he/she will insult you. You are loathsome to that person, who says, 'You are a witch. Why haven't you died?' It is like if you send him/her on an errand, he/she won't go, because you are a witch: all your generation has died but you are alive."[10] The counterargument posed in the songs and greetings was that a long life span came not from malicious witchcraft but from God. As a result, older people deserve care and respect from younger generations.

Despite the celebrations of aging, the aged fellowship groups also suggested that older adults were in need of support and charity, from the church and wealthy congregants. The groups and gatherings provided opportunities for benefactors and patrons to show that they cared about the vulnerable. At the aged meeting in Obo (Kwawu), the organizer thanked the benefactors publicly; most of the benefactors were from Obo but lived in the cities of Accra and Tema (fieldnotes, July 23, 2014). In Akwasiho (Kwawu) and New Tafo (Akyem), wealthy patrons had taken the groups under their wing. In New Tafo, a pharmaceutical businessman had funded their sightseeing excursions, while in Akwasiho, a road contractor had funded the distribution of cloth to fellowship group members at Christmas. Used clothing was distributed at the Akropong meetings. In contrast to the songs celebrating aging, patronage seemed to designate older adults as worthy of charity and pity. Fellowship groups needed these individual patrons because the Presbyterian Church of Ghana is not consistent in supporting aging initiatives, as I discuss in the next section.

Ambivalence from the Church

From my conversations with ministers and elders within the Presbyterian Church of Ghana, religious leaders are ambivalent about their aging programs. Despite the history of founding and running schools and hospitals, most contemporary congregations do not have strong social welfare missions, but instead are influenced by the Prosperity Gospel promoted in the Pentecostal churches, in which wealth is a sign of God's blessings (Mohr 2013). To that end, church construction seems a major goal of many congregations. Many congregations in the towns I visited have rebuilt their older, modest churches and ministers' residences (manses) into spectacular buildings, with tiled floors, glass windows, and wooden

FIG. 4.4 Old church and new manse, Abetifi, Kwawu, July 25, 2014. Photo taken from the doorway of the new, large church.

ceilings, to showcase their power and wealth and, by extension, God's favor on them (fig. 4.4).

Accompanying ministers in Kwawu, I noticed that when two Presbyterian ministers met one another, they quickly entered into a conversation about construction, discussing the price of cement, for example, or commenting on the aesthetics of the floor tiles. For example, the district minister of Abetifi Ramseyer church kindly transported me to the fellowship group meeting in Nkwatia in July 2014. When we arrived at the Nkwatia church, he commented privately to me that the tiles around the forecourt of the church were a mistake, because with the least bit of rain they were slippery and older people could fall. He also said that the tiles did not match the stones in the church building. Instead, he argued, they should have made the forecourt and steps out of cement blocks or just cement. It seemed to me that ministers enjoyed going to one another's churches to see, comment on, and learn about construction and design.

Ministers are transferred from one congregation to another every four or five years. As a result, they had only a short period in which to establish their reputation. Many aimed to literally cement their legacy through fund-raising and building. A Presbyterian friend of mine living in Accra noted critically that pastors are rated on their fundraising ability, not their power to persuade or convert (fieldnotes, July 1, 2015). Sjaak van der Geest notes about Christian church services in Tafo, Kwawu during the 1990s, "the collection represents the zenith of the liturgy" (1997, 540), true for my experiences in Akropong also. Ministers were remembered for building something, which had a plaque on the wall with their name, whereas an ongoing program like the aged fellowship groups seemed less important to establishing a minister's reputation.[11]

Furthermore, if one minister had established or was enthusiastic about an aged program, another minister might replace him (or more rarely, her). The new minister might be less supportive or have another legacy to establish, leading to changes in initiatives at the congregational level. The chairman of the aged program at the Presbyterian Church of Ghana described founding an aged fellowship group at La Presbyterian Church in Accra, but his successor was not interested, and so the fellowship group is no more (fieldnotes, July 4, 2013). The regular transfer of ministers makes lay leaders, including women, important, because they help provide continuity in programs and initiatives in the local congregation.

Within an environment focused on fund-raising and church building, supporting "the aged" looked like a drain on financial resources that should be directed to beautiful tiles and cement blocks. The district minister in Akyem Abuakwa told me that the aged program was expensive because of transportation, and thus he was hesitant to start an aged fellowship program without a strong benefactor (fieldnotes, June 5, 2014). Furthermore, church leaders were interested in attracting young and middle-aged people into their congregations because they are current income earners, who can contribute to church finances, while older women are stereotypically portrayed as devout but impoverished, putting only small coins into the collection boxes. The chairman of the aged program at the Head Office of the Presbyterian Church of Ghana commented to me, "There are those who think that money spent on the elderly is a waste of money, because they don't have a lot of funds themselves. We should recognize that in the past they were our champions" (interview, July 2, 2013). In fact, one minister in Akyem told me that the reason to start a fellowship group for the aged was to remove the older generation from the Men's and Women's Fellowships, because the middle aged would have difficulty belonging to the same fellowship groups as their seniors or taking leadership roles within these groups when their seniors were members (fieldnotes, July 9, 2014). Thus, paradoxically, according to this minister's analysis, the fellowship groups for the aged were a sign not of the church's respect or sense of importance of older congregants, but of their marginalization, so that middle-aged congregants could assume leadership positions on church committees. Thus, "Celebrating the Aged," as the New Tafo's fellowship group's T-shirts proclaim, may symbolize older persons' segregation into less significant arenas of the church.

Finally, the reliance on outside donors or benefactors endangered continuity in programming, as benefactors' goals and motivations shifted. Some of the funding for the aged fellowship groups at the national level of the Presbyterian Church of Ghana came from an African American church in Albany (United

States), through a connection with a Presbyterian woman living in Tema. Although they had been interested in dementia, by 2013, when I had a chance to meet them when a delegation from their church visited Ghana, their interests had changed: they now wanted to build a day care center for disabled children (fieldnotes, July 6, 2013). The view from Ghana was that outside donors were somewhat fickle in their funding, changing direction and being inconsistent in their generosity.

The organizers of the lively aged fellowship group in New Tafo complained about the lack of support from the church for the group, requiring the assistance from an outside patron. Even when the church collects contributions on the day designated by the Presbyterian Church of Ghana as Aged Sunday, the church does not distribute that money to the aged fellowship group. According to one organizer, when the group asked for the Aged Sunday collection, a younger man in the church governance body (Session) asked, "Don't the old people have children and grandchildren to make them happy at Christmas?" Similar to the government's Aged Policy, according to the logic of the younger man's argument, the emphasis on kin care absolved the church of any responsibility of caring for the aged. I heard from one of the organizers that the major patron for the group was incensed by this remark, wanting to tell the church Session to respect the elderly (*bu mpanyinfo*) and that some of the older people in town had been "abandoned by their children and grandchildren" (interview, August 15, 2019). Another organizer said that the problem is that each minister wants to do something that promotes his name and reputation, and that means building projects. The money in the church raised by Aged Sunday went to construction instead (fieldnotes, August 12, 2019).

Advocates for aging within the Presbyterian Church were aware of the ambivalence within the church. A minister in Obo (Kwawu) who was supportive of his congregation's aged fellowship group was upset by how the Presbyterian Church of Ghana gave only lip service to older adults (fieldnotes, July 23, 2014). Yet, there are many advocates for the aged within the church, some of whom have reached important institutional positions. Rev. Samuel Ayete-Nyampong gave a powerful talk at the Synod meeting on the crisis of older congregants in 2007 and later attained the powerful position of Clerk of the General Assembly (2012–2019).[12] I met and heard of several Presbyterian ministers who wrote their seminary theses on aging. However, in general the Presbyterian Church of Ghana's aged fellowship groups seem dependent on the initiative of individuals rather than energized by the church leadership, which remains ambivalent about these efforts at both the local level and the top.

Older congregants criticized the Presbyterian Church of Ghana for its lack of care for them, particularly in Akyem, where many aged fellowship groups were just forming. They used a language of balanced reciprocity to make this argument: although they have contributed to the church in the past, the church does not currently support them. In a group discussion in Begoro, one woman said,

"The church elders don't think about us; we always come to church, but they don't think about us. We even pay their salary, but they don't think of us."[13] In Kukurantumi, a woman complained, "We served the church when we were strong, but today because of our knees, backs, hypertension, and other things, we can only serve the church a little. There will come a time when we can't serve at all. And at that point, it is necessary that the church elders help us and the congregation help us when we can't do anything at all. Because even those with children may not have children nearby. Everyone is on their own."[14] This comment was met with enthusiasm. Another woman built on this comment in the same group discussion: "Someone has served the church but when they are weak, they don't have help from anywhere; some don't have children."[15] The church was therefore viewed as another source of assistance, if children could not help, for precisely the same reason as adult children were obliged to care. Adult children were "forced" to assist because of the help they had received in childhood; similarly, the gifts of time, energy, and money provided by older congregants during an earlier period of the life course should be reciprocated when they were weak and impoverished.

The half-hearted support from the Presbyterian Church for older congregants notwithstanding, fund-raising for a senior day center to be built on the grounds of Christchurch in Akropong began in 2006. A previous minister at Christchurch, Rev. Kwapong, explained to me the impetus for the day center: during Invalid Communion, his presbyters found a woman who was locked in her room when the children went out for the day, sometimes leaving her with food and sometimes without. Christchurch thought that if her children had a place where they could leave her when they went to market, then it would support family caregiving (interview, June 21, 2013). Through Rev. Kwapong's connections abroad, an American Presbyterian minister in the United States helped raise money for the center. Funds were also raised within Ghana by a bank manager in Accra and among the children of aging people who lived abroad or in the urban areas of Ghana (interview, Rev. Nyarko, September 13, 2019). One of the organizers told me in 2015 that many people from Akropong were contributing, because they wanted to be able to leave their parents there for the day (fieldnotes, May 28, 2015). As I discuss further in the next chapter, these migrants are one of the important transmitters of practices about care from abroad because they cannot provide daily care to their aging parents, since they are far away, and they have the financial resources to support the church's initiatives on aging. However, they were not the initiators of the idea, which came instead from church leaders becoming aware of and responding to older congregants' needs through the activities of home visits and giving Communion to bedridden older adults. Many transnational migrants work in elder care in the United Kingdom and the United States, and, having witnessed institutional facilities firsthand, are not strong supporters of them. However, they seemed willing to support a day center, given their concerns about their aging parents and their own absence from Akropong.

Soon after the day center was proposed, a new minister, Rev. Nyarko, came in 2009. Fortunately for fund-raising efforts, he loved the aged program and was convinced that the day center would be a good idea. He agreed with his predecessor Rev. Kwapong: when he visited older people in their homes, the younger members of the household had gone to school and work. The older adults were left alone in their rooms and could not take their medication for lack of food. If they attended a day center, a nurse would be there. In his eagerness, he went by to check on the construction ten times a day (interview, September 13, 2019). However, more recent ministers since 2012 were less enthusiastic.

I heard various visions for the senior day center over the years from different members of Christchurch's aged committee. Some hoped it would provide a free hot lunch, whereas others were concerned about the costs of providing food and thought participants should pay a fee for meals. Sometimes a daily fee for attendance was mentioned; at other times, the program would be free because of the contributions older adults had already made to the church. It was unclear whether the church van would provide daily transportation to the center. All mentioned that there would be nurse on staff, present during the day, and that the main purpose of the center would be sociality, because grandchildren went to school and adults worked during the day. As one organizer explained, the purpose of the center would be for older adults to come together to see their mates and play games. Donated athletic equipment would be located on the second floor, where physiotherapy sessions would take place. Reproducing the discourse of aging advocates across the Presbyterian Church of Ghana as the rationale for their project, the organizer said, "Loneliness kills" (fieldnotes, May 28, 2015).

A prominent building on the grounds of the church was something the Presbyterian Church of Ghana could support, as it expanded the architectural grandeur of the grounds, showing that Christchurch could raise funds from its members and was prosperous due to God's grace (fig. 4.5). An ongoing program was more problematic and expensive, requiring staff and organization, and in some ways was less visible. Although constructed explicitly as a senior center, the building is not designed to be so. It is two stories high and has no kitchen. There are no accommodations for disabled adults, such as a ramp or large washrooms where a wheelchair might turn or a person might accompany another to assist. The function of the small veranda on the second floor was also unclear, unless the building were to serve as a residence. Instead, its façade looks more like a standard contemporary mansion that one might see on the outskirts of any urban area of southern Ghana. As the building reached completion, the lay organizers began to worry that the church leaders would use the building for other purposes and argued, at the least opportunity, including my visits to the church office, that the building was a message that caring for older people can raise money for the church and enhance its physical profile. The fact that the building was completed in late December 2016 but was still not functioning as a senior

FIG. 4.5 Completed senior day center, Akropong, December 29, 2016.

day center spoke to ambivalence among the church leaders about organizing a program to support older adults.

By 2019, the organizer seemed reconciled to the loss of a senior day program. She told me that the risk of family members abandoning their older relatives at the center was too great, which seemed like a strange excuse to other organizers. She said that the aged committee had given permission to the leadership of Christchurch to use the building for other purposes. Even abroad, she said, resources are not sufficient for senior care. She also said that what is important is to give people advice so that they can look after themselves when they are old and be in good shape (fieldnotes, September 3, 2019). Thus, it seemed that the dream of a senior day center, begun thirteen years before, was over. What the church would promote instead was self-care and planning for aging.

Christchurch was not alone in the experience of having aging projects diverted to other purposes. Another Presbyterian church, in the Accra suburb of Adenta, had similarly engaged in fundraising to build a resource center for older adults. However, because they borrowed money to complete the building, they had rented out offices in the building rather than using it as a resource center. Some members of the church worried that those who had donated funds would be upset that the intended purpose of those funds was not realized (fieldnotes, July 1, 2015).

In a religious environment in which the mainline churches have lost their younger members to newer churches, the Presbyterian Church of Ghana is competing with the more popular churches by becoming like them in its rhetoric and programming. Thus, while the Presbyterian Church might be a source of new programs to support older persons, through aged fellowship groups and senior day centers, its voice is muted by competing demands and goals, including concerns about financing and organizing new programs. Some ministers and church elders, because of their personal experiences of giving Invalid Communion, advocate for support of older adults, but others find the focus irrelevant or distracting from the long-term survival and growth of the church, which they view as dependent on the contributions of younger and middle-aged people. The Presbyterian Church does not articulate a clear, strong message on solutions when kin care fails because of its own ambivalence about social welfare for older persons. However, it has generated new spaces—through fellowship groups—for older Presbyterians to articulate and share their experiences and concerns, as we saw in chapter 2. Furthermore, it has helped create an age inscription around senior day centers and aged fellowship groups, despite its failure to wholeheartedly and consistently support them.

Conclusion

In August 2019, I was surprised when not one but two social welfare officers in the neighboring districts in North Akwapim and Adukrom mentioned that they thought each district should support social gatherings for older adults. The town of Akropong, where Christchurch is located, is in the North Akwapim District, and the newly created Adukrom District is further along the Akuapem ridge (and formerly part of the North Akwapim District). The incoming District Chief Executive of North Akwapim in 2019 had asked the social welfare officer about the needs of the district, and she mentioned the needs of older adults as significant. He asked her to propose a plan, and in response, she recommended a senior day center. She imagined a place where nurses could provide basic medical care, so that older adults did not have to go to the hospital; where they ate a hot meal; and where their relatives transported them to the center. A stranger to Akropong, she based this proposal on the day center established by HelpAge in Osu, not far from the national ministries, rather than the much closer Christchurch. Her major reason for recommending a day center was that it would be easier to staff than a full-time residential facility (interview, August 6, 2019).

The Adukrom social welfare officer had a less concrete proposal but also proposed as a solution that the district should have programs where the aged meet and "socialize with one another." They can "share their problems." "A problem shared is half solved." Concerned that older adults are depressed, she thought that a social gathering would help them see that "life is full of living." They will "meet their colleagues and be happy." Then they "will go back home" (interview, August 21, 2019). Nana Araba Apt, who had been involved in HelpAge and was a major advocate for the aging in Ghana, had also proposed to the government, several years before, that a senior day center be run in every district (interview, July 2, 2013). Another social worker I met in Accra also wanted to open an aged center in the neighborhood of La, where she worked, after she became familiar with the needs of older adults. She noted that her superiors discouraged her efforts, saying that there was no problem because older adults are taken care of by their children (interview, July 4, 2014).

For district chief executives, building a center would answer a political need to further their reputation, similar to the Presbyterian ministers in which legacies are established concretely, in visible infrastructure. The North Akwapim social welfare officer had explained to me in 2013 why social welfare activities in the district lacked political support, so that no state support was being proffered to older adults: "The political terrain is very rough." In order to win an election, a political official has to show what he or she did for the district, and new school blocks and clinics are more visible than helping individuals or households. When it comes time to vote, an orphan with a scholarship will not tell others to vote for a particular party, she told me. Speaking as a social worker, she said, "Our work is not seen" (interview, June 20, 2013). Infrastructure, on the other hand, was visible to the public, legitimating claims of capability and connection, in a way that charity was not. Proposing a senior day center was therefore strategic on her part, in promoting social welfare through infrastructure. However, it was not attractive enough: the district chief executive had not yet followed up on her proposal.

Thus, the activity by churches to create social and physical spaces for older adults to gather and socialize seems to have gained currency in some circles. That is, it seems to be an age inscription acquiring the status of an orthodoxy. This idea was being floated in government circles. The problems with the care of older adults were perceived through visiting bedridden, disabled, and frail congregants in their homes. However, the solutions generated within the churches rely on a construction of older adults from which the disabled and bedridden are excluded. Instead, the aged are perceived as social persons with certain kinds of problems, mainly that of loneliness and sadness, who are abandoned during the day by household members busy at school and work. The senior day centers and fellowship groups imagine an aged person to be a generally well and mobile older person with access to transportation, implying a certain wealth or mobility. It is these older adults without signs of a physical disability and who commanded social and economic resources who gained respect as elders and had claims to assistance. For this kind of person, a social gathering is proposed as the solution, allowing for fellowship and sociality and warding off depression and loneliness, which can lead to death. And yet, it is those who are stuck at home through frailty and disability who are most likely to be lonely, without visitors, even if surrounded by an active household (Van der Geest 2002b, 2004b). One of Sjaak van der Geest's older informants concluded a conversation about his poor health with the following adage: "The sick man has no friend" (Ɔyareɛfo nni adamfo)

(2004b, 93). Disabled people's loneliness makes visits by church fellowship groups and by ministers for Invalid Communion particularly welcome. Although the ideas and practices for enhancing sociability among older adults have not been enacted by the state, local officials are aware of them from religious organizations. Officials are proposing similar solutions as they struggle to promote their own initiatives and programs within the state apparatus, to support older Ghanaians whose needs become visible to them.

The comparative history of social welfare policy highlights the importance of borrowing between nations. Lloyd George visited Germany for five days in August 1908 to learn about Germany's national health insurance system before proposing one for Britain (Laybourn 1995). American nineteenth-century reformers borrowed from English and Continental writers "a comprehensive body of charitable theory," as well as formulating their own (Bremner 1980, 323). However, Theda Skocpol (1992) notes that while American reformers attempted to use these ideas to influence American social policy, they were usually not successful. Instead, Skocpol argues that state welfare policies depend on, among other factors, the strategies and goals of politicians and administrators within a political system. I concur with her analysis. State practices of care in other countries had little influence on Ghana. Nursing homes were berated as a heterodoxy by the government of Ghana and those who helped influence its policy. Older adults expressed interest in them, but only because they functioned as a heterodoxy to the status quo—kin care—which was clearly insufficient. What was actually emerging in Ghana depended on the criteria for personal advancement and status in both state and religious circles. Religious institutions have tried, but not fully sustained or institutionalized, certain solutions because of their internal dynamics in which ministers gain a reputation through fundraising and building projects. Yet through their initiatives, senior day centers and fellowship groups have spread as an idea, allowing them to be potentially borrowed by others. Ghanaian state officials are aware of these initiatives, but have not adopted them because visible physical infrastructure wins elections. More invisible initiatives that extend social welfare to older adults, like basic income programs or visiting community nurses, do not carry the same reputational weight and thus find only a few backers.

Part II

Changes in Aging in
Urban Ghana

• •

5

Market-Based Solutions
for the Globally Connected
Middle Class

●●●●●●●●●●●●●●●●●●●●●

In the previous three chapters, I described the changes in aging and elder care in the rural towns of southern Ghana. What is being normalized there are two inscriptions: the idea of senior day centers and the actual practice of fellowship gatherings for older adults. In urban areas, across Africa, in contrast, small, somewhat organized long-term care markets are emerging, caring for the needs of the most destitute through charitable services and for those able to pay, with few organized services for the vast majority of the population (World Health Organization 2017). In Accra, there are some small, struggling nursing homes, but more prominent and popular are home nursing services, provided by numerous agencies, both small, fly-by-night businesses and more well-established operations. The elder care market of nursing homes and nursing agencies is surrounded by a much larger market in which middle-class households contract directly with domestic servants who provide elder care alongside other domestic duties, in exchange for much lower wages than those given to care workers employed by agencies or in care homes.

In general, the aging clients of the commercial care services, both residential facilities and home care, are quite frail. Many are bedridden or otherwise disabled. Some have dementia, requiring constant monitoring, but remain physically healthy. It is the care of these older people that necessitates the most labor, and it is to help with their care that urban, middle-class families generally turn to the expensive services of the commercial care market. As described in chapter 4, church leaders are aware of congregants in similar need of care, but the voluntary and free solutions that have emerged within churches—the fellowship groups—are focused on the more mobile and generally younger members among those considered "the aged."

The urban market in elder care services is being driven by the growth of a middle class in Ghana. The Ghanaian economy has been booming since 2011, expanding the civil service, the traditional occupation of the middle class, as well as the private sector linked to the global economy. In addition, a growing population abroad continues to funnel significant resources to households in Ghana, which has helped support the middle class in Ghana. Women in the middle class are more likely to be migrants, whether to urban areas or abroad, and therefore experience the unwelcome prospect of giving up their employment and relocating to care for their aging parents, a parent's sibling, or their own older siblings in the hometown. If their income is earned abroad, they can afford to pay for commercial elder care in Ghana. The middle class fuels the commercial care market in Accra as employed middle-class Ghanaian women in both urban areas of Ghana and elsewhere in the world try to live up to the obligations of kin care.

Sociologists and anthropologists have often posited transnational migration to be a source of change in family life, with transnational migration replacing modernization as the engine of social change (e.g., Apt 1996). Transnational migration refers to the maintenance of cross-border social and emotional networks and identifications when people migrate across international borders. Two different theories posit how transnational migration creates a commercial care market in the countries from which migrants come. Peggy Levitt's theory of social remittances (1998) argues that migrants communicate the ideas and experiences they learn through their migration to their compatriots in their home countries, thus transferring those practices and concepts as social remittances. Arlie Russell Hochschild (2001) posits that women's migration was stimulated by a global care deficit: as middle-class women in Western countries entered the workforce and experienced a time crunch in balancing productive with reproductive labor, they turned to female migrants as nannies, cleaners, and elder care workers to help them with the labor in their homes. In turn, these female migrants created a gap in care in their own households, replacing themselves with their own daughters or mothers or hiring even poorer women to cook, clean, and provide child care. Both theories suggest that migration is a primary cause of social change in the countries from which migrants come.

What I argue in this chapter is that transnational migration is implicated in the development of the commercial care market in the major urban areas of Ghana but is not the sole cause. In this more subtle argument, I follow Sarah Lamb (2009) and Jennifer Hirsch (2003) who show how changes in family life (in elder care in India and in love in Mexico, respectively) are affected by the diaspora, but also by changes within the country of origin, such as the rise of a middle class in India and intergenerational differences in Mexico. This chapter examines the ways that ideas and practices associated with other societies are adapted by various social actors, as heterodoxies or alterodoxies to maintain the orthodox ideal of kin care. Transnational migration has provided the ideas and capital for commercial care services and enabled some children and kin of older or disabled adults to use those commercial care services because of social and financial remittances from abroad. However, what is adopted seems most affected by the cultural consumption patterns of the middle class in Ghana and by the desire to maintain the orthodoxy of kin care through alternative means. Home nursing services are more popular than other eldercare practices brought from abroad, like nursing homes or hospice services, because of the long-standing use of domestic servants (known as househelp) in urban, middle-class households.

The Growth of a Care Market in Accra

The first home care agency started in Ghana in 1997. The emergence of other agencies thereafter, in the late 1990s and early 2000s, composed part of the marketization and privatization of health care across Africa to serve wealthy and middle-class urban families (Dekker and van Dijk 2010). The four agencies I tracked from 2014 to 2019 were the biggest and most well-established agencies in the care market of Accra. Among those four, the smallest served ten patients and employed twelve care workers or carers (to use the local term based on British usage) in 2019. It did not think it had the capacity to expand beyond that. In contrast, the largest and oldest served forty-five to sixty patients, with fluctuations over the five-year period. I interviewed the owners of three other agencies, one of which had closed just before the interview. Five of the seven total were run by women in their fifties or sixties, and the sixth by a male nurse; the seventh, which had gone out of business, had been owned by three brothers, one of whom lived abroad. Although these numbers may seem small, the six functioning nursing agencies interviewed represented the entire universe of nursing agencies operating in Accra in 2015.[1] Although other nursing agencies emerged subsequently, the four agencies I followed (2014–2019) were the largest and most established. Some agencies were fragile and short-lived; for example, I was told about four additional agencies, all started in the late 1990s, that went out of business quickly. Others have survived by serving as both an agency and a for-profit school for carers; still others started with a school and later created an agency as a side business; others dropped the strenuous demands of training their own employees and simply hired carers trained by self-standing schools. All the agencies struggled to maintain themselves, doing well during economic boom times and cutting back when the local or global economy suffered because many of their clients had children abroad. Agency owners reported to me that they were working hard to figure out how to make the business survive: this meant cutting back on expenses like office space, training, and transportation; figuring out where the owner and manager's time and effort should be directed; and making minimal investments in the business.

The agencies are older and more numerous and serve more clients than the nursing homes. I visited one residential facility, located in a wealthy neighborhood of Accra, for a day in 2015 with six residents, run by a politician's wife. By 2016, it had gone out of business. In 2014 I visited a second one on the road to Akosombo, created as an act of charity, with nine residents, which had been in operation for three years. I lived for a week in 2018 in a third one with twenty-seven residents; I had been visiting it regularly since its foundation in 2015. All had developed in the 2010s. In addition, one agency owner housed one or two residents sporadically in her school or house to see whether she should open a more permanent nursing home. Another agency owner was planning to build a nursing home, but the land she had bought for this purpose was under litigation, as is common in Ghana, thus delaying the start of the project. Another care home in Kasoa, a suburb of Accra, was profiled in the international newspaper the *Guardian*, probably to attract Ghanaians in the diaspora with parents in Ghana. Founded in 2016, it had seven residents in May 2020. The owner reported that it did well only when it began to advertise in English rather than in local languages, indicating that its clientele was among the middle class and elite. Further evidence of this fact was that it priced its services in dollars or British pounds and that all the residents either had children abroad or had lived abroad themselves (*Guardian* 2020). With time, these facilities may become more popular. At the moment, they seem small, fragile, and either in danger of disappearing or having difficulty getting off the ground.

This chapter and the following two are based on fieldwork from July 2013 to October 2019, twenty-eight weeks (or about seven months of research) over six years, in order to track the viability of this market over time. My fieldwork involved interviews with seven owners of commercial nursing agencies, three owners of senior residential facilities, three nurse managers at agencies who directly supervised the carers, eleven patients or relatives of patients, and twenty carers, most of whom were employed by these agencies but two of whom I met independently of the agencies. I also briefly visited twelve households that employed home carers, sometimes accompanying the nurse manager or owner on their supervisory or assessment visits, and sometimes coming on my own to spend an hour or two with the patient and carer. I visited two nursing homes briefly, spending a day there, and stayed a week in the largest and most stable one in 2018, waking at two or three in the morning to help with the bathing of the residents, one of the most important and strenuous daily routines of the institution. I also attended two weeks of classes and three days of final exams at a school for carers run by a nursing agency and attended a morning class at another school. Particularly on the exam days, I was able to chat with teachers and students at a range of different nursing assistance schools in the northern suburbs of Accra. I followed up with the students after their graduation to see where they were employed. I also had conversations with middle-class, urban older people and their children who were not using these services about their thoughts regarding the senior care market.

Private nursing services, whether at home or in a residential facility, constituted a luxury commodity in Accra. Commercial care services in Ghana, as in the United States (Coe 2019a), are a solution only for those with financial resources. Government support would be needed to expand access to care beyond the small number who can currently afford it. At most, the number of patients served by agencies and in nursing homes at any one time during these six years was approximately 200 people, out of a total population of approximately 127,000 people older than age sixty-five in the Greater Accra Region (Ghana Statistical Service 2012). As a luxury service, commercial care services were heavily dependent on urban middle-class consumption patterns, which in turn were affected, in part, by migrant remittances. That children abroad can pay for care services means that they are accessible to a broader group of people than simply the Ghanaian elite. The clients of commercial care services include retired teachers and midlevel civil servants who have children abroad. In Accra and Tema, patients' households tended to be concentrated in the wealthy neighborhoods of Dzorwulu, Ringway Estates, Tesano, Airport Residential, East Legon, and Labone, although there were a few in more middle-class neighborhoods like Mamprobi, Ayigbetown, Ashalley Botwe, and Adabraka. Some patients are return migrants, who came back to Ghana from abroad when they became sick, injured, or frail because greater kin support and cheaper care services were available in Ghana than in their countries of migration like Australia or parts of North America or Europe.

The patients of the agencies I studied were mainly in the Greater Accra–Tema metropolitan area, but the agencies also received requests from other cities and large towns like Begoro and Nkawkaw (both in the Eastern Region), Cape Coast (Central Region), and Sunyani (Bono Region) from relatives working and living in Accra or abroad. One carer I met was sent to the neighboring country of Togo (fieldnotes, July 13, 2018). Another strategy by adult children was to bring their parents from rural areas to the urban areas where their children lived to receive more care from nursing agencies or care homes. For example, in the profile of the nursing home in the *Guardian*, an electronics technician brought his eighty-nine-year-old mother from a village in the Central Region to the nursing home because she was having trouble moving around on the rural roads (*Guardian* 2020). This is similar to the story I told in chapter 3: a daughter brought her mother from a village in the Western Region after she had a stroke. The mother lived in the daughter's house in Accra for several years before the daughter decided to pursue her master's degree and, because of the anticipated strain on her time, placed her mother in a nursing home, where I met her.

The small number of nursing agencies and residential facilities operating in Accra and the few patients they serve may suggest that the phenomenon of commercial nursing services is marginal or not relevant to elder care in Ghana. In my view, however, this new industry provides a window onto broader social conflicts and changes in Ghana, including both class and intergenerational dynamics. Although potential patients cannot always afford elder care services, the interest in them is high among middle-class and elite urban families as a potential option. As discussed in chapter 1, the government has emphasized the role the "traditional" family plays in taking care of its elderly members. In the absence of a widespread state response, the commercial care market shows how individuals with resources are coming up with private solutions as they care for aged relations, in the face of an orthodoxy that no longer corresponds to people's everyday lives and needs to be shored up by alternative methods like those offered by the market.

A Globally Connected Middle Class in Ghana

Historically, in Ghana the middle class has been linked to the civil service or state bureaucracy, in part because of the legacy of colonial administrations (Kuklick 1979; Oppong 1974). As in Europe (Berger 1981; Kocka 1981), the formation of a privileged middle class is dependent, in part, on state political concessions and legal niches that protect this class and distinguish it from others. Considered the primary source of potential opposition in Ghana, the urban middle class has historically won numerous benefits, such as subsidized food prices at the expense of farmers, and engaged in strikes to maintain civil service wages (Opoku 2010). The middle class was educated and employed by the state, which gave it certain privileges such as free housing and transportation, stable employment, and status. Civil servants had access to low-interest loans to purchase cars or pay school tuition, further bolstering their status in others' eyes.

However, the economic downturn of the 1970s and structural adjustment reforms of the 1980s and 1990s resulted in a decline in civil servants' status into a lower middle class as they were retrenched and their wages and benefits eroded; the whole class structure in Ghana shifted downward during this period (Budniok and Noll 2018). Structural adjustment reforms aimed to reduce government expenditure and promote economic growth by boosting the export-oriented sectors of the Ghanaian economy. Imposed by the World Bank and International Monetary Fund, in exchange for further loans, such reforms did not promote an indigenous entrepreneurial class because they focused on highly capitalized export-oriented industries like gold mining, which only multinational companies had the capital to pursue (Opoku 2010). Due to an economic decline and the erosion of state protection of the civil service, many middle-class Ghanaians migrated abroad to maintain their class positions, to Nigeria and Libya to work as secondary school teachers, or to Europe and North America, where they often entered low-wage and low-status occupations (Nieswand 2011). Many early migrants were members of the urban middle class and elite, and they paved the way for more working-class Ghanaians to later migrate (Manuh 2006).

By the 1990s, migration contributed to the expansion of the middle class in Ghana and its greater purchasing power because "social mobility and reproduction are realized in the context of extended families" with remittances flowing across national borders to accomplish these goals (Budniok and Noll 2018, 130). Ghana has a relatively high rate of international migration within Africa (International Organization for Migration 2009). It is estimated that between 3 and 7 percent of Ghana's population has migrated abroad (Twum-Baah 2005; World Bank 2011). Middle-class urban households and many households in smaller towns in southern Ghana have at least one family member abroad. Remittances from abroad were estimated to be $3 billion in 2018 (World Bank 2019a) and compose on average 9 percent of income in Ghanaian households (Mazzucato, Van den Boom, and Nsowah-Nuamah 2008). These remittances particularly help support the local middle class through times of hardship and crisis (Orozco 2005; Quartey 2006), when large and onerous payments, such as for school fees or medical bills, the construction of housing, and the capital for petty businesses, are needed as well as for everyday expenses. Remittances from overseas are mainly sent to households in the richest quintile and those living in the most affluent regions of Ashanti and Greater Accra, from which most international migrants came (Mazzucato, Van den Boom, and Nsowah-Nuamah 2008). Elder care through commercial care services, as a luxury consumption item, is particularly dependent on remittances from abroad.

Ghana's middle class has also benefitted from the country's recent economic growth. Since 2011, Ghana has experienced an economic boom (at 15.3 percent in 2011), its economy growing, on average, 5.1 percent between 2013 and 2018 (World Bank 2019b). Most of the growth was driven by mining and oil extraction (Baah-Boateng 2013). The extraction economy does not produce a local middle class because it employs few Ghanaians. However, the benefits of the economic boom led to an expansion of the middle class in both the private and public sectors (Lopes 2015). In the private sector, the middle class is often connected to multinational companies like telecommunications or banking. The economic growth gave the government further resources, and the civil service has expanded enormously since 2005 (*Economist* 2016).[2] "Ghana's civil service is relatively large compared with other African countries. For instance, based on the 2000 census, the number of public employees in administration, defense, education, and health as a share of the population was 2.1 percent, while the equivalent average for the African region was 1 percent (see also World Bank 2011). A decade later, the number of people working in the formal public sector had doubled from 388,020 to 639,260 people, equivalent to approximately 1 public servant for every 40.6 people" (Resnick 2019, 71, her calculations). Some observers of class dynamics in Africa have argued that the status and economic power of a middle class dependent on the public sector is deteriorating in Africa, while the middle class connected to the private market is becoming more prominent in comparison to its public-sector counterparts, such as in Kenya (Spronk 2014). The reality, however, is more complicated, in Ghana at least. Certainly the middle class connected to the private sector has grown, but the public sector continues to hold its appeal as an employer because those in the private sector work longer hours and have more precarious work. Similar to India, although neoliberalism has resulted in the disengagement of the middle class from the developmentalist state, the government remains significant for the middle class in relation to public-sector employment and education (Donner and De Neve 2011, 15). In Ghana, many people associate public-sector employment with middle-class status.

These different middle classes as routes to the good life (Appadurai 2013) represent "different visions of the state, different modes of capitalist reproduction, and different forms of subjectivity" (Heiman, Freeman, and Liechty 2012, 14; see also Harvey 2005). Whereas the space that typifies the public-sector middle class is the bureaucrat's office, that of the private-sector middle class is the shopping mall and the gated estate. Also, the public and private sectors have different gendered opportunities. In Ghana, the overwhelming majority (90 percent) of civil servants and those employed in the formal sector are men (Heintz 2005). Women in Ghana work at levels comparable to men, dominating the informal sector in trade (Clark 1994; Heintz 2005). Nursing, alongside teaching, has provided one of the few routes by which women can obtain a civil service position. The private labor market is more open to female employment, in part because it is oriented to the provision of services associated with feminine skills (Freeman 2014) and because it overlaps with informal markets in Ghana. However, it is important to note that individuals move between the public and private sectors across their life courses and that the risk of falling out of the middle class is quite real (Kroeker, O'Kane, and Scharrer 2018). The pursuit of master's degrees among middle-class, middle-aged men and women to maintain or improve their class positions has also become prominent in Ghana, further leading to middle-aged women's time constraints.

One of the patterns of consumption in an urban middle-class household is the presence of domestic servants. In Accra, the use of househelp has been quite common among elite households since at least the 1960s (Ardayfio-Schandorf and Amissah 1996; Oppong 1974). Many of the fifty-nine elite families in Accra interviewed by Christine Oppong (1974) had help provided through their matrilineal kin, whether distant or closer kin. Employed middle-class women have long relied on the assistance of other women or girls in balancing household obligations with their employment; it is for this reason that they fostered in their siblings or nieces, as Mercy Amankwah, the retired nurse described in chapter 3, did. Low-income urban households also had domestic servants (Grieco, Apt, and Turner 1996).

Commercial care services operate alongside kin care and domestic service. Several carers described to me their care of kin in addition to their paid care work with an agency. When caring for kin, they received food, housing, and payment for any medical care they needed. As one said, "You are appreciated but not paid" (phone interview, August 13, 2014). One agency owner commented that she is in competition with kin care, "where the family provides care, free of charge" (interview, August 4, 2015). One carer talked about a client who could no longer pay the fees when her agency's rates increased. The client told her, "I can't do it anymore. I will call someone else to take care of my mother, from the village" (taped group interview, June 24, 2014). Yet many clients told me that they chose paid caregivers because of their dissatisfaction with kin care, which created complicated reciprocal exchanges between kin. One client, who had worked for the United Nations abroad, commented that he hired an agency for the care of his wife disabled by a stroke because he found the "extended family" to be "problematic": "they bring problems and the problems hurt you very much." They might talk about him to other relatives, or they might ask him to take care of their child (fieldnotes, June 29, 2015). A daughter of an agency client did not use kin care because "there are problems with relatives. You have to take care of their children and grandchildren. They ask for permission to go to the village for a funeral and there is a funeral every weekend" (interview, June 9, 2015). In the 1960s, Oppong (1974) noted the dwindling sense of responsibility to the matrikin by elite families. In my study, some households seemed to consider kin care unreliable and conflict-ridden.

I argue that the reason home nursing services have taken off, in contrast to nursing homes, is because the middle class in Ghana is used to domestic servants coming into or living in the household to provide household labor. Paid care supplements or substitutes for kin care, signaling the ways that the orthodoxy of kin care is inadequate. However, the potential use of kin labor and the expense of commercial care services make the home care agencies unstable as businesses. In the following discussion, I focus on two kinds of middle-class actors critical to the commercial elder care market: the entrepreneurs who create the commercial care services and the customers who use them.

Entrepreneurs: Active Brokers of Ideas and Practices from Abroad

Many agency owners are return migrants. Three of the seven owners of agencies whom I interviewed had previously lived abroad (in the United Kingdom or the United States), and they opened the agency as a business in order to support themselves in the middle class upon their return to Ghana. Living abroad gave them the financial capital with which to start their business; the agency was their mechanism to make a middle-class living in Ghana. Their experience abroad also gave them cachet (or cultural capital) among their clients and employees as having a particular kind of expert knowledge.

Those who were not return migrants were all middle class, having worked previously in either the private or public formal sector in Ghana, and most had global connections through family or their profession. Among the four agency owners who had not migrated abroad, one of them had worked with a midwifery association in Ghana, traveling extensively for international conferences as part of her work, and she told me that she wanted to help her country with the knowledge of nursing and hospital practice that she had gained abroad. A second, a public healthcare professional, had worked briefly with international development organizations on the millennium health goals in Ghana. A third was a nurse employed in a government hospital in Ghana and had no international experience. A fourth was a pharmacist in Ghana with a brother who worked in health care in the United States and was a partner in the agency business. In contrast to the agency owners who were return migrants, those who had always lived and worked in Ghana had much deeper connections to local institutions, allowing them to obtain referrals from their former colleagues working at hospitals.

Among the three nursing home owners, two were resident in Ghana and were members of the elite. For both, the residential facility was constructed as charity work, although they charged fees from some patients. One, a politician's wife, had numerous other businesses, including a high-end boutique (fieldnotes, June 10, 2014), whereas the other had an NGO she ran that supported widows' clubs and orphans in various regions across the country (fieldnotes, August 1, 2014). The owner of the third residential facility was a working-class migrant in Switzerland, where she worked in a food packaging plant (WhatsApp phone interview, July 16, 2018). Each canton in Switzerland runs a nursing home available to the official members of the canton, and she had persuaded her local one to donate used equipment to her nursing home in Ghana. Since she remained working in Switzerland, she had hired a manager for the nursing home. Although the nursing home operated as a business, charging monthly rates to its residents, it was registered as an NGO, and its migrant owner complained that it required constant infusions of remittances from her employment to subsidize residents' fees. This facility had as many residents as it did because its rates were reasonable and cheaper than home care services, mainly because they were subsidized by the migrant owner's remittances. In 2019, the prices increased rapidly when the remittances dropped, because the migrant owner's husband, then in his late fifties, was furloughed in Switzerland and the owner began to prepare for her own retirement.

I heard from some who worked in elder care abroad about their interest in opening an agency or nursing home in Ghana, as a way of supporting themselves as a return migrant in retirement (fieldnotes, July 23, 2013, and July 19, 2014). While giving a donation to the St. Vincent de Paul Center, an elite woman in Tema expressed interest in opening a nursing home in her own house, for her ninety-two-year-old mother and some other older adults (fieldnotes, June 18,

2015). A nun who had worked as a nursing assistant in the United States for three years after taking a course in hospice in Florida had been trying to open a nursing home in Ghana since 2011 (fieldnotes, June 2013). She opened a small center with two or three residents in 2014–2015 and then sought licensing from the government, so that she would not be blamed if someone died there (fieldnotes, June 18, 2015).[3] There was considerable interest in opening nursing homes among middle-class and elite urban women as a side business-cum-charity but, as far as I could tell, not a lot of success in actually doing so.

Many owners of agencies and nursing homes talked about the care of their own older relatives as providing the impetus for their initiatives. Stella, an owner of a nursing agency, related the story of her uncle who had had a stroke. Her uncle had no kin care because he had separated from his wife, his children were abroad, and his siblings were either elderly or working. Using her social work training in the United Kingdom, she hired and taught a taxi driver to care for him properly (phone interview, July 13, 2013). Another agency owner described bringing her mother to live with her while she was traveling a great deal when working as a trainer for a registered midwives' association. She was the only daughter among her siblings, with one brother living outside Ghana. Her brothers did not give her much help because they felt that as a nurse, she knew what to do. She thinks her mother died of loneliness and lack of companionship, prompting her to start the agency after her mother's death (interview, June 4, 2014). Esther related the story of returning from the United Kingdom to care for her mother, who was dying of cancer, and taking care of her without any help. After her mother's death, she decided to open a nursing agency to serve other adult children with a dying parent to allow them to continue working, as she wished she could have (interview, June 17, 2014). A nursing home owner had started the facility to care for her own father, realizing that there were few elder care resources in Ghana, and continued running the facility after he had passed away (WhatsApp phone interview, July 16, 2018).

Most agency owners, but not the nursing home owners, talked about their role as a cultural change agent in creating a new market. The owners of the agencies were a conduit for new ideas of how elder care might be organized socially and politically and were testing those ideas in conjunction with their clients and employees. Their knowledge and perspective from their experiences abroad prompted a critique of Ghanaian government policy, which had essentially ignored the new market, leaving it completely unregulated, as I discuss further in the next chapter. The agency owners aimed to institutionalize ideas and practices from abroad, in part because their institutionalization would help their business to thrive and enable them to continue to reside in Ghana. At the same time, owners adjusted these ideas based on their personal experiences in Ghana and abroad.

Owners who had traveled abroad varied in their assessment of the elder care arrangements of the West. This variation seems partly explained by the work that they did abroad. The two who were trained and worked in elder care abroad were more enamored of what they learned there. For example, Stella received four weeks of training in home care in the United Kingdom after completing university studies in Ghana. She then worked in a care home for older adults in the United Kingdom and "loved it." Following that experience, she did community care, working in people's homes to support them to live independently, while simultaneously pursuing her social work degree. For ten years, she told me, she worked in the United Kingdom with a range of "vulnerable populations" (in her words): people with learning disabilities, physical disabilities, or mental health problems and older adults. Her experience abroad functions as the gold standard for her: "Some people tell me I brought London to Ghana," she told me proudly. She wanted to reproduce what she learned abroad in Ghana. For example, she would like a regulatory body for agencies and a criminal background check for her employees. She sent her employees to get their fingerprints taken at the police station, but admitted that this measure mainly made employees afraid of committing an offense rather than actually checking their criminal records. Furthermore, she was looking for an agency supervisor trained in the United Kingdom because, she said, "the Ghanaian educational experience does not provide the right skills to do the job. They are not trained in home care settings" (phone interview, July 13, 2013). A year later, she felt even more strongly: "I am reluctant to take a nursing professional from here in Ghana to join me" in the agency (fieldnotes, July 26, 2014). By May 2015, she had hired a Ghanaian British nurse with a strong British accent who was not fluent in a local language because she had lived in Britain since adolescence. The Ghanaian British nurse continued to manage the agency in November 2019.

Another owner of a nursing agency also lived in Britain for many years but had worked not in health care there but instead in the credit collection department of a retail company. Less socialized into British care practices, Esther was more selective than Stella in adapting home care to Ghana. Giving a guest lecture on hospice to a group of students at the School of Social Work in Accra, she emphasized, "We should not look for everything British and American" (fieldnotes, June 23, 2014). Esther told me she decided not to "take from the outside world because the situation is different here. We pick from the developed world, but it is not practical and it doesn't work here. I tailored it" (fieldnotes, June 17, 2014). One of the ways that she had tailored her business was that she gave a lot of budgeting and practical advice to her students and employees, treating them as surrogate daughters, because the income of carers is so low. Furthermore, she was less worried about carer abuse of clients and background checks for employees, than patient abuse of carers because many clients treated her employees as househelp, which infuriated her. Rather than learning about elder care through formal training in Britain, as Stella did, Esther said she learned a lot from caring for her own mother as she died of cancer in Ghana.

Some owners of nursing agencies advocated for an expansion of social welfare programs in Ghana. Stella wished that pensions could pay for carers, the way that Social Services helps older adults in the United Kingdom (fieldnotes, July 26, 2014). Another owner made a similar comment, using Denmark as a comparison (interview, August 4, 2015). Obviously, it is in the interests of home nursing agencies to promote Western-style social welfare policies. If governments pay for these services, home nursing services can be provided beyond the more limited pool of people with access to remittances from abroad, who can barely afford what is seen as a luxury service.

Owners of home nursing services are active brokers of knowledge from abroad, drawing on their transnational migration and experiences abroad. However, they also use other experiences, including their frustrations with caring for older relatives in Ghana. They serve as conduits through which knowledge and information about Western models of elder care—social remittances—flow (Levitt 1998). In Levitt's initial conceptualization of social remittances among Dominican migrants, transnational migrants loomed large as social change agents, bringing new expectations of democracy to the Dominican Republic, just as they send money back home as remittances. Similar to the way that continued research on financial remittances has illustrated their complexity, flowing not only from migrants back home but also *to* migrants from their relatives in Ghana (Mazzucato 2008), Levitt's ideas on social remittances have been tempered by an acknowledgment of the ways that social actors and the local context in the home country affect the ways that ideas from abroad are implemented and institutionalized at home (Holdaway et al. 2015; Levitt and Lamba-Nieves 2011). Thus, Western ideas and practices do not transform societies through the social remittances of transnational migrants; instead, those ideas and practices are shaped by individuals to fit the local context and thus radically transform, as suggested by the concept of the traveling theory (Behrends, Park, and Rottenburg 2014).

These transformations included adapting the business to suit the social and economic practices of the urban middle class. Owners scaled back their dreams: they invested less in the business and cut back on their supervisory and assessment visits that ensured high-quality care. Initially, Esther wanted to open a hospice center and trained her students in hospice techniques. But as her difficulties with running the agency increased, the business contracted to simply providing home care services, without a school. She cut back on home supervisory and intake visits, to reduce the costs of transportation, and she no longer operated an office near a government hospital, but worked, more cost-effectively, out of her own home. Home care agencies could not pay carers well because they were in competition with the vast informal market of househelp and the labor of kin. Investing in the training of employees became less worthwhile for them over time. This realization led them to cut back on labor- and capital-intensive schools to train care workers; instead, they hired workers with a healthcare assistant credential, described in the next chapter, which did not train students in home care. Some raised their rates for home care as high as they would dare, making care services even more of a luxury commodity, in order to retain quality employees and maintain the business. Many owners by 2019 were discouraged by or bitter about the scaling back of their dreams of introducing hospice to Ghana, the inability to provide quality care or to provide care beyond a small elite, or the frustration of their efforts to secure government regulation and support, to be discussed further in the next chapter. On the other hand, they had also not completely given up since it was clear that their services were needed, even though they were too expensive for most urban households.

In the development of commercial care services in Ghana, I would agree with Levitt (1998) that migrants and return migrants play an outstanding role in translating eldercare ideas and practices from abroad. They used that knowledge to create an elder care market in Ghana and hope to expand that market by pressuring government agencies for the regulation and support for their services, without much effect thus far. Their knowledge learned abroad is refracted through their varied experiences, which shape owners' evaluation of how useful those practices and ideas are to Ghana's aging population. Their ability to maintain a commercial care market is frustrated by their clients' expectations of carers being domestic servants and their willingness and ability to pay for senior care.

Adult Children Abroad: Able to Pay and Seeking Reliable Care

Another major actor in the creation of a care market in Accra is the consumers of these services. All of the patients of home care services whom I met had a child abroad. A few, in addition, were return migrants themselves, generally from Europe or North America, who had brought their children abroad with them and then left them behind in the country of migration when they retired or returned to Ghana. Similar to other care contexts, the impetus for commercial care services generally came not from the patients themselves but from their children or other potential caregivers who feel burdened by or unable to provide care.

Transnational migration is significant not only for the transfer of ideas and practices but also in pragmatically changing resources of time and finances within households and among kin. As already discussed, the labor of providing care is increasingly placed on adult children rather than the extended family due to changes in inheritance that privilege children over the extended family. Given the gendered division of labor, daily care provision is associated with women, while the role of managing and financing care is given to men. Migrant middle-class women, whether in urban areas of Ghana or abroad, are increasingly turning to commercial care services to resolve their elder care dilemmas or supplement the care provided by resident kin. As mentioned, many of the patients receiving commercial care services require a great deal of care because of the degree of their physical or mental frailty, which is why kin and househelp sometimes balk at the tasks, perceiving it to be an undue burden. The fact that many households are struggling to care for their aging relations makes them open to new ideas about elder care. Stella talked about one client with Parkinson's disease whose daughter hoped that with the employment of care workers "she could go out and have her life back." Stella found that, unsurprisingly, the daughter did very little for the mother once the agency caregivers arrived (interview, July 26, 2014). These new forms of elder care indicate a shifting of roles in which adult daughters do not provide personal care but instead simply provide the financial support for paid caregivers, as I have discussed in chapter 4 with rural households with urban migrant children. Children abroad take on the role of care managers but generally have difficulty being present to provide personal care (as care providers), unless they return to Ghana in middle age, as Esther did for her mother. Commercial care services have become one strategy by which children "care at a distance" (Baldassar, Baldock, and Wilding 2007).

Because of the exchange rate between the Ghanaian cedi and European and North American currencies, older people's children and siblings who live abroad can quite easily pay for care at rates considered a luxury locally. One friend of mine, a retired journalist, in Accra said he had a former colleague who was cared for by a home care agency, but he thought the services were very expensive and affordable only to those with children abroad (fieldnotes, June 2, 2014). One patient was shocked to learn the price of home care, which her two daughters in the United States had been paying (interview, August 5, 2014).

The adult children abroad, like agency owners, are more likely to be familiar with paid elder care and thus propose it as a possible solution. Medical professionals, whether in Ghana or abroad, also seem to be more open to paid care, whether because of their experiences or their resources as middle-class or upper-middle-class health professionals. The wife of a retired doctor disabled by a stroke discussed how her four daughters, all resident abroad in the United Kingdom and the United States, paid for home care. After her husband's stroke, a daughter who was a community health nurse in Seattle (United States) made arrangements for his care with the agency in Ghana (fieldnotes, June 15, 2015).

Another major source of information about the home nursing agencies is the hospitals themselves, which often recommend agencies when they discharge patients or when admitted patients lack relatives to procure medication, buy food, or provide bed baths. Home care agencies supplement nursing care in hospitals because nurses in the hospital rarely provide bed baths or food, requiring a caregiver to stay with the patient. Home care agencies also help temporarily after a hospital stay because of the lack of rehabilitation facilities in Ghana. Home care agency owners cultivate relationships with hospital staff to maintain these recommendations.

Migrants' knowledge of Western care facilities was particularly important for overcoming the stigma associated with nursing homes and making them acceptable to other kin resident in Ghana. Care in a nursing home is considered particularly shameful, making conspicuous kin's inability or unwillingness to care for an older relative, which the use of home nursing services obscures (Van der Geest, Mul, and Vermeulen 2004). As noted previously, residential facilities, in contrast to home nursing services, are framed as abandonment and the heterodox to the ideal. In the residential facility where I stayed for a week, I was able to observe the admission of an older man in his sixties who was disabled by a stroke. He could not speak, he frequently smeared feces around his room, and he gnashed his teeth constantly, making an alarming noise. His girlfriend who came to visit told me that he had been "sick" (her word) for four to five years. First, he went to stay with a married daughter and her husband in Koforidua, but the daughter was young and her father's care was a burden for her. A son in Accra then took his father in, but the father had a fall there. The son would just lock him in the room during the day (fieldnotes, August 9, 2018). His siblings were concerned that his previous care, under his children in Ghana, had not been ideal. They thus conformed to the older model of care described by Aboderin (2004) in which members of the *abusua* step in to help when the care by adult children fails. What was new was that a younger sister who lived in London proposed transferring him to live in the nursing home. During the sister's two-week visit to Ghana, she organized his admittance, with the support of another brother who was resident in Ghana. She also mobilized the financial support for his nursing home residence among other relatives living in Britain, including his son and nephew living there, who greeted him through WhatsApp calls even though he was unable to respond (fieldnotes, August 8, 2018). The sister compared the nursing home unfavorably to what she knew in the United Kingdom, wishing that there were medical staff on site (and which many older people in Ghana imagined would be available in a nursing home, as discussed in chapter 2). She also said that staff at the hospital where he had gone for a medical exam, necessary for admission to the residential facility, had discouraged her from putting her brother in a nursing home, saying it was like she was "rejecting" him. She was also exploring home care in Ghana but was trying the nursing home for the moment as a kind of experiment. She commented that her brothers liked to make the decisions, but she was trying to direct them "from behind," as the youngest sibling (fieldnotes, August 7, 2018).

Another resident's granddaughter, a young adult, was visiting Ghana from Virginia and, with her cousins, came to say hello. She remarked to me that her grandmother, bed-ridden due to a stroke, received much better care in the facility than in her relatives' home, where her grandmother had lived for twenty years before she came to live in the nursing home (fieldnotes, August 8, 2018). A cousin of another resident commented that the resident had improved during his stay, after suffering a stroke (fieldnotes, August 6, 2018). One of the two residents in the short-lived nursing home run by an agency owner in 2014 was a seventy-year-old nurse, a return migrant who had lived in the United Kingdom for forty-two years. Although she was physically well, she was mentally depressed and suicidal: she did not talk and tended to wander off the premises. Her son who was raised and lives in the United Kingdom brought her to the agency from a care home in the United Kingdom because he did not know his relatives in Ghana (fieldnotes, June 4 and July 4, 2014). In another situation, a daughter in the United States hired a home care agency because she worried that her mother's younger sister, who had moved in with her several years ago and given up her business as a seamstress, was living off the daughter's remittances. Hiring the agency, despite its expense, simplified the reciprocal exchanges, by reducing the claims of the mother's sister on the daughter's remittances. The mother's sister felt unappreciated by the daughters, whom she had helped raise, because they did not send her much money or ask after her (fieldnotes, August 5, 2014, and June 12, 2015). Consumers of commercial care services thus expressed ambivalence about the quality of kin care and the kinds of exchanges that such care might oblige. Transnational migration has therefore created and helped sustain a market for these services, by generating a group of resource-rich and busy clients who need to care for older relatives, whether parents or siblings, across national borders and find commercial care services more trustworthy and reliable than kin. When compared to care services in the United Kingdom or United States, commercial care in Ghana is cheap. Commercial care is a pragmatic response to a time crunch experienced by many professionals around the world—in Ghana as well as abroad—and to greater financial resources, including for care.

In a small facility that subsequently closed, Eunice, a lecturer at a university, explained why she had placed her father, age ninety-six, there. The terrible story tumbled out of her, a situation that remained emotional for her because she had not yet been able to resolve it. Eunice had been living with her father and her brother in her father's house, but the brother began to mistreat the father and consider the father's house his own because he had children and Eunice did not. Eunice's father's sister and her daughter took him to live with them in Togo, but Eunice felt during her multiple visits there that they were mistreating him, feeding him but not bathing him and leaving him locked up in the boys' quarters behind the house. His dementia increased, she felt, as a result of their neglect. Eunice forced his kin to release him to her, and he stayed in the nursing home temporarily, for a few weeks, while she argued with her brother to let her father return to his house. While in the nursing home, her father complained to her, "You have thrown me away" (fieldnotes, June 11, 2015). Yet, it was clear during my stay that the residents of the nursing home were not abandoned, "rejected," or "dumped" by their relatives as was the common lore in Ghana. Instead, they placed them there thoughtfully and anxiously, as a result of the limitations of care by adult children and kin, and visited regularly. And yet, similar to South Africa (van Dongen 2008), as in the case of Eunice's father, older people may end up in a nursing home because of disrupted reciprocity in a family under siege, where younger and older generations fight over material resources like houses.

Older patients themselves usually expect that their own children will care for them and resist the notion of paid care. A university professor described how her mother, debilitated by a stroke, would prefer her own children's care to care from an agency, but the daughter told her mother that she was fifty years old and had a career she did not want to leave. She is so busy that she often does not have much time for her mother, and so for her mother's birthday, the professor just sat with her mother all day, playing games and talking, which her mother appreciated greatly as the best birthday present she could ever have. The mother alternated between living with the professor and her sister, both of whom had careers that caused them to spend significant portions of time outside the house and take numerous trips abroad. They hired carers from an agency to help their mother twenty-four hours a day, paid for primarily by a third sister who lived abroad. After six years of using paid carers, the mother remains unhappy about, but resigned to, the situation (fieldnotes, June 27, 2013). Similarly, some of the residents in the residential facility where I stayed were placed there by overworked daughters. One daughter described her mother living in a village in Akyem with a hired caregiver, but when the hired caregiver left suddenly, the three daughters—"government workers and businesswomen," in the words of one daughter—brought her to the nursing home in Accra, where the eighty-six-year-old mother has been relatively happy for the past two years (fieldnotes, August 10, 2018).

Although those abroad tend to pay for the commercial care, only rarely do *all* of the adult children or siblings of the older patients of the nursing agencies and residential facilities I studied live abroad. According to the owners and the patients I interviewed and the households I visited, many patients have adult children living in Ghana—perhaps even in the same house because of the expense of housing in Accra—in addition to a child or two abroad. The children living in Ghana work outside the house and are often absent during the day, thus necessitating the need for paid care. Because of long commutes due to heavy traffic in Accra, they may leave the house by five o'clock each morning and return late in the evening, around eight or nine. The child (or children) abroad tend to shoulder most of the costs of commercial care as well as expensive, imported items like diapers, equipment like walkers, and over-the-counter medications. In my visits to the clients of home care agencies, I met an older woman, bedridden with a stroke, who lives with her two grandsons, with the costs of agency care workers assumed by a child abroad. The agency was hired when it became clear that two domestic servants could not take good care of the patient (fieldnotes, July 13, 2018). One male patient of an agency lived in his house with his wife and employed son, while other children resided nearby in Accra as well as abroad; he also had two househelp (visits in 2014, 2015, and 2017). A female client of an agency lived with her daughter who worked during the day, moving from her own home for more care in the daughter's house; a son lived elsewhere in Accra and a daughter lived in London (visit in 2014). Many of the patients I met lived in their own homes and served as patrons to the other relatives living with them, although these relatives might claim the house as theirs (as in the case of Eunice's father). Agency care workers served as the primary caregivers but were often supplemented and usually closely monitored by kin caregivers.

Because of the range of other possible caregivers—whether nephews, grandsons, or househelp—consumers were able to put pressure on the agencies to keep the costs of paid care within reach, making agency profits slim (or nonexistent) and care workers' salaries minimal. For example, one agency owner who ran a residential facility temporarily had one resident taken away because the family found a former *waakye* seller to take care of her. The family of the second resident also wanted to take her away, but the agency owner worried that they would not take as good care of her as did her care workers, who offered the patient food every hour to make sure she ate enough (fieldnotes, July 29, 2014).

As Jennifer Hirsch (2003) emphasizes in her study of changing expectations of romance in Mexico, we should not overstate the effect of transnational migration on changes in social norms, which may be changing alongside, rather than because of, transnational migration. The emergence of commercial care services in Ghana arises not only from transnational migration but also from the current and historical prevalence of domestic service and fosterage in urban Ghana, ongoing changes in care reciprocities across the generations, and increased wealth among the middle class in Ghana. The growing commercialization of elder care in Ghana, and perhaps more generally across the Global South (Lamb 2009), I would argue, is the result of a combination of local economic growth, the increased participation of women in remunerative and formal employment in the private and public sectors, transnational migration, and a larger population of frailer elderly. One might consider the commercial care market in Accra a "global assemblage" (Ong and Collier 2005), a provisional social formation generated out of different processes occurring in different locales (such as the United Kingdom and Ghana), in which agency is distributed across multiple people who bring the market into being through their situated, somewhat experimental and tentative, actions (Anderson et al. 2012). The local context affected by outflows of migration and migrant remittances is important, but as Nicola Yeates (2009, 2012) has noted, the migration literature has overemphasized the impact of the countries to which people migrate and the agency of migrants as sources of social change.

What I do not see is the growth of a commercial care market in Ghana due to the employment of Ghanaians in the commercial care markets abroad, although many Ghanaians work in nursing and elder care as a niche employment field in the United Kingdom and the United States. There is not a straightforward global care chain (Hochschild 2001), in which paid domestic labor in households in wealthy countries is performed by female immigrants who left behind their own families in their home countries and then hire care services themselves.

Commercial care services in Ghana are not primarily the result of global care chains, as not all or even most Ghanaian migrants are care workers abroad.

Home Care for the Poor Elderly: Akrowa Foundation

What about the needs of poorer older adults? Commercial care services remain out of reach for poorer older people without international connections, as Sarah Dsane (2013) found in a study of childless elderly women in Teshie, a neighborhood of Accra. Voluntary organizations can provide long-term care, as has been noted in Tanzania (World Health Organization 2017). However, the case of the small NGO named the Akrowa Foundation showcases the downsides of charitable care. Akrowa supported visits to poorer elderly on the outskirts of Accra and the provision of home care services like bathing, massaging, and some physical therapy during their visits. Started in 2006 by a Ghanaian musician who worked in Denmark as a home carer, the NGO relied on three or four Danish students of care work who stayed a month at a time in Ghana, as well as a core of three to four Ghanaian volunteers, the remnants of an initial ten who had been trained in a healthcare assistance school. (I will say more about the healthcare assistance schools in the next chapter.) Most of the Ghanaian volunteers were affiliated with the Young People's Guild of the Abokobi Presbyterian Church.

Although it was featured prominently in a World Health Organization (2017) report as a model program, its scope has declined considerably. When I encountered them, the Akrowa Foundation had a roster of fifty or so frail or disabled adults in the Ga villages on the outskirts of Accra—Abokobi, Akpoma, Pantang, Boi, and Damfa—whom they visited once a week or once every two weeks. I accompanied the Ghanaian and Danish volunteers on two occasions in 2014 and 2015 as they made their rounds: in pairs, they visited ten adults in a morning, staying about half an hour with each one. They provided personal care of bathing and shaving; they checked blood pressure; they massaged limbs and did some physical therapy (fig. 5.1). All of their patients lived with kin, whether nuclear or extended; the primary caregiver was an adolescent daughter, a sister, or a husband.

The NGO also ran a small residential facility in Damfa: three people were resident in 2014, and only one in 2015. No staff lived on site. Instead, a neighbor provided food every day, and the volunteers visited every three days, so the care was inadequate. When I visited the Damfa center with the volunteers in 2014, they set to work with alacrity cleaning dried feces off the floor and a wheelchair, bathing the residents, and preparing a meal.

Although the nursing home was clearly inadequate, because of lack of staff, their model of home care seemed quite appropriate because it attended to the severe needs of bedridden and disabled older Ghanaians. However, as a program dependent on volunteers, the NGO was not sustainable. It had tried to get support from local chiefs as well as the state, without success. Some of the young Ghanaian volunteers were becoming mothers and having to earn money to feed their children.

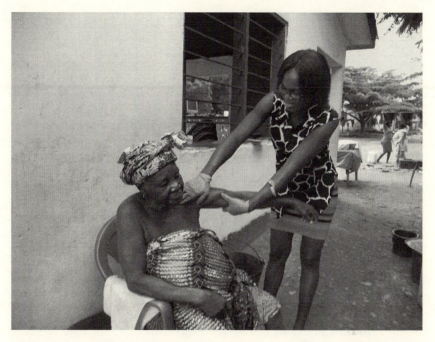

FIG. 5.1 An Akrowa volunteer massaging an older woman during a home visit in 2015.

A third of the original cohort of trained volunteers remained, and they too were drifting off into other lines of work and education. The volunteers could not afford transportation costs between the villages. However, they received respect and appreciation for their work from community members. In general, this model of free home care during periodic visits was much less known than the senior day centers or commercial care services, and seemed equally unsustainable.

Conclusion

To what extent does transnational migration generate social change, including the commercialization of elder care? Much of the literature on transnational migration overemphasizes its role in social change. Initial scholarship posited major changes in family life, including gender and parenting roles (Hondagneu-Sotelo 1994; Parreñas 2004). Later work tempered the impact of transnational migration by acknowledging the significance of changes in family life occurring independently of migration (Hirsch 2003) and of familial repertoires shaped by long-standing urban and regional migration, which are then adapted to international migration (Coe 2013b; Olwig 2007). This tempering of the effects of transnational migration is paralleled in the literature on social remittances, which has evolved to a much more complex and dynamic model than its initial formulation of transnational migrants serving as the vectors of new ideas and practices (Levitt and Lamba-Nieves 2011). Instead, the complex role of other social actors and institutions is acknowledged, as diverting or modifying the ideas and practices brought by migrants. Similarly, the concept of global care chains needs to be modified so that households in migrant-receiving countries are not the sole engines of social change. Instead, the commodification of care is also driven by households in migrant-sending countries, who are trying to meet their changing care needs with new resources. Commercial care services are "assembled" by the uncoordinated actions of multiple people, dispersed geographically, attesting to the fragile and emergent nature of social structures.

Although commercial care services might exist in the urban areas of Accra without widespread transnational migration, migration has helped create and sustain the care market through a multifaceted process involving transnational migrants sending money to aging parents and relatives "left behind," return migrants who open new businesses, and dreams of future migration among young people who seek training in care work, as I discuss in chapters 6 and 7. Return migrants play a pioneering role in introducing and trying to institutionalize new eldercare practices, talking about themselves explicitly as agents of social change. However, they are not united as a body, lessening their impact. As Levitt (1998) suggested, migrants' experiences abroad affect their translation and reflections of these eldercare practices, and agency owners highlight different aspects of "Western" care practices. They also adjust to the economic and social reality of Accra in which their services are in competition with kin and informally found paid caregivers.

Material remittances shaped the adoption of these ideas, by giving families the ability to pay for commercial services, rather than relying on reciprocal obligations within families, generated across the life course but which sometimes seem fragile to an adult child's disregard, time limitations, or lack of economic means, as we also saw in chapter 2. Extended kin can place too many demands on the children of those receiving care, or provide care that others deem neglectful or insufficient. Migrants, as well as health professionals, have been early adopters of paid elder care, particularly nursing homes, and with the ability to make the payments, they shaped care decision making among a wider group of kin. However, they did so in consideration of issues like time and priorities among middle-class households resident in Accra.

It is clear that social remittances include many different kinds of resources. Ideas are the resources usually highlighted, and indeed I often heard the citation of knowledge of British, American, Danish, and Swiss care systems and exposure to concepts like hospice, dementia, and employee background checks. These ideas could not be fully enacted in Ghana. The ideas adopted that became the most popular were home nursing services, not residential facilities, because of their congruence with urban, employed, middle-class women's use of domestic servants and fostered adolescents to help with household labor. Home nursing services are an alterodox inscription to maintain the orthodoxy of kin care.

6

Going to School to Be a Carer

● ●

A New Occupation and the Enchantment of Nursing Education

In June 2015, I was at a secondary school on the outskirts of Accra, sitting with a teacher in the shade of a pavilion in the center of several classroom blocks. Inside the classrooms, hundreds of students from different schools across Accra were writing the examination for a healthcare assistance certificate, after studying entrepreneurial skills, mathematics, and anatomy for the past year. Having observed a class in one school, I was pleased to talk to a teacher from another school about her students and her sense of the curriculum, to compare my field-work insights against her more extensive experience. In the course of our conversation, she commented that the students were "victims of circumstance." She explained that the students were able to pay for their education and were eager to learn, but there is no work for them. As soon as she said this, she backtracked from the forcefulness of her statement as if she found it too depressing, saying that students were in fact learning useful skills that would help them in their own households or as mothers. This goal of improving their domestic lives would have disappointed the students I knew, who hoped to use the certificate to find a job in a hospital.

The genesis of the healthcare assistance certificate was the emergence of the new elder care market created as urban families in Ghana struggled to provide care, described in the last chapter. The story of the healthcare assistance credential illustrates the ways that elder care can reorganize other social relations, which previous chapters have touched on more incidentally. In this chapter, I focus on the tensions between the new care market and the state, whereas chapter 7 illustrates changing relations of social class through home care. The emergence of commercial care services in Accra would seem to illustrate the rise of market forces and the decline of government regulation, a phenomenon guided by the ideology of neoliberalism. Neoliberalism is the doctrine that valorizes private enterprise, to the extent of advocating that the state be run like a business, and the practices associated with this doctrine (Ferguson 2009). At a macroeconomic level, it implies fiscal discipline, a redirection of public expenditure toward areas offering high economic returns, tax reform, a decline of government regulation of trade, liberalization of interest rates and foreign direct investment, privatization of public companies, and secure property rights (Boafo-Arthur 2007). A neoliberal environment is seen as conducive to the growth of capitalism. This ideology can have a profound effect on state care services with its disavowal of the importance of a public or social good (Han 2012; Muehlebach 2012).

From the late 1960s, military coups created political instability, while the economy collapsed, decimating Ghana's hopes after independence. During the 1980s, in an attempt to salvage the country economically, the government of the Provisional National Defence Council (PNDC), and its successor the National Democratic Congress (NDC) (1981–2001) accepted World Bank loans along with conditions known as structural adjustment. In his study of Ghana's structural adjustment experience, Ghanaian political scientist Eboe Hutchful argues that the foreign-led neoliberal interest in structural adjustment and a small state was never passionately adopted by Ghanaian state officials. Instead, "adjustment in Ghana . . . is perhaps more appropriately interpreted as an attempt by the state to recapture and reconstitute its economic base" rather than to promote the liberation of markets and entrepreneurialism (2002, 2–3). Other scholars noted that the Ghanaian officials involved in ushering in structural adjustment programs essentially "ignored the private sector" (Resnick 2019, 72). The private sector has never felt supported by the government of Ghana, even during the height of structural adjustment and economic liberalization (Hutchful 2002). Although the subsequent New Patriotic Party (NPP) government under President Kufuor (2001–2009) "rhetorically committed to a more interactive relationship with business, signified by President Kufuor's call for a Golden Age of Business, observers suggest that this ultimately resulted in more superficial overtures than substantive outcomes" (Resnick 2019, 72). The most recent NPP government of Akufo-Addo (2017–) is also oriented toward business in its rhetoric, but these promises also seem quite shallow.

Thus, the story is more complicated than one of the rise of neoliberalism. Not only have successive governments of Ghana supported an active state, but the state has never been involved in elder care. Elder care services are currently unregulated, without licenses, rules, or oversight. The lack of regulation does not constitute a retreat by the state but rather signals the Ghanaian state's ambivalence about the private sector. As MacLean (2002, 84) argues, the Ghanaian government has long relied on a private-public mix for promoting social welfare: "The Ghanaian government's current desire to reduce its role and promote an augmented responsibility for local government, NGOs, and the private sector in providing social services is not simply a result of the hegemony of the neoliberal development paradigm, but rather a more longterm legacy of colonial social policy in the post-independence era." After independence in 1957, the state rapidly expanded, in a statist-distributional mode of governance, with Nkrumah promising a strong central state that would actively develop the nation and take care of its citizens (Hutchful 2002). Although the postindependence state became committed to providing a range of social welfare benefits, like free or highly subsidized education, health, and housing, particularly oriented toward middle-class and urban populations, it never became involved in the area of elder care.

Furthermore, the Ghanaian government, with different parties in charge, has used economic growth since the 1990s to expand social welfare and the civil service, following the model of a developmentalist, not a neoliberal, state.

> Successive democratic regimes in Ghana invested in a number of broad-based social welfare schemes. Notable among these includes the National Health Insurance Scheme, which was established in 2003 and represents one of Africa's few attempts to implement a universal healthcare program (Blanchet et al. 2012). In 2005, the government also abolished primary school fees and provided schools with a small grant (capitation grant) for each pupil enrolled. Another example includes the Livelihood Empowerment Against Poverty Program (LEAP), which was launched in 2008 and now expanded to all ten regions of the country with more than 70,000 beneficiaries. LEAP is a cash transfer program that provides beneficiaries with direct cash payments and free health insurance (Handa et al. 2013). While all three programs began under the NPP (2001–2009), they were scaled up under the NDC tenure of Presidents Mills (2009–2012) and Mahama (2012–2017), indicating a broad consensus across parties about their importance. (Resnick 2019, 65)

Finally, the NPP government of Akufo-Addo (2017–) made secondary school education free. The expansion of social welfare contradicts the argument about a neoliberal state in Ghana. The National Health Insurance program and the LEAP cash transfer program have benefitted older adults, but as already noted in previous chapters, there are significant limitations to these programs' impact, and older adults feel neglected by the state.

Another wrinkle in the story of the dominance of neoliberalism is that commercial care services repeatedly reached out to government agencies and professional bodies to create standards and regulations for the new services they had created, to help these entrepreneurs make a case to clients about the quality and professionalism of their caregivers and therefore the reasonable expense of their services. The World Health Organization (2017) has emphasized the importance of a legal architecture and standards and monitoring in order to support long-term care services. Esther, the owner of one home care agency, tried for four or five years to obtain accreditation for her agency from the Ministry of Health but was consistently told, "We don't do it this way; we have the extended family" to care for aging persons (interview, June 17, 2014). The lack of current oversight indicates both the government's dismissal of the private sector and markets' need for state support and regulation. Many elder care businesses operate as NGOs because there is no way to become licensed as a nursing home or nursing agency. The growth of the care market illustrates the weakness of state mechanisms and the absence of a government role in the field of elder care. The healthcare assistance credential was the most successful of numerous efforts at legitimating the care market, although it has been a failure not only from the perspective of graduates of the program but also in advancing the interests of the care entrepreneurs. In sum, the government has not supported the emergence and growth of commercial care services. In this it is like many African countries—with the exception of Mauritius, Seychelles, and South Africa—in ignoring the long-term care sector (World Health Organization 2017). Instead, what we see is the entanglement of neoliberalism with a developmentalist state, creating new openings, contradictions, and dead-ends.

The state is a multifaceted institution, with some government bodies more oriented to supporting private businesses, according to the neoliberal model, than others (Gupta 2012). Thus, while one government agency supported the development of the healthcare assistance credential, another government agency tried to thwart it. Students were attracted to the new credential not by dreams of working in home care but by working as a nurse in a government hospital. They found the public sector more attractive than the private sector, in which they would have to work long hours for less pay and in more precarious situations. In order to recruit students, the private educational sector changed the curriculum away from home care skills toward those practiced in hospitals. Those with the healthcare assistance training (HAT) credential acquired hospital-based skills, not home nursing skills. As the healthcare assistance certificate gained in popularity, the nursing profession became increasingly concerned that the credential was undermining the position of nurses. The medical field has historically been closely allied to the government, which is its major educator and employer. Nurses have won concessions from the state because of their importance to the well-being of Ghana's citizens, particularly in maternal and infant care. As a result, the nursing association successfully convinced the Ministry of Health to ban those with the healthcare assistance credential from working in public hospitals. Occupational self-regulation has been one of the main employment protection niches neoliberalism seeks to undo, with Milton Friedman writing an early book about the medical profession as a key example (Standing 2011, 39). The story of the healthcare assistance credential illustrates not the triumph of neoliberalism in Ghana but the ways that the government continues to support a particular strata of the urban middle class—nurses—by employing them in public institutions, rather than responding to the needs of private care and educational markets. As a result, those with the healthcare assistance credential were simultaneously considered untrained by home care agencies and banned from government hospital employment. They could find employment in the larger private healthcare market, which included home care agencies, private hospitals, and pharmacies. Through the contradictions of the state's relationship to the private markets in education and health care, young people entered schools to become healthcare assistants but found that that credential was relatively worthless in realizing their dreams.

The Social Life of a Credential: Forms of Capital in the Making of a Middle Class

What is the value of a new credential? How does an employer or client understand the values of the skills and knowledge of an individual with a new occupation—an inscription—and honor that person through pay and status accordingly? What is the inscription's value relative to adjacent relations, in this case of nurse and domestic servant? Pierre Bourdieu's conceptualization of the forms of capital is useful for thinking through the ways that the care market sought to institutionalize the value of the healthcare assistance certificate and the ways that such efforts were undermined.

Bourdieu (1986) distinguishes between different forms of capital—economic (income and wealth), cultural (cultivation and credentials), social (connections) and symbolic (status)—and illustrates some of the mechanisms by which one is converted to the other. Although the exchange value of capital can be broadly recognized in certain periods, such value is usually the result of fierce negotiation. Cultural capital is the use of high-status cultural resources that affect a person's inclusion or exclusion from high-status positions, including the ability to garner economic resources (Lamont and Lareau 1988). Bourdieu (1977) developed the concept of cultural capital through his work among the Kabyle in Algeria and, later (Bourdieu 1989, 1996), turned to how cultural capital functioned in the intergenerational transmission of social class in France, arguing that the domestic transfer of cultural capital through a family in the dominant class shapes the bodily performances and personal inclinations—the *habitus*—of its young members (1996, 273). Cultural capital is key to the intergenerational transmission of prestige and status within an unequal society.

Yet some social theorists have argued that cultural capital is more fluid, even in Bourdieu's analysis, than is suggested by its use in explaining the reproduction of prestige across the generations. John R. Hall, in his critique of cultural capital, argues that "cultural capital is good only (if at all) in the social worlds where a person lives and acts, and the value that it has depends on sometimes ephemeral distinctions of currency in those particular social worlds" (1992, 275). Similar kinds of cultural capital may be valued differently in diverse social fields or markets, such as education, employment, and marriage (Brown 1985). These differences are themselves subject to social tension and conflict, as different groups seek to convince others to recognize what they value. Mikkel Rytter notes that Bourdieu recognizes that "the rate of exchange between the different forms of valid capital is the result of an ongoing symbolic struggle between more- or less-powerful actors in the social field" (2011, 207). For example, in northern Nigeria, being a Qur'anic student, a previously valued and respected status, became stigmatized in the face of new forms of education associated with modernity (Hoechner 2015). Wage and status bubbles are generated by particular arrangements that temporarily value an occupation highly, until the owners of capital find a way to reduce the value of that labor, such as through outsourcing or mechanization (Sewell 2005). These issues are critical to understanding the status and roles of a new occupation and its positioning in a hierarchical social field of differently valued occupations.

Academic qualifications are an effort by actors to institutionalize the conversion rates between cultural capital and economic capital and thus reduce the diversity and dynamism of interpretations about the value of a particular skill (Bourdieu 1986). To the extent that the state is the major employer of educated persons, as has historically been the case in Ghana, the state provides the equation for converting an academic credential (cultural capital) into a position providing symbolic, social, and economic capital. The formation of a privileged middle class such as nurses or civil servants is dependent, in part, on government political concessions and legal niches that protect a favored class and distinguish it from others (Berger 1981; Kocka 1981). The government has been a key actor in the making and unmaking of the middle class in Ghana through its employment practices and in setting the exchange value of the forms of cultural capital in which the middle class invests (see also Subramanian 2015 for India). Although nursing is currently a privileged occupational niche in Ghana, the assumed stability of this sector of the middle class is illusory (see also Schielke 2012 for Egypt). Nurses' positions may be undermined by an abundance of cheaper workers like healthcare assistants.

Professional organizations, such as medical and nursing associations, have also historically been involved in establishing the exchange value of cultural capital, by maintaining that only people with certain credentials are qualified to assume particular roles in institutions. Credentialing was used to professionalize nursing in the United States and create privileged positions for some, while simultaneously creating subordinate positions to do the "dirty" work of nursing, such as changing beds and cleaning patients (Reverby 1987). Because the government of Ghana recognizes the legitimacy and power of the nursing association, the association was able to undermine the cultural capital of the healthcare assistance credential.

Bourdieu (1996) argued that although educational credentials served as an important form of cultural capital when they were exchanged in the labor market, their significance was to validate the embodied cultural capital transmitted through the family, thus giving the veneer of a meritocracy to social class reproduction. Furthermore, he posited that the transfer of cultural capital through a family in the dominant class cultivated particular bodily performances, aspirations, and personal inclinations—the *habitus*—of its young members, which in school were valued and converted into the cultural capital of grades and credentials. However, I would argue that embodied cultural capital differs from the exchange value of an educational credential. The healthcare assistance credential gave students embodied cultural capital temporarily, demonstrated every day through their uniforms and subjectivities, during the period of their education. The course did have significant effects on students' self-perceptions, status, and knowledge and provided them with the promise of a meaningful pathway. It gave them confidence about their expertise, a sense of purpose that their life was moving ahead, and a self-perception of authority and public mission (which some considered arrogance), at least during the time they were in school. However, its exchange value was determined by the government negotiations with professional bodies and the private sector. Education in general becomes the object of fantasy, swelling dreams, and egos, followed by disappointment and recalibration of the future. Education creates a momentary status with the unmet promise of a stable future but also serves as an instrument for stripping scarce resources from young people as they invest their time, energy, and dreams of a middle-class adulthood in an educational program.

A New Care Market, a New Credential

Esther Amankwah, who originally ran both an agency and a school, worked to create a credential for carers as part of her efforts to legitimize the work and professionalism of her agency employees and differentiate them from untrained domestic servants, whom families were also using to provide senior care. Esther told me that she went first to the Nursing and Midwifery Council, the national nursing association, to see if they would be interested in developing a credential for carers. However, they told her they did not consider care work to be part of nursing. She then turned to the National Vocational and Training Institute (NVTI), which runs vocational schools and supervises certificates in construction, mechanics, electrical engineering, auto repair, dressmaking, and hairdressing.[1] Part of NVTI's mandate is to partner with private industries, and thus it represents a neoliberal wing of the Ghanaian government. James Ferguson writes about the privatization of state agencies,

> Neoliberalism . . . puts governmental mechanisms developed in the private sphere to work within the state itself, so that even core functions of the state are either subcontracted out to private providers, or run (as the saying has it) "like a business." The question of what should be public and what private becomes blurred, as the state itself increasingly organizes itself around "profit centers," "enterprise models," and so on. Rather than shifting the line between state and market, then, neoliberalism in this account involved the deployment of new, market-based techniques of government within the terrain of the state itself. (2009, 172)

NVTI was a government agency used to responding to the private sector and worked with Esther from 2004 to 2008 to develop a curriculum. She was also involved in writing and grading the examinations.[2]

However, Esther found that what she had originally set in motion became a completely different course as NVTI increasingly drew on the expertise of four nurses—who worked in hospital settings and did not understand home care—to rewrite the curriculum. The examinations for "Health Aid (Carer)" in May/June 2004 that Esther had devised—and which she showed me—focused on communication, skin care, diet, wound healing, and bed making. The examinations changed under the nurses' expertise to make them similar to those for nurses, including examples based in hospital settings and familiarity with medical terms (e.g., cerebrospinal fluid). The certificate's name also changed, to Healthcare Assistant Training (HAT).

The focus of the curriculum shifted because NVTI sought to give the certificate greater cultural capital. From an initial two-month course, it expanded to a one- or two-year course (for HAT I or II). The head of NVTI told me that the curriculum "became loaded with other things [unnecessary for home care] because of the interests of the students," that is, to work in hospitals (interview, January 11, 2017). One school owner told me that the course is not particularly focused on aging (fieldnotes, August 4, 2015). By using nurses as experts in the curriculum and the examinations, NVTI responded to students' dreams of becoming nurses, not low-status care workers, and private schools' desire to attract students. Students should "not be tempted by the hospitals," the NVTI director said. Also, he thought some private hospitals were trying to find lower-paid workers and oriented the curriculum toward hospital care. The director of NVTI told me that about one hundred ten private schools offered the certificate in HAT in 2016: forty-eight in Accra, nineteen in Kumasi, and two to three in each of the other regions (interview, June 1, 2015). The schools pay a fee to NVTI as part of their accreditation; one school director complained that NVTI wanted many schools to offer the certificate because of the money from the fees.

Since NVTI began offering the certificate in 2003, by its own estimation, one thousand to fifteen hundred students have obtained it.

Esther's frustrations with the hijacking of the credential she had created led her, ironically, to reject it as meaningful. She criticized the nurse who examined her students in 2015 as talking "rubbish." Esther told me scornfully, "She was so rude to the students, acting as if she was God and saying that she could fail them. I told her off" (interview, June 1, 2015). Esther then turned to City and Guilds in the United Kingdom, which supervises a number of vocational certificates, including in "health and social care," but she was required to pay them in foreign currency, which she did not have. She was desperate to have an outside examiner who could ensure that she was maintaining high standards for her students. Eventually she found training her own students to be too much effort and began hiring HAT graduates from other schools or even people without certificates. Although potential employees with HAT certificates present themselves as "nurses" to her, she finds that they cannot answer her specific questions about home care. Their problem is that they learn arrogance at school, she said (interview, July 10, 2018). She prefers to hire those with "a warm heart," whom she can train as she likes, and whose misguided training she does not have to undo (interview, June 28, 2015). Stella, another agency owner, said that she found she had to retrain healthcare assistants because they were trained in a hospital setting: "They know how to take vitals. But they don't know how to support them in a house. At the induction, I stress that they are social care workers, not just providing medical care. . . . They think of themselves as medical assistants. So playing Scrabble with an elderly person in bed doesn't interest them" (phone interview, July 13, 2013).[3] Other agency owners also discounted the HAT certificate, preferring to give a brief orientation and relying on employees' existing skills learned from caring for their frail or sick relatives at home, in part because investing in skills training for workers who soon depart seemed like a waste of time. Many carers working at agencies and nursing homes did have a HAT certificate, but only because HAT holders could not find work elsewhere; they were otherwise "sitting at home," as Esther reported (interview, July 10, 2018). Because they were oriented toward working in a hospital, they would leave home care suddenly, when they found a better opportunity.

In the meantime, the Nursing and Midwifery Council (N&MC) sought to delegitimize the HAT credential by distinguishing it from nursing. N&MC engaged in "boundary work" (Lamont 1992) to differentiate nurses from carers and protect nurses' middle-class status. I had a series of interviews with N&MC staff over several years to solicit their opinion about home care. In general, they thought the home care agencies should employ only nurses, rather than hiring a health care worker with less training. They accredited home care agencies, but only those that employed solely nurses as caregivers. They told me that carers are not nurses and should not be working in hospitals (interview, July 9, 2018). They told nurses who were "illegally" teaching in the HAT schools that they were "diluting the profession" (interview, January 9, 2017). In response to NVTI's credential, the N&MC developed its own certificate for healthcare assistants, known as the Healthcare Assistant Clinical (HAC), in contrast to the HAT offered by NVTI. Some schools offer both the HAC and the HAT, both as one-year and two-year courses. The head of one school that offers both courses told me that supervision by N&MC was much more stringent than that by NVTI. The HAC course also is more expensive than the HAT (Ghc5,200 vs. Ghc3,600 in August 2015 for the one-year course, equivalent to $1,300 vs. $900 at the time).

As one would expect, given the similarity of their acronyms and names, the general public and students alike are confused about the difference between the two certificates and the kinds of employment these certificates enable. Poorer students are more likely to pursue the cheaper course offered by NVTI. Due to the N&MC's pressure on government hospitals operating under the Ministry of Health, HACs may be employed as assistants to registered nurses in public hospitals, but HATs may not. HATs are eligible to be employed only as ward assistants in public hospitals, a job previously available to men and women with little or no education. A public relations officer at N&MC explained that an HAT could be paid Ghc200, and an HAC Ghc900–1,000, in comparison to a registered nurse who would receive Ghc1,200 to Ghc1,400 a month. HAT students are also prohibited from doing their clinical training in government hospitals.

N&MC thus views the HAT certificate as a threat and maintains the privileged employment niche of nurses by limiting who can be employed in or do clinicals in government hospitals. N&MC considers NVTI to be "duping people" (interview, January 9, 2017). N&MC's consistent denigration of the HAT certificate has put NVTI in a defensive position: it wishes to accommodate N&MC's concerns but also continue the HAT certificate program. Private schools were more angry with N&MC. One private school owner told me that she had invested a lot of capital in building a healthcare assistant school in 2007 and N&MC cannot easily "bulldoze the private institutions." Echoing the neoliberal refrain of Akufo-Addo's government, she argued, "Private-public partnerships develop the nation" (interview, July 18, 2018). The nursing association was powerful enough within the Ministry of Health to reduce the value of the HAT credential generated by another government agency set up to work with the private sector. Meanwhile, private schools and NVTI tried to uphold that value through providing hospital- and nursing-oriented curricula and clinical experiences and giving students a uniform similar to nurses, in order to continue to attract students. Some teachers and school owners assumed that the nursing association would ultimately lose its battle against the HAT certificate, as private hospitals could reduce their costs by employing lower-paid healthcare workers in the place of nurses.

The HAT credential emerged from an assemblage of neoliberal processes, including the creation of commercial home care services and the growth of private schools within a neoliberal educational context. These initiatives were uncoordinated. However, the story of this credential also illustrates the limits of neoliberalism. The private educational market failed to increase valuable skills and enhance graduates' incomes; it also failed to put pressure on civil service wages. Nurses unfamiliar with home care services became the experts in setting the curriculum and examination for the HAT as NVTI sought to raise the cultural capital of the credential, thus orienting students toward the most valued places of employment: hospital settings, not home care. At least for the moment, professional organizations like the N&MC control the kinds of credentials accepted within the government hospitals, thus limiting the value of the HAT educational program developed by private schools. Thus, students were trapped between, on the one hand, the exuberance of private schools and a care market eager to expand and, on the other hand, a professional organization closely tied to the most preferred employer, the government.

The Enchantment of Nursing Education

Many of the healthcare assistance students hoped to become nurses. Nursing, alongside teaching, has traditionally provided one of the few routes by which women can obtain a civil service position. The middle class in Africa has mainly been defined by its employment sector, along with education (Lentz 2016). In the past few decades, nursing and medical personnel have been somewhat sheltered from other public service reductions and retrenchments, as the Ghanaian government tried to stem the international migration of government-trained nurses, which was quite high in the 1990s until it slowed by 2006 (Abuosi and Abor 2015; Appiah-Denkyira et al. 2013). The government of Ghana also considers nurses critical to national development, particularly in the promotion of maternal and infant health to meet the Millennium Development Goals (to be attained by 2015). Although nurses feel underpaid for the hard work they do (Böhmig 2010), their salaries had risen since the early 2000s and were at about $400 a month in 2015 (Appiah-Denkyira et al. 2013; Darko 2015). During the coronavirus epidemic, Ghana's health workers received a 50 percent pay raise, similar to some other countries that offered extra benefits to health workers because of their risks of infection, and attesting to government health workers' privileged status (Paquette 2020). As nurses' benefits, status, and pay have increased, and because it is seen as a stepping stone to international migration, nursing is an increasingly popular profession among young Ghanaian women.[4] As a result, there is great demand for nursing education.

Entrance to government nursing schools is extremely competitive, with three thousand applications for two hundred and fifty positions. To be admitted to a nursing program, students need to have a high enough score in three core subjects (English, integrated science, and mathematics) and three elective subjects on the secondary-school examination (WASSCE). Fewer than half of secondary school graduates taking the WASSCE in 2016 passed, with pass rates in the subjects of integrated science and mathematics particularly low (*Ghana News* 2016c). Many students retake the exam over several years to try to improve their scores.

After the government allowed private nursing schools to open in 2003—to help address the nursing shortage, reduce the high population-to-nurse ratio,[5] and meet Ghana's Millennium Development Goals, particularly in the areas of infant and maternal mortality—Accra and other urban areas witnessed an explosion of private nursing schools. In Ghana, as in other parts of the world, private schools have focused on vocational courses of study oriented toward seemingly fast-growing and attractive careers like IT and health care. Private schools in Ghana are founded by entrepreneurs who see them as a profitable venture, and they have grown increasingly popular at all levels of education in urban areas. Whereas during the 2010–2011 academic year there were thirteen public and four private nursing colleges (ISSER 2013), the number had doubled to twenty-three public and ten private nursing colleges by 2016 (National Accreditation Board 2016). The N&MC also published a list of twenty-five unaccredited nursing schools in August 2016 (*Ghana News* 2016b). Many schools offer not only nursing programs but also programs for lower-level positions in health care, including the HAT supervised by NVTI and the HAC supervised by N&MC. Revealing the degree to which the new programs in the private sector relied on existing institutions, the teachers at the healthcare assistant school I followed were primarily employed at other schools, both public and private, including a mathematics instructor from a nearby private senior high school and an anatomy instructor from a public nursing school. The teachers taught in the healthcare assistant school for extra income, sometimes arriving late or inconsistently because of their other teaching or administrative responsibilities.

Educational programs are advertised on the radio and television as well as through posters plastered on public transportation and on fences and walls. The advertisement for a private nursing school offering a HAT supervised by NVTI depicted in figure 6.1 illustrates an ideal image of a medical professional: a well-groomed, neat, and happy young woman, wearing a uniform and carrying medical equipment of a stethoscope and chart (or book), depicting her literacy and technical skills.

Word-of-mouth advertising through existing clinics and hospitals is also important. The students I met through my fieldwork heard about the certificate courses from relatives or spouses, some of whom already worked in health care. These key individuals, in addition to remittances from migrants, paid for students' expensive course of study.

The attraction of both healthcare assistance certificates among students is due to their association with nursing. Many healthcare assistant students would like to become nurses and fantasize that healthcare assistance is a step in that direction. One young woman working as a carer wanted to become a midwife. Her WASSCE scores were not high enough, so she pursued a certificate in healthcare assistance, paid for by her parents, a pastor and teacher in the Volta Region.

FIG. 6.1 Sign advertising healthcare assistance education at a private school on public transportation (*trotro*), Accra suburb, January 2017.

She then went to work as a home carer for an agency, and now hopes to study pharmacy and open her own pharmacy shop (interview, July 19, 2018). Another carer working for an agency told me that she got healthcare assistance training because she thought she was training to be a nurse. She worked for a private hospital for some time as a ward assistant, mopping the floors and helping with admissions. When she had trouble with her boss,[6] she learned from a friend about home care and became employed by an agency (fieldnotes, June 15, 2015). As in the United States (Ducey 2009), where the training of lower-level healthcare workers toward radiology, nursing assistant, or medical billing does not count toward nursing education and medical education, a year or two of healthcare assistance training has no exchange value for further education. Students who want to pursue a nursing education would be better off retaking the relevant examinations of the WASSCE to obtain a higher score rather than enrolling in a healthcare assistance certificate program. Young women are enchanted by the occupational promises of the certificate, but then disappointed by its occupational reality. One agency owner who also ran a school commented that many of her students thought they could go abroad with a healthcare assistance certificate, like the nurses, but the credential does not translate abroad in the same way a nursing degree does (fieldnotes, July 6, 2018).

Although faith in schooling has been present at least since the time of independence in Africa, particularly in its capacity to transform society (Vavrus

2003), neoliberalism in the form of private schooling is revitalizing educational enchantment. By educational enchantment, I mean the ways in which schooling becomes *the* vehicle for fantasies of the future. As Jeannett Martin, Christian Ungruhe, and Tabea Häberlein (2016) note, young people appear to be unshaken in their belief that going to school and university will help them to rise socially (see also Laube 2016 and Maurus 2016). By enchantment, I am referring not so much to the mystical or occult forces that Jean Comaroff and John Comaroff (2001) see as mobilized to explain millennial capitalism, but instead to the false hopes engendered by schooling, despite the social realities faced by educated youth. Lauren Berlant (2011, 122) discusses the powerful forces that lead to misrecognition, in which "fantasy recalibrates what we encounter so that we can imagine that something or someone can fulfill our desires." There is an everyday desire to be enchanted and have hope, born out of struggle and the need for direction and movement. Although Arjun Appadurai (2013) distinguishes between fantasy and the imagination, in which fantasy is individual and imagination is collective, I find it difficult to differentiate between the two because of the ways that persons take up hegemonic imaginations for their own personal projects. Educational programs are explicitly oriented to the future (Stambach 2017) and powerfully shape young people's aspirations (Mains 2011; Martin, Ungruhe, and Häberlein 2016; Maurus 2016). In a precarious world, all steps feel uncertain and full of risks, and thus enchantment is necessary to move in any direction.

Relying on the private sector leads to enchantment of schooling through marketing, public relations, and overblown promises (Nisbett 2013). In many ways, these images mobilize a nostalgia for a past that existed, if at all, only for a generation that came of age around the time of Ghana's independence, in which education led directly to state employment. Although this developmentalist model never truly worked in reality for all young people, neoliberal educational dreams rely on one aspect of this model—that schooling promotes social upward mobility to the middle class, in this case, of nurses. As such, neoliberal governance scavenges the developmentalist infrastructure, an infrastructure that it aims to replace through the market. The certificate enchants students with dreams of stable professional positions that were produced by state investment in a middle class. Catherine Bolten (2020) notes the importance of credentials in transforming a young person into an adult in Sierra Leone. Yet, simultaneously, young people can collect numerous educational credentials that are not, in fact, recognized as signifying talent and knowledge by employers and other powerful adults. New educational programs, designed for private labor markets, mobilize the infrastructure, labor, and visions built by the developmentalist state because the private sector offers only precarious, service-oriented labor to those with only secondary education in Ghana, such as in elder care. These new forms of education marginalize young people. Thus, those with the credential ended up being considered untrained by home care agencies and banned from government hospitals, leaving them with the option of working in the private healthcare market or finding another occupation. Through the contradictions of the state's relationship to the private markets in education and health care, young people entered schools because of dreams of becoming nurses but found that that credential was relatively worthless in realizing that dream.

The Contradictions of the Curriculum, Clinical Training, and Exam

What I witnessed by attending a healthcare assistance school in an Accra suburb in 2014–2015 was that the curriculum and examination of the HAT certificate were oriented toward public health, maternal and infant care, and hospital-based health care, rather than what might be useful in home care, such as geriatrics, first aid, and stroke and dementia care. The syllabus produced by NVTI lays out the following vague objectives for the certificate:

1 To demonstrate a broad knowledge base incorporating Healthcare concepts.
2 To demonstrate knowledge of the theoretical basis of practical skills.
3 To demonstrate knowledge in numeracy, literally [*sic*], and skills in Healthcare. (NVTI 2010)

As at other levels of the Ghanaian educational system (Coe 2005), the examination questions drive the course content. The four written exams in 2015 included a general one, given for all NVTI certificate programs, from auto mechanics to hairdressing, in entrepreneurial skills, mathematics, and English language; and three exams specific to health care—trade theory, trade drawing in anatomy, and trade science and calculations. Question formats were multiple-choice, matching, or short essay.

Exam questions were mainly oriented toward the hospital and involved knowledge of medical terminology. For example, a sample math problem stated, "Mr. Kweku Manu, a 76-year-old farmer, was admitted to the emergency room after sustaining an injury to his left lower leg with a blunt cutlass. The doctor prescribed capsule clozamzin, 500 mg p. o. qid x 7 days. Clozamzin is dispensed in 250 mg capsules. Calculate how many capsules he will take in a day, and calculate how many capsules he will take for seven days." The trade theory examination asked a variety of questions concerning communication ("Confidentiality means . . ." "When caring for people from different cultures you should try to . . ."), first aid ("In case of fire in a patient's room, the first action to take is . . ."), medical terms (define "bed cradle," "aphasia," "hyperthyroidism," and "cerebrospinal fluid"). The trade theory examination was similar to what Esther had devised ten years before, but with a greater attention to medical terms and technical language.

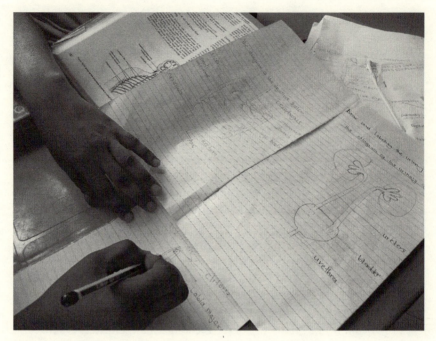

FIG. 6.2 A student practicing drawing the urinary tract, June 2015.

Trade drawing asked students to draw ten organs of the body over a two-hour examination period. Students received specific drawing instruction in class and practiced their drawings often over the last few weeks of the course (fig. 6.2). One of their anatomy instructors in the school, a trained midwife, told me that she considered it more important for students to know the *functions* of organs, rather than their abstract depiction, but she felt she had to teach them how to draw, given the examination questions (fieldnotes, May 29, 2015). My understanding is that "trade drawing" was included in the healthcare assistant examination because it was an important component of the examination of other trades like mechanical and electrical engineering, administered by NVTI, whose current head was an engineer.[7]

Trade science asked a number of different questions concerning home care, hospital care, and public health. For example, a man has just been discharged from the hospital after suffering a stroke; how will you prevent bedsores and feed him with a NG (nasogastric) tube? Or, you are educating a group of food vendors about food safety; state the points you will make to them. Or, define standard precaution. Or, educate new mothers on the importance of breast milk.

In addition, students had to pass a clinical examination, in which they were asked, one by one, to answer two or three questions orally and conduct one practical activity. On the day of the clinical examination, I was able to speak briefly to the school's outside examiner, a nurse who worked in a government clinic. HATs were not hired there, and she did not have a clear sense of what HATs ought to be able to do. She said, vaguely, when I asked her, that what is important is that the HATs "assist" the nurses and "learn more" (fieldnotes, June 17, 2015). She did not have any sense that HATs might be providing home care. As a result, many of her oral questions to students (as they reported to me and one another) concerned malaria prevention and antenatal care, reflecting the value placed on maternal and infant health as a result of the Millennium Development Goals. None concerned the care of older adults. As practical activities, she asked one student to make up a food tray for a patient and another to fill out a medical chart, activities associated with hospital-based settings rather than home care. In comparison, the owner of the school, who also ran a home care agency, felt that the most important practical skills in home care were lifting, turning, bedsore prevention, and management of stroke patients (fieldnotes, May 27, 2015). A manager of a nursing agency commented that those with the healthcare assistance certificate do not know how to give a bed bath, and so she teaches them during their orientation (fieldnotes, June 19, 2015).

Traces of the original home care syllabus remained but were accompanied and superseded by questions derived from hospital care and public health. Questions posed by the clinical examiner were oriented toward general public health—like malaria prevention and maternity care—rather than the care of older adults struggling to manage dementia, diabetes, heart problems, or disability caused by a stroke, because she, like so many others, was unclear about the purpose of this certificate. In general, the course oriented the students in confusing ways. This incoherence allowed students to maintain their initial goal of becoming nurses working in a hospital, with the status and authority of that role, rather than working in home care assisting older and frail adults.

Embodied Cultural Capital: Going to Healthcare Assistance School

The healthcare assistance school gave students embodied and symbolic cultural capital during the time they were in school. The daily activity of going to school gave students a feeling of agency, authority, and status. Being in school provided a reason to get up in the morning, a reason for their actions, and a sense that they were moving forward. The activity of education felt full of purpose and progress and thus was enchanting. Sitting around and doing nothing at home are stigmatized, although many young people have to do so while awaiting examination results or placements. Thus, these students received, from their healthcare education, "social belonging, a public identity, a sense of well-being, and future aspirations" (Millar 2014, 35). The key features that gave HAT students this sense of identity and status were their uniforms and their healthcare knowledge, both of which were used by the schools to attract students.

NVTI required HAT students to wear a uniform. The uniform was very similar to that of nurses in Ghana (see fig. 6.3). This uniform gave them a public

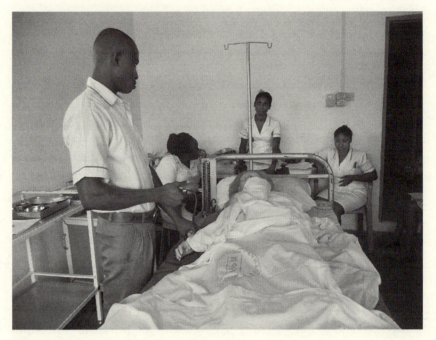

FIG. 6.3 A view of students' uniforms while practicing for the clinical examination with a dummy, June 2015.

identity as they commuted long distances to and from school across the congested and sprawling city. Clothing functions as a social skin for youth across Africa, performing their status and identity to others and in which they make substantial investments (Bolten 2020; MacGaffey and Bazenguissa-Ganga 2000; Newell 2012). As a result of their uniforms, healthcare assistant students reported being viewed as nursing students by their friends and families, and they were asked for medical advice. This public identity also spurred them to identify as nurses and with the mission of nurses to train and help the public. For example, one morning, when Millicent arrived at school, she recounted to the other students an accident she had seen on her way to the school that involved a motorbike. At first, the students discussed the prices of motorbikes. Then Bella said, "As a nurse, you have to get down." Mary illustrated what a nurse should do by calling out, "Driver, wait! Let me help!" (fieldnotes, June 12, 2015). They developed "a heart for the work" (Wendland 2010), in which nursing was a calling to serve the public.

Part of being an educated person was also buying prepared food during the break in the classes. Students frequented snack kiosks up the road or traveled over a swampy area to a restaurant on a main road where they could get a substantial Ghanaian meal of stew or soup over fufu or banku. Afterward, they would stop at a small kiosk to get various imported items like a cold bottle of soda, sweets, or other small items. Once, two students went to get their hair done at an upscale salon nearby, where they complained about the price but lounged on the seats in the luxurious atmosphere (fieldnotes, May 27, 2015). After the second day of the examination, walking back to the main bus station, they stopped at a restaurant to have fried rice and chicken, considered a non-Ghanaian dish (fieldnotes, June 10, 2015). I was surprised that students were able to afford eating out, and two students did consistently forgo buying meals, one because of her high transportation costs and the other who supported his family in northern Ghana. For the others, buying food in restaurants signaled their student and professional identities. The women who ran the establishments they frequented treated the students with respect and recognized their uniforms.

Through their course of study, HAT students came to identify with nurses and were treated as persons on the way up. They hoped to further develop the skills and subjectivities they had gained in the course in their employment. However, although they gained embodied cultural capital through being in "nursing school"—in the form of authority, status, and respect—their credential did not have much exchange value in the labor market.

Becoming Enchanted by Hospitals and Recalibrating the Exchange Value of the Certificate

The students in the course and whom I met at the examination site overwhelmingly aspired to be nurses who work in hospitals, particularly government hospitals. Many agency owners and NVTI director also commented on the intensity of this aspiration among students. The NVTI director said that students see "care as a stepping stone to nursing. It is not" (interview, June 1, 2015). Similarly, Esther, the owner of the home care agency, said that the students want to "show off" and are "excited to work in hospitals." However, "they are being deceived because there is no work for them" (interview, June 1, 2015). Although students at the school I followed had clinical experiences for two weeks in home care and seven weeks in a private hospital, they spoke only of their hospital clinical in their conversations in the classroom, unless prompted otherwise by me.

Hospital work was preferred to home care for several reasons. First, working in a hospital gave one status whereas working in someone's home was similar to domestic service. Hospitals were associated with educated professionals and domestic service with the nonliterate. Nurses and carers act differently in relation to patients. Nurses in Ghana are known to be rather abrupt and curt, giving orders that patients must obey (Böhmig 2010). A nurse who was teaching at the school for carers that I attended told the students, "Don't shout on patients as some nurses do" (fieldnotes, June 3, 2015). Similarly, an owner of a small nursing home was recruiting a nurse for her facility but simultaneously criticized nursing training, saying that nurses were not friendly to their patients but just shout at them (fieldnotes, August 1, 2014). In most hospitals, family members, not nursing staff, do "the dirty work" of bathing and feeding the patient. In a patient's home, in contrast, carers must follow the household rules and do the menial work that hospital nurses avoid.

The students were enchanted by their hospital experience and spoke often of their colleagues during informal conversations in the classroom, even though they had been insulted by the nurses, who had shouted at them and used them as low-status errand runners for food and lab results.

> They talked about a nurse [they met through the clinical training], who was training to be a doctor. They did not like her because she was arrogant. She told Bella to fetch her doughnuts (*bofrot*) from a place far away. She told Brilliant to go to the lab to check the results, and Brilliant refused, so the nurse complained to Brilliant's supervisor. Brilliant told her supervisor that when the lab staff had the results, they would send them back, so it was no use going to the lab to bother them. The supervisor, impressed, asked what Brilliant would like to do. Brilliant said she would like to follow the doctor on rounds. When she did so, she learned a lot about different cases. Bella continued the conversation about the nurse by saying that she did not think this nurse had the heart to be a doctor. (fieldnotes, May 26, 2015)

Observing the healthcare professionals around them carefully, the students were choosing whom to model themselves after. The nurses seemed part of the middle class, because of their autonomy, status, and power in the workplace, in contrast to home care, which looked more like being a domestic servant working for the rich and powerful. Such talk about nurses whom they had met at the hospital was an important part of their occupational self-identification.

Second, rates of remuneration differ, with hospital staff receiving a monthly salary linked to stable professional work and carers a daily rate associated with precarious, informal employment. Nursing assistants in hospitals were paid a monthly wage of Ghc800–900 (or about $200–225 in August 2015, approximately $1.67 an hour for a forty-hour work week). In contrast, in 2015, home carers were paid a daily rate of around Ghc20 (or $5) for ten hours or Ghc30 (or $7.50) for twenty-four hours, with some receiving Ghc500–700 a month if they worked many days. Because of the monthly salary, hospital workers are seen as more autonomous in their schedules, important for young women with child-care needs. Millicent, newly married, said she wanted to work in a hospital because they close at two in the afternoon, whereas one works much longer hours in care (fieldnotes, May 29, 2015). As one carer working for an agency told me, "I would rather struggle for a government appointment where I could work eight hours and go home. Here [in home care], I work twenty-four hours [a day]. In comparison, the government job is far better" (interview, July 17, 2018). The owner of a school said about her students, "They like their freedom and they don't want to have to work hard. They don't want a boss or supervision" (interview, May 22, 2015). Students perceived that they would be more tightly supervised in home care, by the patients and their relatives, than in a hospital, and felt constricted by the daily rate.

Finally, the students said, they thought the hospital was a place where they could learn many things from those around them and through the variety of cases they encountered, which would not be possible from taking care of one patient with the same illness. They could continue learning and "move ahead" in a hospital. They hoped to move up in the hospital hierarchy through their skills, in neoliberal fashion, since they lacked the right credentials. Joanna told me proudly that during her hospital clinical, a nurse told her to give an injection to a patient. Although Joanna had not received instruction on this technique, she had watched the nurse do it, so Joanna said she could do it and did so (fieldnotes, May 26, 2015; on the significance of imitation in education, see Coe 2005). Joanna also dressed wounds during the hospital clinical that were much worse than those she had dressed at home while caring for her mother, disabled by a stroke. Hospital-based work, and what students learned there, excited them during their training, and they oriented themselves to working in a hospital.

However, the HAT students were concerned about the limited employment and educational opportunities available to them. After they had completed the written examination and were studying for the clinical examination, the students shared their future plans, using a mixture of English and Twi, as is common among senior high school students.

> Florence said anxiously, "*Mihia* certificate *no* [I need the HAT certificate]."
>
> Bella said, "I don't want to re-sit [the certificate if she fails]." She said she would not go on to do the second-year HAT course; rather, she would re-sit the WASSCE and do general nursing. She explained why: "*Carer nyɛ* effective *wɔ Ghana ha. Wobɛbrɛ saa ara. Ghana nye* [Home care is not financially viable in Ghana. You will be so tired (doing the work). Ghana is not good (in terms of remuneration for employment)]." She felt it was okay to do home care abroad, however, because one would be better paid.
>
> Millicent argued that if you completed the second-year HAT course, the hospitals will take you, like Nyaho Clinic [the name of a private hospital serving the elite]. Another student is doing her attachment there, she said as proof.
>
> Bella responded, "They call them health assistants [meaning, they are not nurses]. The best thing, if you get the chance, is to be a community health nurse or a general nurse." They then discussed the respective pay of a community health nurse and general nurse. (fieldnotes, June 12, 2015)

On another day, Brilliant looked up the word "carer" in a nursing dictionary bought for the course. She read aloud, "Carer: A non-professional," and commented, "It's a pity-*o*" (fieldnotes, May 29, 2015). Another noted, "There is no job for this work," prompting a discussion of other educational opportunities among her peers (fieldnotes, May 27, 2015). Toward the end of the course, they socialized one another to dampen their aspirations and plan other courses of study.

Thus, some of their education during the HAT course involved recalibrating their expectations, as a result of peer and teacher comments. When the anatomy instructor, a midwife, criticized the past examination questions as confusing or inaccurate, Millicent argued back that the "Nursing Exam Council" set the questions, but the teacher corrected her that it was in fact NVTI, not N&MC, that administered the course. The teacher told them that they were going to be "healthcare providers," so they have to collaborate with the nurses, but would not be in "great control" as nurses are. Brilliant responded, "That is why we have trouble getting jobs" (fieldnotes, May 29, 2015).

As they approached the end of the course and their exams, students increasingly realized that their credential might have little exchange value: their best option was as a ward assistant at a private hospital. Even home care agencies did not value the credential because it was oriented toward hospital-based skills and subjectivities and did not train the students to give bed baths, transfer patients, or prevent bedsores. Thus, for insiders in the field of health care, the credential of HAT carries little cultural capital, even though students' friends and kin consider it symbolically impressive as a "nursing credential" and the school a "nursing school." As students moved from being outsiders to insiders in health care, they too learned the lesson about the relatively worthless credential for which they had studied.

I followed up with seven of the students from the course in December 2016—six months after they had passed the exam—and in August 2018 and heard news of the others from those I was able to visit. None of the fifteen students in the class—fourteen women and one man—actually worked in home care for which they were officially trained, although the four agencies I followed in Accra mainly employed those with HAT certificates. Three had found work by December 2016. The best student, Millicent, was working in a small private hospital recently founded by a surgeon and his wife, but was paid a small monthly stipend of Ghc200 (about $50) because of the paucity of patients. Although her salary was very low (initially she told me she was paid nothing at all), she wore a nursing uniform to work and had high social prestige. She lived with her family in a suburb of Accra and was supported by her husband, a soldier who had completed many international tours with the United Nations peacekeeping forces and with whom she had recently had a baby. Two other graduates, Brilliant and Bella, were working in private pharmacies, one using her social networks to obtain the position and the other with previous experience in a pharmacy prior to her HAT training. Joanna was planning to embark on another course, this time in cosmetology, funded by her husband as her HAT training had been. The sole male student showed me photos of his further training in the fire service, in which he and other men posed in all-black uniforms, looking macho and like they were fast friends, in contrast to his experience of being the only male student in the healthcare school. However, he found the pay of the fire service too low to live on and was currently pursuing entry into a new program, a government-sponsored youth employment scheme. Two students relied on their husbands' international remittances; one husband hoped his wife would soon join him in New York City to work in home care. Thus, the students seemed to have recuperated quickly when their dreams died, mobilizing themselves for another project like marriage, migration, or further education rather than being depressed (see also Bolten 2020 and Laube 2016). Young people were eager to become re-enchanted by another project by which they could attain respect as well as income.

Conclusion

Entrepreneurial movements have created a change in the educational and employment possibilities in many countries in the Global South. Entrepreneurs created an elder care market for the middle class and wealthy in Accra, whose services they wanted to legitimate through state regulation and to which they needed to recruit skilled workers. Some entrepreneurs opened an agency and a school, both of which they hoped would be profitable businesses. An attempt to legitimize the care market generated the healthcare assistance credential, but the credential was quickly transformed to become more similar to nursing and oriented to hospital-based settings, and thus more attractive to students unable to gain admittance into nursing programs. Educational entrepreneurs relied on misleading promises, a misrecognition of the possibilities, using the images of a middle class tied to civil service employment to promote training for precarious, relatively low-paid work in the private healthcare sector. The credential's popularity incurred a counterstrike by the nursing association and the most sought-after employer, government hospitals, which negated its exchange value, at least at the present time. A new inscription—the occupation of home carer—sought cultural capital. Through negotiations over many years between a professional organization and different state agencies, it was denied cultural capital. It became clear, officially for those in the healthcare field, if not always beyond it, that a carer was not a nurse. The new occupation of carer represents the development of precarious service work for educated young women, an occupation that many HAT graduates enter from a lack of other employment options.

The story of the HAT certificate speaks to the confusions generated by a transformation to neoliberal governance, in which a government agency partnered with private employers and private schools to create licenses for healthcare paraprofessionals, but in which the major employer, the state, is reliant on professional organizations that are interested in maintaining the privileged occupational niche of nursing under the developmentalist model. Neoliberal processes have introduced new dynamics in state-dominated education and health sectors but are not completely dominant because they rely on the infrastructure of the developmentalist state to generate value. Neoliberal processes are assembled through and entangled with an older model of the social order, which does not go away entirely. These different interests collided, and the HAT students became "the victims of circumstance," dreaming of state hospital employment and ending up in a more precarious private healthcare services or other fields through their social networks. In the wake of their disappointment, using their optimism and creative persistence, healthcare assistant graduates sought alternative pathways to get ahead, whether through private employment, other educational opportunities, or state youth employment programs. This chapter illustrates how elder care is intertwined not only with social relations within kin groups but also with relations between the state and markets and between the generations, as young people sought to gain the status of a stably employed nurse through an educational credential originally designed to train home care workers for older adults.

7

Carers as Househelp

● ●

Aging and Social Inequalities
in Urban Households

This chapter continues the argument developed in chapter 6 that changes in elder care are intertwined with wider social changes, affecting them and responding to them. This chapter examines how changes in social inequalities are reflected in changes in domestic labor (Rollins 1990). An expansion of wealth or the growth of a middle-class class brings new kinds of servants and new varieties of domestic services (Colen and Sanjek 1990; Sassen 1998). In the United States, with increasing income inequality, the growth of commercial elder care services in the past three decades has enabled a reflourishing of gendered, racial, colonial, and class hierarchies (Coe 2019a; Glenn 2010, 1992). In urban Ghana, a prosperous middle class has emerged after years of economic growth and transnational migration resulting in remittances. "The skewed income and wealth distribution in the country has sharpened as a result of market reforms," writes Ghanaian political scientist Kwame Boafo-Arthur (2007, 11). Neoliberal economic reforms deepened inequalities in the regional distribution of wealth, with the Greater Accra Region benefitting the most (Ninsin 2007). This is one reason why so many people continue to migrate to Accra, leaving behind their aging parents in the rural areas and why those parents are dependent on migrants' remittances. In addition, increased resources allow the urban middle class and elite to hire more servants, including those with specialized training as eldercare workers.

The new inscription of carer reflects and instantiates emergent forms of social inequality.

Home care services bring young people into unfamiliar, middle-class and elite households in a new role, as carers. Given youth unemployment and underemployment in Ghana (Baffour-Awuah 2013), young people are looking for a way to make a living, and one way to do so is by providing domestic services to middle-class and wealthy families. Carers are mainly young women in their twenties, although a few young men also work in this field and are in demand to help older men. Carers are considered somewhat educated since many have a secondary school diploma in addition to training as a healthcare assistant.

Social changes in aging not only result in changing intergenerational reciprocities between parents and their children but also complicate hierarchical relations *within* households. These new hierarchies build on and reconfigure previous hierarchical domestic relations between kin, foster children, slaves, and domestic servants, as well as with professionals like nurses. The new occupation of carers, as an inscription, are often filtered through these adjacent relations. These confusions with adjacent roles have repercussions on carers' status, pay, and treatment by patients. As a result, I argue, carers attempt to navigate their status in relation to the adjacent roles, engaging in symbolic boundary work (Lamont 1992) to establish their relative status. They position themselves as professionals like nurses against the category of househelp through wearing uniforms, teaching biomedical and scientific knowledge, and emphasizing their educated status. However, these forms of cultural capital are not always recognized or valued by older patients and other household members, including househelp. This chapter, by examining the experiences of a new kind of worker, explores how new configurations of inequality emerge between and within households, within the context of an aging population and changing intergenerational reciprocities.

A New Occupation, a New Inscription

All the owners of commercial care services, whether agencies or residential facilities, complained about their difficulties with recruitment and retention of reliable, knowledgeable, and caring employees. The oldest agencies initially trained their own staff and opened schools to accomplish this purpose. These schools were a source of profit in addition to the revenue from the agency business. However, for three of the four agencies I followed over time, these schools became a significant organizational challenge and expense for the owners, requiring the rental of a building and the employment of instructors, generally retired nurses or part-time instructors from other institutions, although Esther was determined to teach her students herself. Two of the three owners ended up closing their schools because of the organizational complexity and expense, in order to concentrate on the agency as a business. During the 2010s, as the postsecondary credential in healthcare assistance described in the last chapter became popular, it created a pool of young people who approached agency owners for employment because they could not find work in hospitals as they would have liked. Although they were not well trained in home care, as I discussed in chapter 6, the agency owners hired them as a willing and available source of labor. However, because those employees aspired to be nurses working in government hospitals, they often left suddenly when another opportunity arose. One agency owner commented that she had "lost the cream of the crop of the people trained," mainly to private hospitals but also to migration abroad (interview, June 17, 2014). Another said she was having trouble finding trained workers—they did not know what they were doing, and because they wanted hospital work, they "run off" suddenly (interview, June 25, 2015). This situation was visible to perceptive clients: one client's daughter commented that the care workers wanted to be health assistants in hospitals, so while working in home care, they were waiting for another opportunity to come along (interview, June 27, 2013).

In order to retain a reliable workforce, the agencies had to offer better working conditions, namely better pay and respect for their employees. One agency owner said that to pay carers more, she needed to increase what she charges the clients, but she had to be careful about doing so or she would lose clients entirely (fieldnotes, August 6, 2014). Another agency owner said that she wanted to keep the fees to patients low so that the clients were not just "the upper class" but also people in her own middle-class level (interview, August 4, 2014). A third agency owner complained that she cannot increase her prices because her clients complain that they pay their househelp Ghc100 a month, when she is charging Ghc20 a day for home care (interview, July 26, 2014).

As noted in the last chapter, in 2015 carers were paid a daily rate of around Ghc20 (about $5) for ten hours or Ghc30 ($7.50) for twenty-four hours; some receive Ghc500–700 a month if they work almost every day in the month; others who work fewer days might receive only Ghc200–300 monthly. Carers can make a living through the work, but only if they work long hours. When they have children, many drop out of the profession, as they find it difficult to continue to care for their children and work simultaneously, given the long hours of work necessary to make a living. Carers compared their pay to what they would receive from working in government hospitals, where they would receive benefits in addition. As one carer told me, "The money is not much compared to the hospital, so it is not encouraging" (interview, June 30, 2015). "The pay is nothing," said one carer (taped group interview, June 24, 2014). Another working in home care said she would gladly continue to do this work if it paid more (interview, September 13, 2019). The residential facility in particular paid very poorly (Ghc450 a month in 2018, or about $112), to keep its rates acceptable to residents, and as a result had trouble attracting and keeping staff. The owner emphasized that she was subsidizing the facility with her working-class wages in Switzerland. Because of difficulties with staff retention, those employees who remained were overworked in addition to being poorly paid, leading to low morale. They were physically exhausted from turning and bathing patients, with many suffering from back pain. Commercial care services vary in how much they charge patients and how much supervision they provide, but as in other countries, they take a large cut of carers' pay. A government social worker in a poor neighborhood of Accra tried to organize an association for care workers because she was concerned about their maltreatment at the hands of both agencies and clients, but she did not get much support from her bosses for doing so (interview, July 4, 2014).

Carers' pay is further reduced by the cost of transportation, as they travel from their homes to their patients' residences across the sprawling and congested city of Accra. Housing costs are cheaper on the outskirts of Accra, as well as in its slums. The neighborhoods where care workers live are usually far from the leafy residential streets where they work. Commutes can be time-consuming and expensive. Carers usually spent between a fifth and a third of their income on transportation. A care worker in a residential facility paid Ghc10 a day in transportation, which consumed a little less than half of her pay of Ghc450 a month (fieldnotes, August 5, 2018). Another home carer earned Ghc800 ($200) a month by working five days a week, but spent Ghc160 ($40) during the same time period on transportation (fieldnotes, July 13, 2018). Some carers prefer to perform live-in work, to reduce the cost of transportation, although staying overnight in the household has the down side of positioning them as householp, increasing their share of domestic work, and reducing their autonomy.

In chapter 1, I discussed the significance of adjacent or contiguous relationships in allowing the replacement of daughters by other persons considered like them. Here, I use the concept of adjacent relationships to explore how a new occupation, like carer, is understood in light of other occupations or roles and is built out of those understandings of other relations, through opposition and similarity simultaneously. In other words, a new inscription around the occupation of carer is being generated. By setting care work in opposition to similar and familiar occupations, patients and carers negotiate the role expectations, knowledge, skills, and class status of this inscription.

The major problem for commercial care providers was that they had to justify their costs of care—and, by extension, the status of their employees—to patients and their families, in comparison to other labor from domestic services, fostered adolescents, or extended kin, the adjacent relationships to carer. These competing labor sources put downward pressure on commercial care providers' rates and thus made it difficult for them to offer attractive salaries to their workforce, thereby reducing their ability to recruit and retain skilled and reliable staff. Agency owners had to ensure that the occupation of carer had cultural capital. Different people define what qualifies as cultural capital variously and thus how much economic and social value to place on a particular skill, connection, or experience. The new occupation of the carer is emerging at a time in Ghana when norms of cultural capital are shifting and multiple occupations are undergoing changes in their prestige levels, due to changes in education, economic trends, and migration. Although "household work always operates in situations of inequality, and . . . through household work the multiple axes of inequality dividing household workers and employers intensify and harden" (Colen and Sanjek 1990, 10), those axes of inequality are constantly being negotiated and contested in everyday life (Adams and Dickey 2000). The position of carer is very much in flux. Although officially the policy guidelines of the Nursing and Midwifery Council clearly differentiated carers from nurses, as discussed in the last chapter, the categories are still actively being negotiated in interactions between patients who rely on home carers, carers themselves, the agency owners and managers, and the domestic servants in the middle-class and elite households that employ carers. The remainder of this chapter explores how carers deploy their cultural capital as a claim that carers are nurses, not househelp, and how such claims are interpreted by patients and the differentiated members of patients' households.

(Not) Househelp: Education, Control, and Respective in Adjacent Relations

In my research with the nursing agencies in Accra, carers supplement or replace the care provided not only by daughters, wives, and younger sisters but also by more distant relatives, domestic servants, and househelp. Although the care of a daughter, wife, or sister is idealized, her care in urban areas of Ghana has long been supplemented by adolescents fostered in the household, women hired informally, and more distant relatives. Thus, carers can easily be confused with those adjacent relationships.

As I discussed in chapter 3, daughters living in larger cities and even in towns in southern Ghana often have responsibilities that compete with household duties and also have access to cash to hire domestic servants. Such daughters may become care managers in delegating the work of daily elder care—including companionship and cooking as well as more strenuous household tasks like washing—to more extended kin or househelp in rural towns like Begoro and Akropong. Thus, what makes care workers new and different in the provision of care is not their non-kin status, for non-kin are already providing elder care in some households. Instead, they are a more expensive form of domestic help, an expense justified by their specialized knowledge and education.

As has been noted about care work in other parts of the world such as the United States (Buch 2013; Stacey 2011), kinship idioms are used to incorporate and domesticate paid carers into the household's hierarchical relationships, as is done for househelp also. For example, one older male patient I visited, a retired doctor, said that his carer, a young woman, was "like family." On hearing this, his carer laughed, as if she did not think it was true but did not want to contradict him outright. (When I asked her about this comment later, in private, she confirmed this interpretation.) He continued, calling her his great-grandchild. One of his complaints about one agency he used was that they continually rotated their carers, which made it difficult to become familiar with the carers and make them "like family" (fieldnotes, August 6, 2014). Another patient's wife said that the carer was like a daughter, but the carer responded privately to me that she disagreed: "The food they give me is different than the food they eat. We eat on different plates and drink out of different cups. They eat a lot of vegetables in this house; we don't eat vegetables. We don't drink milk here. They give us porridge without milk.... We are just like househelps. They group us together" (fieldnotes, July 17, 2018). Although kinship idioms based on generation and seniority are used to naturalize the hierarchical relations between carers and their patients, carers do not put much effort into distinguishing themselves from family members. Despite the two comments above, the fact that these were the only comments I heard on this topic suggests that carers' non-kin status was not, in fact, under negotiation in determining their status, similar to the experiences of paid caregivers in rural areas whom I described in chapter 3.

Instead, carers focus their energy on showing their difference from the adjacent role of househelp. Carers' age and gender are similar to those of fostered adolescents and househelp. What makes them novel is their rate of remuneration, their biomedical training, and their supervision and management by an outside institution, the agency, rather than by the household members, particularly the most senior woman in the household. It is precisely these issues that form the basis of conflict in the exchange of care services. For example, although households expect househelp to modify their norms of cleanliness and conduct to meet the household's expectations, home carers see themselves as having forms of expertise about biomedical knowledge and proper care, which family members are not expected to possess. Modeling themselves after nurses working in a hospital, carers attempt to set the care standards in the home, although they are not always successful because they are instead treated as househelp who should conform to household norms around food, cleanliness, and routines.

Two elements of care work stigmatize home carers: one, the nature of the work and, two, the location of their work in other people's homes. These characteristics affiliate home carers with househelp, work befitting an uneducated young person. In terms of the nature of the work, carers lift patients from the bed or a seated position; they bathe them; they clean them after toileting; they change beds and clothes; they clean the patient's room and area; they help feed them; they give them medication; they provide companionship through games, prayers, songs, or conversation; and they are at the patient's beck and call during their shifts, whether day or night. One agency owner complained that she interviewed many potential employees, but they did not stay once they learned of the nature of the work: "Many people think that once you get to be a certain age, you don't sweep. But in this job, you sweep" (interview, December 30, 2016). Shellee Colen and Roger Sanjek (1990) note, "Household work in all class societies results in a measure of stigma. Household labor . . . is seen as lowly, devalued work, associated with dirt and disorder" (5). The tasks carers perform are "dirty work" (Palmer 1989), and as such degrade the performers of these tasks. Educated adults view the nature of the work as lowering their status. Employers of such workers can avoid the degradation of "dirty work" and maintain their status.

The location of the work further stigmatizes carers. Stella, an agency owner, said about her employees: "They are expecting to work in a hospital, and it is hard for them to work in a home. It is also about status. They want to work in an environment recognized by others. If they are asked where they are working and they say 'Korle-Bu [Hospital, the flagship government hospital in Ghana],' then the response will be 'Oh, Korle-Bu' [said with appreciation and respect]. But if you are working in someone's home, then it is like you are a maid or householp" (phone interview, July 13, 2013). Even if they are doing the same kind of work—cleaning and feeding people—as a ward assistant in a hospital, being able to say that they work in an institutionalized setting allows the respondent to imagine a more prestigious occupation.[1] Stella joked that she should rename her agency the United Nations so that her carers would be pleased to work for her. Work in a person's home, on the other hand, is associated with domestic service and the degraded status of householp. One carer who had worked in caring for two years told me that home care is "not a good job" because she changes diapers and sees older people's private parts. So she has not told anyone about the job she does. Her sister, with whom she lives in Accra, does not like the job she does, and she tells her mother in the Bono Region that she works in a hospital because otherwise her mother would be "disappointed" (interview, June 19, 2015). The staff of the residential facilities, even though they were not working in a hospital, did not encounter the status threats with which home care workers were preoccupied. One carer also noted the difference in worker autonomy in residential facilities and home care, saying that she hoped to open a residential facility where she could work "without any hindrance." In contrast, when she worked in someone's home, she is "not comfortable there. They are always watching you." For instance, while she is giving a massage to a male patient, his wife will think she is hurting him (interview, June 5, 2015).

Home carers frequently expressed that they are viewed as householp by their patients: they claim they are not respected as human beings, not trusted, and given tasks that they feel are beyond their scope of work. One agency owner complained that her workers were not given treated water in the household (usually in plastic sachets), but rather told to "drink from the tap." Or the patients served them cold porridge, the remains of what they had eaten (interview, June 17, 2014). A carer from this agency reported the same concern about sachet water, telling me in an interview, "I challenged [the patient]: 'You [yourself] are not taking the tap [water], but you want someone to take care of someone, and what happens if I am sick?'" (taped group interview, June 24, 2014). As noted above, the provision of food and drink, of the same quality as the patient's, is a key symbol of respect and appreciation, including whether the carer is considered a kin member or househelp. Fostered children similarly use food and drink to determine whether their foster parents care for them like their own children (Coe 2013b).

Carers also report a lack of respect for their work. In a discussion I had with two carers, they said,

AGNES Clients can ask, "Why are you doing this job? Go to nursing training." It discourages you.
FLORENCE They look down on you.
AGNES I say [to the patients], "This is what I want to do."
FLORENCE In this part of the country [in this country?], they don't know what it means to be a home nurse. They don't understand. (taped group interview, June 17, 2014)

Thus, carers and agency owners feel that they have to educate patients about the nature of their work and roles. As one carer said, "[Only] a few people understand that care is a profession. A lady said, 'I can have four housekeepers [househelp], but I still need a carer for my mom. The cook will not see how the grandmother was breathing badly'" (taped group interview, June 24, 2014). She felt that this client understood and respected her work, unlike many others, because she could see she needed a carer in addition to her cook.

Carers are often asked to perform the tasks of househelp in addition to providing care to their patient. One carer told me that the patient and his or her relatives ask her to perform ordinary domestic chores like heating something up for them. They take advantage of her. They can be "abusive" (group interview, June 17, 2014). When I asked another carer about the challenges of the work, she said that the clients "want you to help them with house chores. They will impose their house chores on you. So I will do it. I take it as we are all family" (interview, July 13, 2018). An agency owner wrote in the patient contract that the carers were only responsible for cleaning the patient's room. They could heat water and boil rice or other food like *ampesie* (boiled plantain or yam), but not cook stews and soups (fieldnotes, August 4, 2014). Stella, an agency owner, said,

Sometimes clients want caregivers to be househelp. I let them do some light cleaning here and there, but not for the whole house. We had a situation where one of our best caregivers was doing some housework but wouldn't do all of it. The client's relative said that she [the carer] should not step into the house again. When I protested, saying she was one of our best caregivers, the relative said that she hadn't swept under the table in the kitchen or cleaned the fridge well enough. We took the caregiver away. The client [the mother] asked about her when the new caregiver showed up, saying that the first caregiver was very patient. She wanted her to come back. So we spoke to her daughter, and the first caregiver came back, and another caregiver did the housework. The relations think the caregivers are there for them also, not just the clients. It is a challenge for the caregivers and very frustrating. It is hard to distinguish caregivers from househelp. (phone interview, July 13, 2014)

A carer in this agency spoke about a similar situation, where she was doing the cleaning for a patient who was also very heavy and hard to lift. She complained to the patient's daughter:

"Are you going to pay me extra money for the housework?" Because I was asked to take care of the mother. I want to have time for the person [patient]. If I do this [house]work, I won't have much time for her. The daughter told me, that she is grown more [older] than me, and so it is not fair that she should sweep and mop when I am there. She could have given birth to me, she told me. I told her she had to hire househelp, but because I needed this job and I didn't want to stay at home [not working], I said yes. I agreed to do the housework. (interview, June 19, 2015)

In both cases, the carer and agency capitulated to the patient's requests because of the economic capital of the patient, but with tension and resentment. It is important to note that the patient's daughter used her seniority in age in her argument that the carer, a young woman, should do the dirty work. The carers' relative age, in comparison to patients and their children, positions them as similar to househelp or young kin members who should do the most physically strenuous tasks.

The performance of household tasks rankles carers, but so does the fact that patients and their families can order them to do things in the house as they would househelp. A carer said, as a home carer, as opposed to a hospital worker, "You have to abide by their rules" in the house (interview, June 30, 2015). Another one said, "I have to dictate what you eat, what you wear, everything" in a hospital, but in home care, the patient determines what he or she will wear. If they are diabetic and want to drink Coke, then you have to convince them that it is bad for them (taped group interview, June 24, 2014). For patients and their relatives, the position of "nurse" is associated with ordering others around. Treating carers like househelp was part of the attraction to potential employers, as noted in one interview with a patient's daughter, a university professor. She said that her partially blind mother was "furious and angry" at the notion of an agency when it was first raised by her adult children. "She'd heard that the nurses control you and order you about," so the professor warned the agency to send someone who would listen rather than command. As a result, six years later, her mother has accepted her carers, in part because they enable her to live in her own home with which she is familiar, so that she can move around despite her blindness, rather than having to move in with one of her adult children living in Accra (interview, June 9, 2015). In general, the professor is satisfied that the carers do not behave like nurses in trying to dominate the situation and her mother.

Finally, carers, like househelp, felt that they were not trusted by household members. Agnes, for example, said, "They think you want to steal or take advantage of them" (group interview, June 17, 2014). One carer I knew was fired after a robbery of the house where she was working, probably because she was assumed to have collaborated with the thieves (phone interview, August 14, 2013). The trust at stake—a concern for property and money—arises from the anxiety generated by the vastly different social and economic positions of the househelp, carers, and patients. In particular, poorer persons are living in the intimate spaces of much wealthier persons: in their houses, their wealth is visible and on display, provoking jealousy or greed on the part of those who do not have it. Patients position carers in an economic and social stratum similar to househelp and feel some of the same class anxieties about them. Carers were also affected by the class distinctions, talking about feeling inspired by their patients' homes to do better for themselves and set long-term goals for investments and savings (this was particularly the case in Esther's agency, where she encouraged her caregivers to do so). Deborah, for instance, described how seeing the sumptuous homes of her wealthy patients made her "crave to be somebody" (interview, July 19, 2018).

The confusion between carers and househelp means that one of the key relationships that carers have to manage within the household, in addition to that with the client and his or her relatives, is with the househelp. Househelp are important in terms of carers' experience of working in households, and carers strategize about how to maintain good relationships with them. Unfortunately, I did not elicit the perspectives of househelp, only those of carers and patients. Many househelp are similar in age to carers, as young women; although occasionally, there are differences, as when househelp are much older than carers. Carers are usually better-educated than househelp, who are more likely to have nine years of schooling or less. As one patient's daughter astutely noted, there is competition between househelp and carers, with petty jealousies, gossip, and tale telling to the patient by both parties. She observed, "If one party is not cooperative, they get very particular about who is supposed to do what. No one is willing to go the extra mile. There is some rivalry too: they are the same age. But the nurses [carers] are glorified househelp. [She raised her arms and elbows in front of her, like a powerful chief, to indicate their sense of themselves as persons of high status]. The househelp get upset when the nurses won't wash their own plates" (interview, June 9, 2015). From the perspective of this patient's daughter, the source of the tension between two similarly situated groups—househelp and carer—was that the carers thought that they were better than the househelp.

The carers' perspective on this same tension is that the househelp feel anxiety that their jobs will be taken away because the carers will replace them in the household. At the same time, long-term househelp have knowledge about the family and its habits that the carers do not have, which puts them in a superior position to the carer. One carer said that in one patient's household, the househelp refused to cook for her, so she had to bring her own food. The househelp refused to do so, the carer explained, because the carer was hired after the patient developed bedsores in the househelp's care. The househelp worried that the carer would take away her job, even though the househelp was kept on through the carer's employment and her salary remained the same. Sometimes this same househelp refused to help this carer lift the patient because she did not feel that it was her task to perform. The carer said that she knew that lifting was her job, not the househelp's, but lifting can be difficult and gave her back pain, and it would be nice to have some assistance once in a while (interview, June 28, 2015). Sometimes househelp replace carers, after observing them for some time, as was true for one young woman who came to interview with an agency. She had been the cook for a woman whose mother was previously cared for by the agency, and she took care of the older woman when the agency left. Now, finding the work too difficult, she was seeking work at the same agency (fieldnotes, July 10, 2018). Stella also complained that one client had terminated the contract after the househelp had watched the care worker perform her duties, and "when she became good at it, she didn't need us. They could pay her less than they were paying us" (phone interview, July 13, 2013). Househelp, by watching and imitating care workers closely, could thus acquire caring skills without the expense of a credential, but also without its salary. One carer managed her relationship with househelp by telling them, "I will teach you if you want to learn" (interview, June 24, 2015).

Another carer talked about how she handled the relationship with househelp, so that these rivalries did not arise and househelp would cooperate with her. In particular, she addressed the househelp's concern about job security directly, did not gossip with them, and respected the househelp's knowledge about the family based on long-term joint residence:

> First, we [carers] washed [clothes]. When you do their washing for them [the patients], then they will let their househelp go. You spoil someone's job, and that is her daily bread. They [the patients] treat you anyhow, just as they treat you like the househelp. [Now] I tell the househelp, "I am not coming for your work. My job is your Madam. You are doing your own thing. If you prepare the food, you do it and I feed her. Yours is the washing and ironing." So though we are in the same place, there is different work. You don't go to them conversing and gossiping about their Madam, [and] you will be fine. They know a lot. They will tell you a lot about the person. [If you complain,] they will take your insults to them [the patients]. They didn't go to school. They see you, "Eh!" they are [feel] betrayed. They will do whatever it takes to destroy the relationship. You take them as a colleague, but not so you insult people to them [which the househelp is likely to report to the patient]. You go professionally; then you are free. (taped group interview, June 24, 2014)

Another carer said about househelp, "They think they know better because they have stayed with them for a long time. The agency tells me not to be close to the househelp, so I am not free [open and friendly] with them. Sometimes they watch you from a distance and then decide you are okay, and then it is fine" (interview, June 5, 2015).

Another carer said that if the househelp knows the patient very well, she recommends, "lower yourself to learn what the person knows," so she can do the job better (interview, June 29, 2015). When I visited one patient's household with the nurse supervisor of the agency, the househelp, a woman in her thirties, said that she had been in the household for ten years and teaches all the carers what to do and how her patient likes things (fieldnotes, June 24, 2015). Her greater knowledge of the patient as well as her seniority to carers helped her manage the carers who cycle through because of turnover at the agency.

Thus, there can be conflicts between househelp and carers because of the confusion about their respective roles, job security, status, and intimate knowledge of the household. Carers have to manage their relationship with househelp carefully so that they are allies and not enemies in accomplishing the work and pleasing the patient and family, on whose approval the continued employment of both parties depends. At the same time, they do feel superior to househelp and signal such status through their dress, education, and biomedical knowledge and discourse.

(Not) Nurses: Carers' Biomedical Knowledge, Dress, and Education as Uncertain Cultural Capital

Agency owners report a number of strategies they use to differentiate their workforce from househelp. Esther makes sure that her patients are not paired solely with one carer because a single carer encourages the patients, she feels, to forget about the agency's role and treat the carer like househelp (interview, June 17, 2014). Another agency makes the carers' food the responsibility of the carer, rather than the patients, since employers are responsible for providing food to househelp (fieldnotes, June 15, 2015). Many agencies require that carers wear a uniform to differentiate them from househelp. Stella said, "Sometimes they look to us [agency employees] as the househelp or maid. This is why all my caregivers have uniforms, to distinguish them from a maid or househelp" (phone interview, July 13, 2013). The uniform was usually a blouse or top, printed with the agency name, rather than an entire outfit, although one agency had a uniform similar to a nurse's with white trim, as in figure 7.1.

This sartorial distinction affected patients' interpretation of the professionalism of the carers and the quality of the agency. A patient's daughter said critically about one agency she used, "At one agency, the girls were just like househelps, dressed in their own clothes" (interview, June 27, 2013). She was not happy with this agency for many reasons, including the lack of supervision and the high costs,

FIG. 7.1 Carer in uniform with her patient in the courtyard of his house in Accra, August 6, 2015.

but ordinary clothing also suggested a lack of professionalism in her eyes. A uniform thus serves as cultural capital for the carers, clients, and agency.

Carers often report using their biomedical knowledge, completion of secondary school, and healthcare assistance certificate as forms of cultural capital in their interactions in the household. These forms of knowledge are not always recognized in households, which causes agency owners and carers to complain bitterly. In the healthcare assistance school I attended, the anatomy instructor, a midwife, strongly emphasized the importance of biomedical knowledge in contrast to "culture" in inculcating the public health mission of nurses: "Equip yourself with proper knowledge" so that you can change your community, as you yourself have been changed (fieldnotes, May 26, 2015) and, a few days later, "You are knowing things that they don't know. Teach them" (fieldnotes, May 29, 2015). Carers' biomedical knowledge is set in contrast to the lack of knowledge of fostered adolescents and domestic servants, which comes from their families of origin or their years-long stay in a household. Ironically, in carers' practice of care, their formal training and education may matter less than their warmth, patience, knowledge of the person's habits and tastes, and previous experiences of caring for a sick or elderly person in their own families or households, the same font of knowledge from which househelp draw their skills. Quite a few carers had in fact taken care of a sick relative, whether a father, mother, or grandmother, before being hired as a carer or entering healthcare training. Many of their own relatives had suffered from a stroke, which is also a primary reason why patients and their relatives seek an outside agency's assistance with care. Although the carers often relied on informal knowledge to accomplish their tasks, they positioned themselves as having access to biomedical knowledge because that was key to their status in the patient's household.

Nursing agencies trade on biomedical knowledge and other forms of knowledge to raise the status of the carers as a profession vis-à-vis other kinds of household workers. The conflictual process of raising the status of the female-dominated nursing profession has been well documented in the United States and France (Reverby 1987; Schultheiss 2001). The status of nurses has been dependent on the creation of a strict hierarchy within the nursing profession, in which a few have gained high status and pay but many lower levels have not. Similarly, in Ghana the training of carers justifies the higher pay and status of the carer in comparison to "uneducated" and "rural" househelp and sometimes in relation to the patient and their kin—for example, in giving carers authority to dictate care practices to family members rather than being ordered to perform certain tasks. Owners of nursing agencies emphasize, as part of their marketing, that as a result of carers' knowledge and attention, patients live longer than they do under the care of househelp.

Biomedical knowledge and training are critical to the carers' sense of professional self. The key ways that they deployed this knowledge was in terms of using equipment like latex gloves, writing notes, mentioning medical terms for diseases and bodily processes, reading medication labels, and having some information about diabetes, strokes, and blood pressure; but they were generally not as fluent in these matters as trained nurses are. The training in biomedicine helps them feel pride in their work and allows them to differentiate themselves from househelp. One carer described how she recognized her patient was dying, and how she called the doctor to come. "If I wasn't a professional, I wouldn't know" (taped group interview, June 24, 2014). Another carer in the same group interview told me,

> In the olden days, if someone is ill, the aunty [who] is in a village somewhere not doing anything will come and take care of the person. So they have the perception that the work is not for those who are educated. They think you are not educated, because you are changing a diaper. We had to let them know that this is not just someone from the village, but we learned something from the class. You have to wear uniforms, and you have to wear gloves to change a diaper. We know the medication. They realize they [we] are not villagers. They know you are a professional caregiver. You sign in and out, and write what happened that day, so the next carer comes and reads [what happened on the shift]. (taped group interview, June 24, 2014)

Biomedical training is the key distinction between carers and their adjacent role, househelp, and it brings carers closer to the adjacent occupation of nurses. Such knowledge is signaled by everyday, visible practices like clothing, accessories, and literacy.

Carers' knowledge was key to their employment, as one patient's daughter described it. She used to rely on househelp for the care of her eighty-two-year-old mother, partially blind from glaucoma. However, she then needed "someone more knowledgeable" to help with her mother's medication. She noted that the househelp had mainly not completed junior secondary school. In her words, the agency provided "partially trained nurses" who could "dispense medication" (interview, May 31, 2015). In her mother's house, the carers work only during the day, leaving her mother to the care of the househelp in the evening and night.

Because training and education are key to status enhancement, they are cited in the humiliation of carers, when patients or their relatives are angry at them. One carer talked about a difficult relative of a patient, who insulted her, "You are nothing! Where is your certificate! Where did you train!" (taped group interview, June 24, 2014). A relative of a man who had previously used an agency said dismissively about the carers, "They call themselves nurses," even though their training was awful (fieldnotes, July 15, 2018). Feeling that these sentiments were not always articulated by patients, carers explicitly emphasized their training, literacy, and use of equipment like latex gloves in the home to bolster their position and sense of self-worth.

Carers were generally perceived by their own friends and neighbors as being nurses. Some hid their actual profession as a home care worker out of shame; others did not. One middle-aged woman working as a carer and living in a slum in Odorkor did not tell her friends and neighbors the exact work she was doing; she said that they think she works at a clinic (interview, June 23, 2015). Another carer reported feeling respected as a medical professional in a household where she worked. In a household in the middle-class neighborhood of Mamprobi, she reported, the patient's relatives called her to tell a neighbor's child about "this or that," for example, about drinking cold things when one has asthma, using the carer as an authority figure to support the instructions of the child's mother. The patient's sister also asked the carer to check her blood pressure (interview, July 2, 2015). Another carer, living in the slum of Nima, told me that although her family knows the work she does, because her mother and her sister also worked for the same agency, no one else does. The people around her think she is a nurse because of her uniform, and so they ask her what they should do for headaches, for example. She has not bothered to explain her occupation to them (fieldnotes, June 23, 2015). A fourth carer living in Nungua said about her father and friends, "They see you as a nurse" (interview, June 29, 2015). The uniforms help in this regard, and carers wear them as they travel to and from work.

A confident young male carer told me that he managed to convince another househelp of his status by talking about his knowledge and showing his health-care assistance certificate to her. The househelp was a young woman of about twenty who just completed secondary school and cooked for his client. He reported, "She doesn't respect us [the carers]." The cook told him about home care, "This work, I would never do it, even if I had no job." He was quite insulted by this statement, which implied that his job was lower than hers: "She thought we were nobody." Later, he was teaching the patient's son and his wife, who live in the patient's house, about hypertension and medication. The cook asked him, "Do you want to go to nursing school?" He told her, "I have completed nursing school," by which he meant school for healthcare assistance. The patient, over-hearing this, was also surprised and asked to see the certificate. The next time the carer went to the house, he brought his certificate. He reported that the cook started showing him more respect as a result, although the patient, a difficult man, did not, perhaps because, with his higher education, he recognized that healthcare assistance was not equivalent to nursing (interview, June 30, 2015).

Carers contrast what they learned at school to caring knowledge acquired by other means to shore up their precarious position in patients' homes. I was able to see this dynamic in action one day when I visited an older man who was bed-ridden as a result of a stroke. His carer was a young woman in her early twenties who had been working with him for less than a month; this was her first patient after completing healthcare assistance school. Because the patient could barely speak, I ended up chatting mainly with the carer and the housekeeper who cooked the patient's food, a woman in her fifties. It turned out that the house-keeper had been taking care of the patient since he had had the stroke, a year and five months before, until the man's children had hired the agency four months ago. The carer was eager to show off her medical knowledge—of catheters, for example—and also to learn medical information from me, which I resisted, as I was unqualified to give it.

As we continued our conversation, the carer and the housekeeper began to spar over what constituted proper treatment of the patient. The housekeeper emphasized her long-term, personal knowledge of the patient in making her arguments. For example, she said that these days—during the rainy season, in July—the weather was cool and he could sleep well, but when the weather was hot he itched a lot, and she has a cream that she gives him. The housekeeper continued by saying that when she took care of her own grandfather, her mother taught her medicines which took care of bedsores. The carer challenged her on this issue, saying that she learned in school that bedsores are avoided by the sheet being flat and without any particles like sand on it. She stood up to brush the patient's sheet to demonstrate. She looked to me for confirmation, and unfor-tunately, I found myself nodding, recalling my own short course in nursing assistance in the United States a few years before. She went on to say that bedsores were avoided by having a "hygienic environment" and changing the patient's position. The carer was impressed with the way the blood pressure medi-cation kept the patient very healthy—she checked his blood pressure regularly—whereas her own father, also a stroke patient, took many different medications without positive results. The patient has not gone to the hospital all year, she said, which she attributed to the blood pressure medication. The housekeeper thought that perhaps the patient should reduce his medications since he is now feeling better, but the carer argued in response that it was the medications that were keeping him healthy. They also had a more minor disagreement about salt in the patient's food (fieldnotes, July 29, 2014).

From my vantage point, the different caregivers in this household seemed to be competing with one another over who was better qualified to take good care of him, with the much younger carer using her school-based knowledge to her advantage. Although she managed to silence the much older housekeeper, at least in my presence, it was not clear to me that she had convinced the housekeeper that her medical knowledge was superior to the housekeeper's home-based remedies and long-term knowledge of the patient.

The training and certificate are attempts by carers to position themselves as educated and medically trained "nurses," rather than as "househelp." Those attempts are usually not successful, but occasionally they are, generating requests for medical advice from neighbors and respect within their patient's households. Some patients, as the quotes above illustrate, call carers nurses and consider them like nurses, but others conceive of them as glorified and arrogant househelp, "partially educated" or badly trained.

"Ghana Is Not Good" for Care Work: Care Work and the Global Horizon

In the previous chapter, I reported on a student in the nursing assistance school who said to her peers, toward the end of their course, "Home care is not financially viable in Ghana. You will be so tired (doing the work). Ghana is not good" in terms of remuneration for home care.[2] Many employed carers would agree with this assessment, and as a result, they dreamed of migrating abroad, where they imagined, unrealistically, that elder care paid better.

Carers, whether working in the home or a residential facility, have difficulties making ends meet. The long working hours, necessary to make a living, are tolerable for many carers when they are single and childless. However, when they get married and have a child, the job becomes less attractive, as young women cannot balance their household responsibilities and the expectations of their husband with the irregular and long hours of the job. One dedicated carer complained about how she was not earning enough money from her work to cover childcare costs and so had stopped working for the past two months. But she was thinking about going abroad to do the same work: "I know that if I go abroad, my husband will sacrifice," which he was not willing to do for the same work in Ghana (taped group interview, June 24, 2014). Many care workers initiated conversations with me about what care work was like abroad and told me of their dreams of going abroad. The newly minted carer who sought to lord it over the more long-term housekeeper, discussed in the last section, had a long conversation with me about her brother's willingness to give her money to migrate abroad because of her carer skills (fieldnotes, July 29, 2014). Another carer told me that when she tells others about her work, they respond, "Oh, you have money!" to which she laughs, because she had just complained to me about the pay. When I responded with some confusion over this expectation, she explained that it is because "people outside [abroad who do this work] have money" (fieldnotes, July 13, 2018).

The romance of abroad compensates for some of the frustrations of the care market in Ghana. Carers enter the profession in Ghana in part because it is seen as a remunerative profession abroad. They plan to begin work in Ghana, gain some experience, and then migrate, perhaps in the same line of work or for further education as a nurse while working abroad. Entrepreneurs in elder care highlight their international connections to attract students to their schools and to the new profession of carer. The owner of a large private nursing school in Accra— with two to three hundred students a year—had an exchange program with Denmark, and she trumpeted to me how many of her students were currently in the United Kingdom and the United States (interview, August 4, 2015). One graduate of an agency school reported that most of her cohort of students—who graduated three years before—had traveled outside the country, to the United States, the United Kingdom, the Netherlands, and Australia (taped group interview, June 24, 2014). Carers have also gone abroad temporarily with their globally connected middle-class and elite patients, resident in Ghana, on family visits to the United Kingdom and India. Migrants abroad pay for their relatives to take healthcare assistant classes in preparation for bringing them abroad to do elder care work, as was true for two of the fifteen students in the school I followed. However, there is no clear pipeline leading from the care market of Accra to the care market of New York City or London: carers would have to be retrained and relicensed in the country of migration, although their course might be only a few months in duration and relatively cheap in comparison to other forms of further education.

In their interest in going abroad, carers are following the lead of the nursing profession in Ghana, after which they model themselves. In 2009, 24 percent of nurses trained in Ghana worked abroad, primarily in the United Kingdom and United States (International Organization for Migration 2009). Carers are aware that many Ghanaians work in elder care in these countries (Arthur 2008; Coe 2019a). When I observed Esther give a lecture about aging to social work students, a young man reported on a phone conversation with a friend who worked in home care in the United States: as they were talking, the student heard screaming in the background. His friend told him that his patient had dementia, a new concept to the student. The student told Esther that he was not sure he had the temperament to do care work because he is very emotional (fieldnotes, June 23, 2014). Thus, information about care markets abroad—including knowledge of disease states and work conditions—siphons through the social networks of carers, potential carers, and their friends. These social remittances both attract and deter potential care workers from working in care.

Knut Graw and Samuli Schielke (2012) note that even nonmigrants are affected by "the global horizon" or an awareness and imagination of other societies, in which migration looms as *the* route for success at home (see also Fouron and Glick-Schiller 2002). Like high-tech and factory work financed by multinational capital in the Caribbean or Southeast Asia (Freeman 2000; Sassen 1998), care work prompts young people's onward migration by putting workers in touch with households with connections abroad while simultaneously denying them a livelihood in the local context that allows them to realize their dreams as wives and mothers.

Carers are interested in a Western model of elder care only in that it creates an established care market that provides stable employment and remuneration. Social welfare programs create a larger care market in Europe and North America than is present in Ghana, and shortages in direct-care workers in the West mean that work in this field is available for new immigrants (Institute of Medicine 2008). Exchange rates between currencies mean that poverty wages in the United States from home care employment translate into the possibility of making real estate investments in Ghana, as I have documented among Ghanaians retiring from decades of home care work in the United States (Coe 2017, 2020).[3] Owners of home care agencies are both pleased that their former students and employees find work abroad and dismayed that they lose the skilled workers they have trained. To the extent that carers attain their goal of migration, they reduce the possibility that an elder care market will be viable in Ghana.

I met two carers in Ghana who managed to go abroad, and both trips were strikingly unsuccessful in comparison to the experiences of care workers I met in the United States. Neither landed in Ghanaians' most highly ranked and remunerative migration destinations of Europe or North America as they hoped. After working several years for an agency in Accra, which was no longer giving her work after a dispute, Faustina went to Kuwait in 2015, borrowing money for the airfare. Working as a maid for a childless couple for several years, she endured her passport being seized and her wages not being paid until she ran away to a shelter. Through the intervention of the Ghanaian embassy, she was able to return to Ghana with her passport. Faustina has had difficulty finding work since her return to Ghana. In 2019, she was considering going to Vietnam to teach English or joining the fire service in Ghana if she could mobilize her political connections to obtain this civil service position (WhatsApp conversations in 2014 and 2015, and an in-person interview in 2019). After being trained by and working for Esther's agency in Accra, Deborah went to South Africa for ten years when she was in her mid-twenties. She found work as a nanny and later a beautician, but, without work papers, she found it difficult to make a living. Ultimately, she was rescued by Esther. Deborah returned to work in home care for Esther, feeling that she had lost ground in comparison to her same-age peers (interview,

July 19, 2018). Employer abuse of immigrant domestic servants is common in the Gulf (Gamburd 2000), and immigrants from other parts of the African continent often experience violence and harassment in South Africa (Steinberg 2015), so these experiences were not unusual for these migration destinations. Neither Faustina nor Deborah came back with the resources or capital with which to support themselves, resulting in a return to care work or unemployment in Ghana. As documented in other research (Graw and Schielke 2012; Mains 2011), underemployed and unemployed youth in Africa see migration as the route to attain success, but that success may be elusive.

Conclusion

In the context of demographic changes and growing inequality, both in Ghana and between Ghana and other countries, a new kind of work is emerging that is open to young people: elder care. Positioned in relation to the low-status, poorly educated, young, rural-in-origin role of househelp and the high status and authoritative role of nurse, the occupation of home carer is ambiguous for carers, their friends and family, and the patients and their relatives alike. Care work has the potential to complicate hierarchical and social class relations within households. Household labor is being reorganized among younger and older women in different social classes as middle-aged and wealthier women are shifting some care work to younger and poorer women, both househelp and carers. Increasing economic inequalities are reflected in social inequalities in households, generating new kinds of social tensions around education, status, and authority. Educated persons, rather than becoming middle-class civil servants with authority and status, are instead becoming servants to others.

Carers and agency owners tend to inscribe carers as similar to nurses, with the cultural capital of biomedical knowledge and education. This positioning happens not only among carers' neighbors, friends, and family but also to the significant members of the households in which they work—patients, their relatives, and househelp. The characteristics of being like a nurse are signaled by their uniforms, professionalism, literacy, the possession of biomedical knowledge, and the use of biomedical equipment. However, the adjacent role of househelp constantly threatens the occupation of carer: the kind of work performed and the location of work make home carers seem very similar to househelp. Furthermore, the age of carers also means that they are often junior to patients and their relatives and sometimes even to the resident househelp. Because they seem like "glorified househelp" to some patients, carers often do not receive the respect and status they feel that they deserve. Their cultural capital of education is not valued, or not as valued as they would like. Their desire to present themselves as professionals does not fully convince those who observe their work.

This chapter speaks to the limited options for young people with a secondary school education and to the disjuncture between their aspirations and the employment available to them in Ghana. Cultural capital—in which they have invested their time, energy, and dreams as well as their relatives' capital—disappoints in its exchange value in local employment markets. As noted in research on young men in Ethiopia (Mains 2011) and in a fishing village in Ghana (Lucht 2011), disconnections between personal aspirations and actual opportunities in the local social context create a desire to go abroad. As carers in Ghana find that their expectations for employment are not met by reality, they begin to idealize work abroad as a place where they imagine care work is better compensated and respected. Many carers feel ambivalent about care work in Ghana because of its low pay and associations with domestic service, but the possibility of it being a stepping stone to migration abroad overcomes the stigma for some workers. Their disappointments with the cultural capital of carers in Ghana may propel them into even more precarious servitude in a new social hierarchy abroad, as for Faustina and Deborah, subject to additional indignities of being an immigrant and racialized as Black or African (Coe 2019b). This chapter illustrates the struggles of young, urban, secondary-school-educated, mainly female Ghanaians to find work with status, respect, and pay to support themselves and others. The care market in Accra is one place where they land, but it offers them employment that positions them as householp, disappoints them, and fuels their imagination of more rewarding care markets elsewhere.

Conclusion

● ●

The world population is growing increasingly older, meaning not only that individuals are living longer, often with chronic conditions that require care, but also that many societies around the world are experiencing the overall aging of their societies, with a lower proportion of children and young adults and a greater proportion of adults over sixty years old. African countries are also undergoing these demographic changes, although they remain primarily youthful. Because age is a major social category by which societies decide how to distribute power and resources, the growth in the older population and its need for care—along with urban and transnational migration and social inequality—can prompt other social reconfigurations. These reconfigurations are occurring within kin groups and beyond kin groups. These changes have repercussions on the intergenerational exchange of financial and cultural resources and the terms by which people are entitled to those resources.

According to the orthodoxy, in southern Ghana, elder care is primarily in the hands of "the traditional family." This differs from the reality, in which "the family" is defined not as the siblings, nieces, and nephew of the aging person who are significant in matrilineal and patrilineal systems but more narrowly as the adult biological children of older adults who were looked after into successful adulthood. Within that small group of adult children, the division of care labor is gendered, with a daughter expected to provide care on a daily basis to an older person or group of older persons. Sons and successful daughters take on the role of care managers, remitting from both abroad and within Ghana to support care provision. Kin are finding both care management and provision difficult. They may lock someone with dementia in a room for the day or provide only food to an older person, while forgoing companionship and medical care.

Changes in Care has examined processes of social change through the lens of aging in Ghana. Both quiet, unnoticed transformations and highly visible changes in the orthodoxy of kin care for older adults are happening in different social circles. Among the middle class and elite in Accra, home nursing services offered by commercial agencies are increasingly popular, and residential facilities (such as nursing homes or care homes) are actively discussed, although only a few with small numbers of residents are in operation. The mainline churches, which cater to older congregations in rural towns, are experimenting with voluntary associations like aged fellowship groups and, to a lesser extent, senior day centers, focused on providing sociality for relatively active and well older adults rather than everyday care for those who are bedridden and disabled.

In contrast to these visible initiatives, quieter alterodox changes negotiated among kin are under way. For instance, rather than middle-aged daughters moving to care for their mothers in the hometown, sometimes mothers move in with their daughters, negotiating changed relationships with their sons-in-law, in a house considered his, in towns where few people know them. Sometimes, adult children hire a more economically vulnerable woman as a servant for pay or arrange for a foster child from a more economically disadvantaged household to live with an aged person in the daughter's stead. Neighbors are also important in looking out for and feeding older adults. These practices pass under the radar; not discussed, they are enacted at the level of practice.

Other possibilities are more discursive, floated as ideas that may gain traction as practice one day—or not. For example, some older adults advocated for balanced reciprocity with the state or church, rather than with their adult children: because they have contributed to these institutions when they were strong and had income, the institutions should contribute to them now that they are weak and frail. Another idea floated is a more individualistic approach, in which older adults are encouraged to plan for their own retirements, rather than relying on their children.

These innovations in care are happening in fits and starts, in episodic and scattered ways, visible in certain circles more than others, speaking to the uncertain and contingent nature of social change. Various groups have tried models of care that have not succeeded. Churches became aware of the needs of the bedridden through their monthly practice of Invalid Communion, but directed their resources to well and active older adults, who tend to be more visible and powerful. Home care agencies have tried to obtain state support and regulation to expand their field of action beyond a small group of elite and middle-class urban households with access of remittances from abroad, but the state has ignored them and protected nurses, to whom carers are seen as competition. For the most part, these initiatives are alterodoxies that either are subsumed into the orthodoxy of "family" care or are not seen as a threat to it. Even in the face of social failures in creating new infrastructure, institutions, and practices, the ideas travel and find new ground within Ghana, such as a senior day center floated by state officials charged with social welfare, or as the carer credential transforms into a credential for nursing assistance, generating a disaffected workforce in elder care. Not all social changes happen through inscriptions, but they are an important process by which social change occurs, in less visible ways.

Through changes in care, two axes of inequality are also shifting. One axis is a gerontocratic one, in which some people gain authority and power through seniority and in which children and young adults are the main providers of household labor and, therefore, the daily provision of care. This axis of inequality across the life course is becoming less significant but has not completely been replaced by an axis organized around social class, in which status is permanent, no matter which age one may be. Rather than domestic labor (including elder care) being associated with age, particularly with adolescent girls, care becomes a class-based relation of domestic servitude in which women struggling to eke out a living are employed in more prosperous and educated households to provide care. This inequality results in tensions over caregivers' status in households, as discussed in chapters 3 and 7.

Furthermore, rather than aging being a source of power, including the negative power of witchcraft, the perception of aging is also changing. Aging is becoming increasingly associated with frailty and weakness. Patrons can gain status and visibility by supporting the vulnerable, in which the aged are clumped with orphans. Such support is welcomed by older adults in the absence of state benefits and neglect by churches and kin groups, but also positions them as passive and in the role of recipients of charity. The social category of "the aged" or *mmarisiwa* generated within the church aims to rehabilitate aging into a reflection of God's blessing, rather than a source of lament and pity or, worse yet, a sign of older people's spiritual malevolence against the younger generation.

Transnational migration plays a role in these changes in senior care. Many of the commercial nursing services are founded by return migrants, who are using economic and cultural capital from abroad to start care businesses in Ghana. Adult children abroad are also less likely to return to care for an aging parent; many of the users of commercial nursing services in urban middle-class and elite circles rely on the remittances of their children abroad to pay for them. Another major subset of users of commercial nursing services are return migrants, some of whom returned to live in Ghana, leaving behind their adult children in the country of migration, when they became ill. Furthermore, images of an idealized "West"—where the aged are imagined (wrongly) to be cared for properly—are used to propel social change in Ghana, to try to put pressure on the government to do more for older adults. Finally, some carers are attracted to care work by the possibility of going abroad, since they know that many migrants from Ghana work in senior care abroad.

However, this is not the whole picture. The increased importance of women's formal work—which urban and transnational migration intensifies—is another major factor, in which women experience more time pressure and less incentive to begin a period of reduced economic productivity in the hometown to care for a mother or father. The historical increase in the felt needs required by children and adolescents—in which adolescents are no longer a major source of household labor but have rights to many years of education—also makes "family" care less available. These issues are related to class, in that middle-class and elite households are more likely to feel these changes connected to women's and children's roles and therefore employ or take in women and children from poorer households to provide labor in their stead.

Home Care

Given Ghanaians' increasing longevity and the increase in chronic problems and disabilities due to strokes, high blood pressure, and diabetes, families desire forms of support beyond kin care. Home care is likely to be more attractive to Ghanaian families than nursing homes, given the number of extended family and househelp living in middle-class and elite households in urban and rural areas and the stigma attached to visibly moving an older adult into a facility, associated with abandonment. The agencies in Accra are older and more numerous than the residential facilities, providing toileting, dressing, feeding, and companionship to older persons in their homes while their children are away at work or are abroad. This suggests a pressing need for home care services in the decades ahead.

The commercial care services provide a new source of employment for young women, and some young men, with secondary school education, which is quite salutary given the high rates of unemployment among youth, including educated young people, in urban Ghana. The urban senior care market has created a need for care workers who are skilled and passionate about their work. These are not currently available in Ghana. As described in chapter 6, an agency owner worked with a government agency to create a credential for care workers, so that, on the basis of their skills, she could justify charging her clients and paying her employees a wage higher than that given to househelp. However, under pressure from private nursing schools hoping to attract students and students hoping to become nurses, the carer curriculum changed over the course of a decade, from an emphasis on home care to a use of hospital-based examples. On examinations in June 2015, students were asked about maternity care and general preventative measures, rather than geriatric care, and in clinical examinations, were asked to set a tray and other hospital-based procedures, rather than perform the routine tasks of home care. As a result, the agencies find that neither students with the healthcare assistance training (HAT) certificate administered by NVTI, nor those with the competing nursing assistance clinical (NAC) administered by N&MC, are equipped for home care. Furthermore, the students are not happy to care for older people in their homes, but instead seek work in government and private hospitals. Thus, carers pursue opportunities elsewhere as soon as they understand the nature of the job. Both students trained in healthcare assistance and the agencies are frustrated, the students by entering a field associated with domestic service and the agencies by employing ill-trained people. These issues lead to low-quality care for the patients, whose families are often sacrificing large sums of money for care. The current situation is not meeting the needs of patients, young people, or commercial care services.

Home care agencies should be involved in creating the curriculum for carers, to be sure that the training of the students meets their needs for skilled workers who care about older adults. The government agency supervising the carer credential, whether NVTI or N&MC, needs to coordinate more closely with the sectors that are in a position to employ graduates. The work of caring entails a holistic approach to health care, comprising social work and psychology in dealing with those with memory loss, depression, and dementia as well as routine practices of caring for physical and aging bodies such as lifting, bed baths, bedsore prevention, and handling the paralysis and weakness that follows a stroke. It is not clear which government body, whether N&MC or NVTI, should regulate the program, but they should cooperate more closely with each other in running it. Even if NVTI is the supervisory body, nurses with an understanding of home care will need to be involved in the training and supervision of carers. So too will other professionals like social workers and geriatricians.

Carers need to be valued, not only in terms of routine practices of respect, but also in terms of their pay and other compensation. They should have opportunities for further training to become nurses in the future. At the same time, carers' curriculum should be sharply distinguished from nursing, by focusing on the skills necessary to provide good care to older and disabled people in their homes, where the carers will have to operate relatively independently, unlike nursing assistants who work in the hospitals under the direct supervision of nurses. The course should be short, from a few months to no more than a year, to make the financial costs of a carer education accessible to a range of students.

These recommendations would result in a more coherent system in which patients and their relatives are pleased with the quality of care, carers are interested and invested in elder care, and agencies are able to employ dependable young people whose skills increase year by year. However, these reforms will still not allow care services to be available beyond a small group of older adults who have a child working in a professional capacity abroad. Many rural and peri-urban poor families face similar needs for care services, as the voluntary work by the Akrowa Foundation, discussed in chapter 5, attests. However, they will obtain it only if the state becomes involved in subsidizing or wholly funding senior care services.

The Contradictory Role of the State

Why have African countries neglected the needs of older adults? Isabella Aboderin and Monica Ferreira (2008) consider one of the key drivers for such blindness to be the assumption that families take care of older adults adequately, which this book has demonstrated is not always the case. Another basis for state neglect is sub-Saharan African governments' focus on development. Older people are assumed to be nonproductive members of society even though many remain economically active as long as their health allows. The government of Ghana is thus very much in line with the subcontinent as a whole. For example, Nigeria is in a similar position to Ghana, with little attention paid to the needs of the aging population (Adisa 2019). The government of Ghana's official position is that older adults are taken care of by their families. The focus on family care by the government has made it relatively absent in the initiatives discussed here, even as it becomes clear to older adults and their relatives that family care might be insufficient to ensure an older person's well-being. Its silence has led to the alterodox inscriptions noted above.

Ghana's government illustrates the contradictions of neoliberalism. The Ghanaian government, in general, is not a state dominated by neoliberal ideology. Instead, it is an interventionist government in other aspects of social welfare. Much of the state budget is directed to infants and children because of the international funding available to support the Millennium Development Goals, which became the focus of state efforts in Ghana in the 2000s (Aboderin and Ferreira 2008). Rev. Dr. Samuel Ayete-Nyampong, a major advocate on aging and former moderator of the Presbyterian Church of Ghana, considers the focus on young people to be determined by the interest of outside funders, who "think old people are cared for in the family unit—or that is what they would like to have happen." These outside partners then drive the government of Ghana's attention to women and children (interview, June 26, 2013). This international agenda is one way that a global project has reoriented national infrastructure and institutions (Sassen 2006).

In addition to a national health insurance program instituted since 2007, a major government initiative has been the expansion of free education to primary and junior secondary schools in 1996 (reinforced in 2005) and to secondary schools in 2017. As a result, the Ghanaian government spent 18.6 percent of its total domestic budget on education in 2018 and 6 percent on health in 2017 (World Bank 2019c, 2019d). The Department of Social Welfare, which is the government agency most concerned with the needs of the poor and aged, has very few resources and staff. The District Assembly Common Fund, which should be used for social welfare and poverty alleviation, including for older adults, is instead used for other purposes. The focus on young people may be appropriate given that the Ghanaian population is overwhelmingly young. However, this policy emphasis arises not from a concern for demographic majorities but rather from the ageist assumption of the greater productivity and dynamism of young people, and that support in old age is less valuable for national development than investment in the education or health care for the young (Barrientos 2002). It does not make sense to pit generations against one another, as this book shows how well-being across the generations is inextricably linked. The care of older adults can be a source of paid employment for young people and adult women, and the productivity and financial resources of the middle-aged generation are often directed into elder care. Some women become economically inactive to provide care to a mother or mother's sister. Better provision of preventative and therapeutic care for older adults (as, for example, after a fall or stroke) might lead to less long-term disability of older adults, who would then require fewer social and financial resources from their kin and possibly remain economically active. In sum, leaving it to families seems most apparent in relation to Ghana's aging population, but not in other spheres of government activity, in which social welfare has expanded. Still, neoliberalism, combined with a discourse about Ghana's "tradition" and a historically hands-off approach to social welfare (MacLean 2002), has buttressed the government's neglect of aging issues and emphasized the development focus of government budgets.

The state has both promoted and stymied the commercial market in home care services and schools to train carers, creating a contradictory assemblage. The government of Ghana has not responded to the agencies' desires for regulation and standardization. Its response to the care market's request to create a credential to give care work cultural capital has been ambivalent, promoted by one government body (NVTI) that is familiar to responding to the skilled trades market, but squashed by a more powerful professional association for nurses, which is closely tied to the Ministry of Health, which operates the government hospitals. Thus, the state continues to protect a key sector of the civil service in line with a developmentalist model.

The people most hurt by the state's neglect are the least visible and the least able to advocate for themselves: the not-wealthy bedridden older adults in the rural areas without living children or spouses. They are also the ones least served by the current initiatives among rural churches, which organize well and mobile older adults, and urban commercial services, which help disabled and bedridden adults who have social and financial resources through their kin group.

When they think about aging at all, public officials seem most primed to follow what the mainline churches have proposed—senior day centers that would provide a hot meal and some routine medical tests to older adults who are healthy or wealthy enough to transport themselves there. In other words, the older adults visible to social welfare officers seem to be the healthy ones who suffer from loneliness during the day when they are left alone in the house by school-going children and working adults. The bedridden and those with dementia, who one might argue need the most care and are the greatest burden on families, would not be helped under this model. Thus, a disconnect exists between the most serious needs of older adults and the families that care for them and the inscriptions that have gained some traction and seem to be becoming the new orthodoxy. Although the senior day centers run by the churches since the 1990s are no longer thriving, and the one built in Akropong never became operational, this idea, even in its failure, may rise again, in part because a senior day program seems more possible—from an organizational and budgetary perspective—than a full-fledged residential facility. Furthermore, in adding to the built environment, a day center meets the needs of politicians to make their public service visible to their constituents.

In other parts of Africa, another orthodoxy, of the basic income grant, has emerged. Under neoliberal auspices, new ways of expanding social welfare are gaining traction in southern Africa, generating new models for the state's relationship to its citizens (Ferguson 2015). In Botswana, Lesotho, Mauritius, Namibia, Senegal, Seychelles, South Africa, Swaziland, Tanzania, and Zambia, state efforts on the aging have concentrated on the expansion or introduction of a social pension (Aboderin and Ferreira 2008, 7; Fröhlich 2016; United Nations Population Fund 2012), in which the pension is not dependent on contributions from lifetime earnings. Uganda also makes small grants to senior citizens (Whyte 2020). In January 2018, Kenya was the latest country to launch a social pension scheme, which gives a small monthly income to those over the age of seventy (Burrows 2017). In South Africa, the social pension has led to a reduction in poverty in households containing a pension recipient (Case and Deaton 1998; Ferreira 2006). Spending on social pensions in Namibia and South Africa is 2 and 1.4 percent of GDP, respectively, and estimates of the amount of spending to reduce poverty in older adulthood range from 2 to 5 percent of GDP (Kakwani and Subbarao 2007). (In OECD countries, the range is 2 to 3 percent.) One simulation by Kakwani and Subbarao (2007) found that targeting households headed by an older person would result in greater reductions in poverty than a universal basic pension, based on an analysis of fifteen sub-Saharan countries, including Ghana. Even a small social pension can make a huge difference in poverty reduction, not only among older adults, but in the general population, because of the ways that the monthly sum is distributed between the generations and through social networks.

The expansion of the social pension in South Africa did not emerge from a political movement, in which older adults were galvanized to demand care (Case and Deaton 1998). However, older people's sense of rights was important in the expansion of the pension scheme to Africans in South Africa in the 1940s (Sagner 2000). A pension, if widely adopted and distributed, can create an identity related to age and an age-related movement, as has happened in the United States through Social Security. In order for the Ghanaian government to adopt a more proactive stance toward the needs of older adults, whether in the direction of a senior day center or a social pension, it may have to be pushed in that direction by a political movement led by vocal older adults.

Are Older Adults in Ghana a Political Force?

Supporting James Ferguson's argument that we are witnessing "new kinds of political claims-making and new possibilities for political mobilization" in Africa

(2015, 14), this book illustrates how older adults in Ghana are articulating a vision of a caring community and nation, as they encounter the aging process and cope with new aging trajectories and intergenerational reciprocities.

Since 1997, on Republic Day, July 1, the government of Ghana has held an annual gala for older adults, at which they are given food and drink and they dance to music. Rev. Ayete-Nyampong described this event dismissively: "There is very, very little on aging, except for 1st July, where the elderly get a bottle of Fanta [a soft drink]. The government doesn't want to talk much about it, because they feel guilty" (interview, June 26, 2013). Rhetorical promises regarding government actions and state displays of respect for older adults are made on this celebratory occasion. For example, on Republic Day in 2018, Vice-President Mahamadu Bawumia stated, "The plight of the aged is something that we must be at all times work tirelessly each day to help address" (Takyi-Boadu 2018, 6). Like Rev. Ayete-Nyampong, many consider these events to be only symbolic. In general, the aged take a passive role, listening to the speeches of government officials and consuming the banquet. The most wealthy and politically connected older adults, such as retired civil servants, are those invited. However, opportunities for political voice are opened up by these proceedings, in which state officials appear before a group constituted by a putatively shared identity, as the aged who have sacrificed in the past on behalf of the nation. In one meeting held in the regional capital Tamale in the Northern Region in 2018, older adults asked for a stronger social safety net (Jafaru 2018). At another, in the Upper East in 2018, they asked for the expansion of the list of medications covered by the national health insurance scheme (NHIS) because it did not cover chronic diseases associated with aging like hypertension or diabetes (*Daily Graphic* 2018). As noted in chapter 2, the price of medications not covered by NHIS was a concern also mentioned by older adults I met in rural areas of the Eastern Region.

The aged fellowship groups within the mainline churches seem particularly poised to become a political force, in part because of their frustrations with the church leadership over recognition and financial support. In their regular gatherings, like the annual Republic Day celebrations, the aged fellowship groups provide a forum for expressing a critique of the state and the church over the treatment of older adults. For example, during a group discussion in Begoro (Akyem), a woman said harshly, "The government doesn't recognize our pitifulness [or doesn't take compassion on us]."[1] She advocated for a small sum to be received by older adults every month, like a social pension, and her remarks generated enthusiastic clapping by others in the group. In Kukurantumi (Akyem), after an older man discussed how the government took care of its retired workers, another man publicly complained, "You and I have served the church for so long, that the church should do the same for us."[2] Both thus argued for financial contributions to older adults, drawing on the model of pensions for civil servants.

However, it is not clear that older adults will become a political force in their critique of their neglect by the state and other significant social groups. Lois

McNay (2008), drawing on the work of Susan Gal (2003), argues that although people may recognize injustice and identify systematic domination and common interests, they may not be able to devise strategies for action and feel able to act. In the contemporary moment, older adults in Ghana recognize their common interest and propose solutions by the state and by other social institutions like the church to address their neglect. However, they have not been able to harness the symbolic elements of neglect and balanced reciprocity to engage regularly in explicit political advocacy outside of certain contexts in which they gather together in age-defined groups. Instead, the heterodox and alterodox discourses simmer within their local networks without gaining traction more widely. Furthermore, the everyday care needs of those least able to advocate for themselves—bedridden older adults without strong kin connections—also tend to be overlooked in these advocacy efforts by younger, more mobile older adults who define their care needs differently. Finally, in Ghana, these concerns and solutions are currently trivialized by those who have not confronted the care of an aging person or their own aging. It is the eye of the beholder that determines whether "the aged" matters and is consequential (Enloe 2013). These concerns would need to be framed in the language that the powerful find reasonable and significant, probably around economic development.

Home care agencies and nursing homes are also deeply involved in advocating for greater state funding for their senior care services, using the history of state incorporation of and support for private organizations, like schools, and the current political rhetoric about the importance of public-private partnerships in Ghana. The commercial care services run by elite and middle-class urban women with professional and transnational connections continue to reach out to the state for regulation and subsidy, and their efforts may one day be successful, although they have not been thus far.

The advocacy may ultimately result in pressure for the state to care for its older people in ways it has never done before. Ghana might mimic the social pensions adopted by other middle-income countries in sub-Saharan Africa, after seeing that it is possible in peer countries. The establishment of free or low-cost senior day centers for older adults, whether by churches or by the state, would be a form of wealth redistribution. Visiting home care services through community health nurses might be expanded from the care of infants and mothers to include bathing and physical therapy for older adults, along the lines of the work of the Akrowa Foundation. Any of these would redefine the obligations of the state to its aging population and constitute an important expansion of care for the vulnerable in Africa and elsewhere in the Global South.

In Ghana, solutions to care for older persons seem very much in flux, with a variety of moral imaginings and no dominant patterns of care. "Family" care remains the ideal, but in practice it is often inadequate, frustrating, and filled with conflict. This is a space where the care of older adults can be reimagined. Given what is at stake, older persons are willing to explore solutions beyond kin care. They reconfigure the orthodoxy of "the traditional family" to make claims for other institutions like the church and state to provide elder care in ways considered "modern" and un-Ghanaian. Extending the notion of balanced reciprocity, forged in the context of senior-junior relations, they argue that their previous contributions require, in return, care and support from groups beyond the family, including the nation as a whole.

Acknowledgments

This book has been long in the making. It began with a moment of surprise in 2013, at finding that the building being erected behind Christchurch in Akropong was intended to be a senior day center. That moment launched me into studying aging, but there were many twists and turns in my flight path. Initially, I thought research on aging in Ghana would connect to my ongoing research on Ghanaian immigrant care workers in the United States. Ultimately, these projects became different books, even when they informed one another, as the transnational connections between care work in the United States and Ghana were not dense enough to warrant consideration together. This book was delayed when I wrote about Africans working in American home care first, driven by the urgency of being relevant in a changing policy environment around health care and aging in the United States. I was also diverted by trying to find another way to tell these stories through film, feeling that books were not accessible to my research participants and did not have a broader impact on the issues with which they struggled. But finally, in the midst of the coronavirus epidemic, like many others, I was stuck at home, and a book came into being.

The reason the senior day center struck me was not only because of its innovation but also because so many of my friends in Ghana were aging. Visiting them over the years to converse about their life struggles and mourning their passing composed the main pleasure and pain of my coming to Ghana, as I had been doing since 1997. I salute their powerful spirits and hold onto their idiosyncratic personalities and quirky mannerisms in my heart. They enriched my life, and enrich me still.

Numerous people helped me in this research along the way. In Accra, I stayed with Aunty Emily Asiedu, who was a model of active and wise aging. I used her house as a base to travel three or four hours across Accra daily for my fieldwork and return in the evenings spent and hot, to be received by her good humor and generosity. In Akropong, I lived with Mrs. Christie Afari Amoako, Ms. Gladys Ohene, and Brigadier-General and Mrs. Adu-Bediako, learning about the complexities of aging and family life from our coresidence.

The District Ministers of the Presbyterian Church in Akyem Abuakwa and Kwawu, Rev. Paa Bawua-Bonsofo and Rev. Ansa-Peasa, hosted me very well during my short stays. Other Presbyterians facilitated my research, including Mr. Fred Ateko in New Tafo; Gladys Ohene-Temang, Eleanor Aboagye, and Joe Banson in Akropong; and Rev. Seth Agidi in Ho. Rev. Ayete-Nyampong always gave freely of his time for a conversation in Accra. Erdmute Alber and Tatjana Thelen had valuable conversations with me about my research in 2018, including when they visited me during my research stay in the nursing home and Tatjana accompanied me during interviews of healthcare assistance students. While studying in China, Rogers Krobea Asante transcribed the focus group discussions from Akyem and the aged fellowship meetings from Kwawu, including the more complicated songs, jokes, and riddles. Joe Banson helped clarify my translation confusions. Over the years, research support was provided by my home institution, Rutgers University, through the Research Council, as well as by an International Senior Fellowship from the University of Bayreuth in Germany.

Earlier versions of these chapters were presented at different conferences and workshops, including the African Studies Center at Harvard University, the Critical Research on Africa lecture series at the University of Pittsburgh, and at Teachers College, Columbia University. I am grateful to many colleagues for their thoughts in response and in subsequent conversations: Erdmute Alber, Jean and John Comaroff, Nicole Constable, Pamela Feldman-Savelsberg, Michele Gamburd, Casey Golomski, Tabea Häberlein, Ursula Read, Jennifer Riggan, Tatjana Thelen, and Sjaak van der Geest. Erdmute Alber gave me the push I needed to start writing the book in October 2019, and the introduction was workshopped by her postdoctoral and graduate students at the University of Bayreuth. Jennifer Hasty read and gave excellent comments on several chapters of the manuscript. Members of my family also provided inspiration and support in numerous ways, including with the writing: Robert P. Coe, Jane Meleney Coe, and Cheryl Shipman read the entire manuscript for clarity and organization. Sarah Lamb, as editor of the series on Global Aging, remained a strong supporter throughout. I am grateful to two anonymous reviewers for their excellent comments and suggestions, as well as to Jasper Chang and Kimberly Guinta at Rutgers University Press.

I never expected to grow old myself, feeling that I was hurtling through life too quickly, but now I have reached an age where I have to admit that I will not die young. Like Barbara Myerhoff, a pioneer anthropologist of aging, I am grateful to those who have aged before me—both in Ghana, where half of my heart lies, and in the United States, which I have learned to make my home. They have given me a model for how to age, and die, well.

Notes

Introduction

1 Major parts of this introduction were first published in Coe and Alber (2018), with different examples.

2 Grounded in a praxeological approach, inscription as used here does not resonate with the way the term is used in philosophical scholarship inspired by Jacques Derrida, in which it is part of mimesis and the production of the double body (see a summary in Irwin 2010). The aim is also not to detect differences between scripts guiding performances and the back stage in the sense of Erving Goffman (1986) but to figure out how people's feelings, actions, and changing assumptions are producing new practices and discourses.

3 "*Sɛ wo maame anaa wo papa anaa obi a hwɛ wo na wo se yi aba de a, edu baabi hwɛ no na wei* [pointing to his teeth] *no ntutu*" (interview, July 27, 2005).

4 "*Me nso megyina ha a aka bɛɛ bosome bi na madi aduoson mmeɛnsa. Na mmerɛ a.. me sɛnea mehuu sɛ mmerɛ a na meyɛ ababaawa no na me ho yɛ den. Metumi kɔ baabi ara, metumi kɔ afuo ansa na mabɛsen akɔ sukuu, metumi yɛ biribi ara. Nso menyini duruu aduosia a mereba no hodwodwo aka me, wɔ me kotodwe, me sisi, me ho nyinaa. Adeɛ kye koraa na meresɔre koraa wobɛka sɛ maye adwuma anadwo no a, wobɛka sɛ makɔyɛ adwuma a menhu me ho ano, enti na mayɛ bɛtɛɛ*" (group discussion, July 9, 2014).

5 "*Mepɛ sɛ mekyerɛ sɛ meyɛ aberewa*" (fieldnotes, September 3, 2019).

Chapter 1 The Orthodoxy of Family Care

Two of the four substantial sections in this chapter were previously published in "Negotiating Elder Care in Akuapem, Ghana: Care-Scripts and the Role of Non-Kin," *Africa* 87, no. 1 (2017): 1–18. The argument has become more nuanced and the sections revised accordingly.

1 I will discuss these fellowship groups further in chapter 5.

2 Doxa is so commonsensical as to constitute tacit knowledge.

3 About half of all households in Ghana's national surveys receive remittances from migrants, whether inside or outside Ghana (Quartey 2006).

4 "*Oow Awurade Nyankopɔn hu me mmɔbɔ oow, me mma yi oow, baabi a wɔmo wɔ biara wo na woyɛ ɔdɛɛfoɔ, hwɛ wɔmo ma me na yɛ sei . . . wɔmo nya bi di a na wɔmo nso wɔmo ayɛ deɛn, na wɔmo nso abrɛ wo bi ama woadi*" (fieldnotes, July 24, 2014).

5 HelpAge has had an interesting history as an organization. It was begun in 1988 by the elite in Accra, organized into zones, who as volunteers visited older adults in their homes. However, there was high turnover among the volunteers. The group, in affiliation with the Catholic Church, started the Derby Avenue day center in 1992 and another day center in Osu in 1993. It became affiliated with HelpAge International, as part of the process of NGO-ization of indigenous community organizations in Ghana, which made them more dependent on, on the one hand, the state and, on the other, international funding and agendas (Hutchful 2002). By the 2010s, when I encountered the organization, HelpAge was almost exclusively involved in advocacy work with the government.

6 For example, the African Union (2014) also recommends that states "identify, promote and strengthen traditional support systems, including medical home based care, to enhance the ability of families and communities to care for older family members."

7 In contrast, the African Union policy switches between "the children" and "the family" as the source of support for older adults, covering both bases.

8 "*Me nena no onni obi a ɔsoma no enti ɔse mentena ne nkyɛn na wasoma me*" (interview, August 12, 2008).

9 In contrast, Hanrahan (2018) discusses how Konkomba daughters in northern Ghana, among a patrilineal group, may return home to care for their mothers as a nonnormative practice because of neglect by their brothers' wives, thus creating conflicts with the husbands whose homes they have to leave. Older men were generally cared for by their much younger wives.

10 All names in the book are pseudonyms, except for those who are already public figures.

11 "Okay, *time a me maame ɛkaa baabi no na kyerɛsɛ obiara nni fie, na me* sister *nso wɔ Accra. Okay, mebaa ha kakra, mebɛtenaa ha . . . , na mewɔ kurom ha but na mente fie ha. But me maame wui no obiara, mmɔfra no nyinaa, yɛn mma no wowo enti obia nso mpɛsɛ ɔbɛtena fie ha. Enti na kyerɛsɛ, obiara nni ha ɛnyɛ fɛ, enti na ɛkyɛ sɛ mebɛtena ha. Na saa* time *no na yɛn* cousin *baako wɔ ha, ɔno nso yare obiara nni ne ho, ontumi nsɔre mma abɔnten, na obiara nni fie a na ɛnyɛ fine. Enti na ɛkyɛsɛ mebɛtena ha na mebɛbɛhwɛ no. ɛno ka ho na ɛma me bɛtenaa ha ɛna mebɛhwɛ me* cousin *no, a year ni a owui. . . . Enti na kyere sɛ mee mabɛtena ha a na me ba nso ɔpɛ sɛ kɔyɛ adwuma, otu kwan ɛwɔsɛ mehwɛ . . . . ɛheen, mehwɛ ne mma no wɔ akyi*" (joint interview, September 12, 2008).

12 "*Enti ɛyɛ saa wo no aa woyɛ ɔpanyin no wo na wobɛba na nkwadaa no nso akɔbɔ wɔn ho mmɔden apɛ biribi de abɔ wɔn bra.*"

13 "*Me* brother *panyin, nea medi n'akyi. ɛna ose obia nni fie ha ɛna maame no nso ne nkoa wɔ fie ha saa a biribi si a obia nni hɔ enti ɛsɛsɛ meba na me ne mmɔfra no nso bɛtena sɛ ɛbɛyɛ a ɔno nso n'ani bɛka. ɛno nti na ɛma mebɛtenaa ha.*"

14 "*Enti sɛ metumi a, na mafrɛ me nuanom na meka kyerɛɛ wɔn sɛ matena me maame nkyɛn a, mabrɛ enti me nso mekɔ akɔpɛ adwuma ayɛ. Tese Suhum anaa sɛ Tema, anaa Kumasi na seesei, mɛkɔ a, menya obi a ɔde me bɛkɔ anaa sɛ biribi a ɛte saa adwuma wɔ hɔ a, menya sika na mede aba, ɛneɛ menya sika de a, na mede bi abrɛ me maame na ɔde bi ahwɛ me ba anaa sɛ biribi a ɛte saa. Sɛ me ne akwadaa no nso na ɛbɛkɔ a na menya bi a na mede bi abrɛ me maame bi. Eno nso deɛ, na kyerɛsɛ me nuanom, wɔn nso wɔaba, yɛ dɔɔso*" (interview, September 9, 2008).

15 *"Kyerɛ sɛ, me papanom na wɔyɛ mmɛrema nko aa, wonni obiara, wonni ɔbea a wɔ hɔ a ɔbɛhwɛ wɔn maame enti wɔma me bɛtenaa ha"* (interview, September 9, 2008).

16 Roth (2007) describes a similar phenomenon in urban Burkina Faso, in which marriage serves a strategy of aging among older men.

Chapter 2 Heterodox Ideas of Elder Care

Some of this chapter was previously published in "Imagining Institutional Care, Practicing Domestic Care: Inscriptions around Aging in Southern Ghana," *Anthropology & Aging Quarterly* 39, no. 1 (2018): 18–32. This chapter is a considerable expansion of that published piece, with the addition of material from more recent research in 2018 and 2019 as well as unused material from 2013 and 2014.

1 The film, *Making Happiness: Older People Organize Themselves*, is available at: https://doi.org/doi:10.7282/t3-thke-hp15.

2 Woman 1: *Wonni ba a, obiara nni hɔ a, ɔbɛhwɛ wo*. Woman 2: *Wo ba koraa, ɛtɔ da bi koraa, ɔnhwɛ wo*. Woman 3: *Wo ba koraa, ɔnhwɛ wo* (group discussion, Begoro, Akyem, July 9, 2014).

3 *"Eduru saa berɛ yi a me me fa mu no, kyerɛ sɛ woawo mmɔfra no bebiree, nso eduru saa berɛ yi a na wɔn nyinaa agya wo hɔ rekɔyɛ adwuma wɔ baabi na aka wo nkoa na wowɔ fie"* (group discussion, New Tafo, Akyem, July 11, 2014).

4 *"Wo nkoa na wowɔ hɔ a sɛnea obi dii kan kaae no, wo mmanom nyinaa agya wo hɔ kɔ, ne wo nananom nyinaa. Gyesɛ ebia afe so ansa ɛna ebia wobɛhu wo ba bi anaa wo nana"* (group discussion, New Tafo, Akyem, July 11, 2014).

5 *"Me nso me deɛ ne sɛ ɛduru yɛn mpanyinfie nso saa ara ɛyɛ a na yɛn mma ne yɛn nananom nyinaa wɔ akwantuo mu. ɛno enti ɛyɛ a na aka yɛn nkoa wɔ fie, yɛ* feel very lonely" (group discussion, Kukurantumi, Akyem, July 11, 2014).

6 *"Nkodaa no nyinaa ahwete, obira rekɔpɛ ne paa bi adi."*

7 *"Me nananom no obiara ɛrehwɛ ne ba enti ɛha sukuu no, wɔmo se ɛha sukuu no enye enti obiara ba wɔ nkyɛn. Enti menni obiara. Obiara mfa ne ba mbrɛ me"* (group discussion, July 9, 2014).

8 *"Me mma nsoso wɔn nsoso wɔawo mma, wɔn nso wɔwɔ akwantuo mu. Wontumi nyi . . . ayɛ den enti wɔntumi nyi sika no mfa mma me enti gyesɛ me* force *kakra ansa na me nso manya me ano aduane"* (group discussion, July 9, 2014).

9 *"Bebree no wonni nnipa a wɔbɛhwɛ wɔn so. Sɛ ɔrepɛ nsuo koraa anom a ebia ɔbɛtwee a ama obi bɛpue a na ɔte sɛ obi rekasa a na ɔafrɛ na ɔde nsuo ama no. ɛɛ ebi nso wɔ hɔ a aduane koraa ɔbɛnya adi no. Mekɔ sra obi ɔse aduane koraa no ɛyɛ den ma no* because menni *the next meal a me nsa bɛka"* (group discussion, Asamankese, July 12, 2014).

10 *Waakye* is a street food for breakfast or lunch made with beans and rice and served with a spicy sauce like *shito*. *Burkina* is a drink made from millet and milk. Brought from northern Ghana, it is sold as a snack on the streets in southern Ghana.

11 *"Mpo sɛ yɛwɔ mma ne nananom a wobu yɛn sɛ yɛyɛ abayifoɔ"* (group discussion, July 9, 2014).

12 *"Sɛbe, onwoo. ɛyɛ ɔdo a wɔde brɛɛ, ɛnyɛ* force."

13 *"Na awerɛhoɔ nso menim sɛ ɛno nso sabisabi ɛno nso ɛkum nnipa. Enti saa mmerɛ no a yɛn mma no anyini a wɔmo agya yɛn hɔ wɔ fie no ɛyɛ a na yɛn ani ngye, yɛn ho kyere yɛn"* (group discussion, Kade, Akyem, July 12, 2014).

14 *"ɛmesɛ faakotena sɛnea na obi reka no ɛho asɛm no ɛyɛ ahomete, onipa sunsum ɛkɔ fam. Enti sɛ ebia obi wɔ hɔ a na ne classmates nyinaa wɔn awu, wɔn a wɔ ne wɔn ɛbɔ so no"* (group discussion, Kade, Akyem, July 12, 2014).

15 *"Adwendwen nso ma onipa yare"* (group discussion, Kyebi, Akyem, July 8, 2014).

16 *"Bere biara sɛ ɔkɔm nso wɔ hɔ a na ama adwendwen nso ne adeɛ yi na ama yareɛ no nso ɛkɔ soro bebiree"* (group discussion, Asamankese, Akyem, July 12, 2014).

17 *Kenkey* is made from fermented corn. A starchy ball, it is eaten for breakfast because it is so heavy and filling.

18 *"Me nkoa ɛna mete fie saa. . . . Enti aduane no, menfeel mpo sɛ mɛdidi efiri sɛ ɛyɛ a na me nkoa na kyerɛ sɛ awerehoɔ nso ahyɛ me mu kakra"* (group discussion, Begoro, Akyem, July 9, 2014).

19 *"Ɛyɛ a na ɛberɛ wɔde ma wo aduane wɔ fie no etumi pa ho a obi kɔ adwuma koraa ɔmba ntɛm, ɔkɔ afuo mu nso a ɔmba ntɛm, enti ɔba na ɔyɛ aduane no a ɔde ba a mendi"* (group discussion, Kade, Akyem, July 12, 2014)

20 In 2010, there were 581,865 Ghanaians over the age of seventy (Ghana Statistical Service 2012).

21 *"Wokɔ hospital a yɛsɛ tɔ aduro. Sika bɛn na mede rekɔ tɔ aduro no? Yenni bi"* (group discussion, July 9, 2014).

22 *"Yenni sika enti yɛntumi ntɔ aduro no, aduro no ne boɔ yɛ den. Ebia wokita 1 cedi, aduro no wobɛkyɛ beyɛ sɛ 10 cedis. Ɛhen na worekɔ nya 9 de abeka ho de ayɛ 10? Wonkɔ nya na enti na woakɔ tena fie. Na kyerɛ sɛ hospital no koraa wokɔɔ no kwa"* (group discussion, July 9, 2014).

23 *"Ɛha wokɔ hospital a wɔkakyerɛ wose ɛyɛ old age so they give you only paracetamol and you return"* (group discussion, July 9, 2014).

24 *"Baako a ɛwɔ hɔ bio ɛyɛ sɛnea yɛn ayaresabea no ɛteɛ no ama woduru ɛɛ wei bi a wompɛsɛ wobɛkɔ hospital. Esiane sɛ wobɛkyɛ a enti wobɛba na woabere. Enti ɛɛ ɛma bebiree no a yareɛ no bɔ wɔn a wɔmo de tena fie a na ɛnɔ̪ mu na bebiree . . . megyedi sɛ bebiree fa so na wowu. Enti ɛɛ anka me mafa mu de ɛ government no ɛwɔ sɛ y ɛnya preference ɛma mpanimfoɔ. Sɛ yɛduru hɔ ara pɛ a na anka ebia wɔama kwan ama yɛahwɛ mpanimfoɔ no"* (group discussion, July 12, 2014).

25 *"Yɛhia sika, yɛhia sika paa na ɛɛ yɛn mmerewabɔ mu yi ɛɛ sɛ woayɛ aban adwuma na woapɔn, sɛ woanyɛ aban adwuma na woapɔn na wote fie, once a woanya aduoson ɛde rekɔ no wo asetena woayɛ mmɔbɔ paa. Berɛ biara you are weak. Woda nyane koraa wontumi nsɔre, woda mpa mu saa gye sɛ wɔsɔre bɛbisa sɛ nana ɛnɛ wo ho te sɛn ɛna ɛfaa hen na ɛkɔ sii hen. Enti yɛnyɛ mmɔbɔ, yɛhia aduro a yɛbɛnom a ɛbama ama yɛanya apɔmuden. Even sɛ woantumi ankɔ hospital koraa na wowɔ fie a wonya sika na wokɔ tɔ aduro no a wote fie a wobɛnom no nkakrankakrankakra na ɛreboa wo"* (group discussion, July 12, 2014).

26 *"Na baabi wɔ hɔ a tesɛ Aburokyiri sei yɛwɔ baabi a wonyini na sɛ obiara nte wo ho a yɛtumi de wokɔtena hɔ tesɛ sukuu a wo mane wo, yɛwɔ dɔkotafoɔ, yɛwɔ wɔn a wɔnoa aduane, biribiara. Wobɛhyia wo classmate, enti ɛma wo ani gye, enti ɛma wo nyini kyɛ. Saa adeɛ no ebi nni Ghana ha titiriw ɛne yɛn mansin mu ha enti yɛn haw ne no"* (group discussion, Old Tafo, Akyem, July 11, 2014).

27 *"Ɛha aban yi wɔ dwene, woanyin a ɛmfa ne ho. Wonni obiara a ɔbɛboa wo"* (group discussion, Begoro, Akyem, July 9, 2014).

28 *"Ɛna sabisabi aban nso nhu mo mmɔbɔ"* (group discussion, Kade, Akyem, July 12, 2014).

29 *"Ghana yenni system a yɛde boa mpanimfoɔ. Sɛ obi renyini a, na ayɛ sɛ yɛagya ne ho saa ara"* (group discussion, Asamankese, Akyem July 12, 2014).

30 *"Mobɛsi dan bi koraa ama yɛn a yɛbɛhyia wɔ mu. Anaa sɛ mmerewa no yɛnnom sei a yɛntumi nyɛ hwee no, yɛbɛtena mu na mobɛboa yɛn"* (group discussion, Begoro, Akyem, July 12, 2014).

31 *"Asafo no nso ndwene yɛn ho, yɛba asɔre daa, wɔndwene yɛn ho. Asafo no yɛn koraa na yɛtua sika, wɔndwene yɛn ho"* (group discussion, Begoro, Akyem, July 9, 2014).

32 "Yɛn ho yɛ den no a ɛsɛsɛ yɛyɛ investment bi a ɛbɛhwɛ yɛn no yɛanyɛ. Yɛfaa no sɛ yɛn ho yɛ den no, yɛn sika no a yɛanya no ɛno ara na ɛsɛsɛ yedi na yɛbɔ yɛn bera. Na yɛn werɛ afiri yɛn nkɔkoraa berɛ mu sɛ yɛrebɛnyin, mmerɛ bi rebɛba a honam no rebɛpopo, ɛntumi nyɛ adwuma enti ɛsɛsɛ anka yɛtumi sie ɛtɔ fie na yɛsiesie yɛn akyi yie na yɛyɛ mmera a yɛa fall on that na aka akyire. . . . Ɛnɛ akodaa biara nni hɔ a ɔno bɛtena akɔkoraa ho sɛ ɔrehwɛ no enti sɛ ɔansiesie wo akyi yie na ɔamfa biribi anto hɔ a, a wo nkɔkoraa berɛ ne wo mmerewabɔ mu no wobɛ fall on a na wobɛka sɛ wobe depend upon wo nana bi anaa wo ba bi a na ayɛ haw" (group discussion, Old Tafo, Akyem, July 11, 2014).

Chapter 3 Alterodox Practices of Elder Care

Some of this chapter was previously published in "Imagining Institutional Care, Practicing Domestic Care: Inscriptions around Aging in Southern Ghana," *Anthropology & Aging Quarterly* 39, no. 1 (2018): 18–32. The chapter is a considerable expansion of this article, with the addition of material from more recent research in 2018 and 2019 as well as unused material from 2014.

1 "Ɛmesɛ sɛ wo ani bɛgye wo mpanin berɛ mu a na efiri wo abrabɔ a wobɔɔ wɔ wo mmabaawa anaa wo mmerante berɛ mu. Wo mma no a wonyaa w ɔn no ɛsɛsɛ wotete w ɔn ɛde Nyamesuro nso hyɛ wɔn mu ɛma wɔn nya ahomɔbrɔ ne tema de ma nnipa. Enti sɛ ɛba no saa na sɛ wo mma no wɔnya baabi si deɛ a . . . wotumi boa wɔn na wɔnya baabi si a wɔn bɛnya tema ɛda ama ɛna no. Mpo sɛ wonni hwɛfoɔ koraa a ebinom tumi fa obi ɛbɛtena wo nkyɛn. Wɔmo bɛtua no ka, wo adidie mu, wo biribi a wɔmo bɛhwɛ sɛ wo nso wo asetena mu ɛbɛyɛ yie. Enti anigyeɛ no deɛ ɛbɛba a ɛwɔ berɛ a wowɔ ahoɔden no ɔkwan a a wofaa so a wode ɛhwɛɛ wo mma" (group discussion, July 12, 2014).

Chapter 4 "Loneliness Kills"

One section of this chapter was previously published in "Beyond Kin Care? Institutional Facilities in the Imaginations of Elderly Presbyterians in Southern Ghana," *Africa Today* 65, no. 3 (2019): 69–88. The rest is original material.

1 My thanks to one of the reviewers for this insight.
2 *Oware* is a game played with seed pods and carved wooden bowls.
3 I decided not to focus my research on Shepherd's Center, as I do not speak Ewe, the language of these groups.
4 The eleven-minute film, *Making Happiness: Older People Organize Themselves*, can be viewed at https://doi.org/doi:10.7282/t3-thke-hp15.
5 "Ɛma yɛn vibrant ɛsɛn sɛ first no ara, other churches ne ade . . . wɔtete hɔ saa ara boom boom" (interview, August 13, 2019).
6 "Yetumi kanyan yɛn ho" (group discussion, July 11, 2014).
7 "Generally, sɛnea wotie a mfie aduosia ɛrekɔ no, after 50 years, 60 years ɛyɛ ɔhaw nkoa" (group discussion, Asamankese, Akyem, July 12, 2014).
8 "Meyɛ ababaawa no na me ho yɛ den. Metumi kɔ baabi ara, metumi kɔ afuo ansa na mabɛsen akɔ sukuu, metumi yɛ biribi ara. Nso menyini duruu aduosia a mereba no hodwodwo aka me, wɔ me kotodwe, me sisi, me ho nyinaa. Adeɛ kye koraa na meresɔre koraa wobɛka sɛ mayɛ adwuma anadwo no a, wobɛka sɛ makɔyɛ adwuma a menhu me ho ano, enti na mayɛ bɛtɛɛ" (group discussion, Begoro, Akyem, July 9, 2014).

9 *"Woyɛ deɛn a* from 70 going *no wonya wo ho tɔtrɔtɔɔ da, wobɛyare kakra"* (group discussion, Begoro, Akyem, July 9, 2014).

10 *"Wobɛsoma no no a, wobɛsoma no no baako mmienu mmeɛnsa ɔse oow, na wo ho ayɛ no ahi. Wo ho yɛ no ahi a ɔse oow woyɛ ɔbayifoɔ, wo nso wonwu da ɛna wote hɔ. . . . Kyerɛ sɛ wosoma no a ɔnkɔ, woyɛ bayifoɔ, wo afoɔ nyinaa awu na wote hɔ"* (group discussion, Begoro, Akyem, July 9, 2014). A person interviewed by Barbara Stucki in a rural Asante village made a very similar comment in 1990–1991 (1995, 27).

11 Building a house is an important way for individuals to gain status and respect from others, and they may narrate their biographies through their houses (Van der Geest 1998). Houses are visible and promote sociability. Thus, church leaders may be doing the same with church buildings as individuals do with their own houses. Catherine Bolten (2020) notes the efforts that youth in Sierra Leone put into building projects to prove their seriousness.

12 He too was moved by the plight of older congregants through giving Invalid Communion, in Kumasi. Like Reverend Agidi, he has an NGO on the side that helps older adults (interview, July 28, 2014).

13 *"Asafo no nso ndwene yɛn ho, yɛba asɔre daa, wɔndwene yɛn ho. Asafo no yɛn koraa na yɛtua sika, wɔndwene yɛn ho"* (July 9, 2014).

14 *"Sɛ wowɔ ahoɔden no woasom asafo no. ɛnɛ yi a yɛn kotodwe, yɛn sisi,* hypertension *ne nyinaa yɛgu so nkakrankarankakra yɛde bɛsom ɛwɔ asafo no mu. ɛbɛduru berɛ bi no na afei deɛ wontumi nsɔre koraa, koraaa. Na saa berɛ no ɛna ɛsɛsɛ anka asafo no nso wɔmo nso ɛyɛ mmoa bi ɛde boa saafo ɔno a wɔmo nso wɔmo ntumi ɛnyɛ hwee bio no. Obi wɔ hɔ a ɔbɛtenaa ha koraa ebia wowɔ mma nanso wo mma no obiara nni hɔ a ɔbɛn wo. ɛnɛ obiara fa ne adeɛ a waa"* (group discussion, July 11, 2014).

15 *"Ɔasom asɔre no a aduru mmerɛ a ɔayɛ merɛ, ɔanya mmoa mfiri baabi ara, obi wɔ hɔ onni ba."*

Chapter 5 Market-Based Solutions for the Globally Connected Middle Class

This chapter is a substantial reformulation of "Transnational Migration and the Commodification of Elder Care in Urban Ghana," *Identities: Global Studies in Culture and Power* 24, no. 5 (2017): 542–556. It has a new argument, and all the information about the nursing homes is new.

1 These six were the only ones mentioned to me in interviews and conversations with owners of nursing agencies and friends in Accra who had explored private nursing care for their relatives.

2 Nonetheless, a loan from the International Monetary Fund accompanied pressure to reduce government spending, with the Ghanaian government announcing that in 2017 there would be no openings for government positions, with a few exceptions (*Ghana News* 2016a).

3 These concerns about who would be blamed for a death were reasonable. Staff at a residential facility were aware of how they were held responsible for a resident who died in a nearby hospital, where the nurse told the resident's child that the death was the residential facility's fault (fieldnotes, August 10, 2018).

Chapter 6 Going to School to Be a Carer

Much of this chapter has been published as "The Enchantment of Neoliberal Education: A Healthcare Certificate, Elusive Adulthoods, and a New Middle Class in Ghana,"

Children's Geographies 18, no. 6 (2020): 601–613, although I have reframed the argument and organization slightly as well as added new information.

1 Although the addition of home care to this list of offerings might be surprising, the education of similar workers—social and healthcare assistants—is done by vocational institutes in Denmark and the United Kingdom (Cort 2002).

2 Although a year might seem a long time given the six- to fifteen-week training for certified nursing assistants in the United States, it is similar to Denmark's social and healthcare helper course of a year and two months.

3 One of her long-term clients enjoyed playing Scrabble in the afternoons.

4 A nurse trained in Ghana can work in the United Kingdom, but he or she would have to pass an additional nursing exam to work as a nurse in the United States. As a result, many nurses from Ghana work in lower level healthcare positions, including as nursing assistants (Coe 2019a). Even in the United Kingdom, nurses from West Africa experience a loss of status and professionalization (Aboderin 2007).

5 As of 2010, there were almost 25,000 nurses in Ghana, with a nurse-to-patient ratio of 1:971 (Ghana Health Service, 2010, 19). Of trained health professionals, 70 percent are in urban areas, while health delivery in rural areas is mostly by unskilled health workers. However, there have been improvements: more health professionals have been trained, and there have been efforts to retain skilled health workers, which have reduced the rate of out-migration (ISSER 2013).

6 This may be an oblique reference to sexual harassment from her boss.

7 Nursing students used to have to do two drawings on their examinations, so this idea may have been modeled on the nursing exam, but this requirement was dropped in the most recent nursing examination.

Chapter 7 Carers as Househelp

Some of this chapter was previously published as "Not a Nurse, Not Househelp: The New Occupation of Elder Carer in Urban Ghana," *Ghana Studies* 19, no. 1 (2016): 46–72.

1 Moving out of domestic service and into caring and cleaning work in institutional settings was a significant step for the whitening and social class mobility of Irish women in the United States (Phillips-Cunningham 2020).

2 "*Carer nyɛ* effective *wɔ Ghana ha. Wobɛbrɛ saa ara. Ghana nye.*"

3 In the United States, the average income of home health workers, both live-in and live-out, is $13,300 annually, with one in four living below the poverty line and over half relying on public assistance (Paraprofessional Healthcare Institute 2016).

Conclusion

1 "*Enti aban ɛnhu yɛn mmɔbɔ*" (group discussion, July 9, 2014).

2 "*Wo ne me yɛasom asafo yi a bɛduru bere yi a yɛte mu yi, ne a ɛsɛsɛ asafo no yɛ ma yɛn no*" (group discussion, July 11, 2014).

References

Abel, Emily K. 2000. *Hearts of Wisdom: American Women Caring for Kin, 1850–1940*. Cambridge, MA: Harvard University Press.

Aboderin, Isabella. 2004. "Decline in Material Family Support for Older People in Urban Ghana, Africa: Understanding Processes and Causes of Change." *Journal of Gerontology* 59B(3): S128–S137.

———. 2006. *Intergenerational Support and Old Age in Africa*. New Brunswick, NJ: Transaction.

———. 2007. "Contexts, Motives, and Experiences of Nigerian Overseas Nurses: Understanding Links to Globalization." *Journal of Clinical Nursing* 16(12): 2237–2245.

Aboderin, Isabella, and Monica Ferreira. 2008. "Linking Ageing to Development Agendas in Sub-Saharan Africa: Challenges and Approaches." *Journal of Population Aging* 1(1): 51–73.

Abu-Lughod, Lila. 1991. "Writing against Culture." In *Recapturing Anthropology Working in the Present*, edited by Richard G. Fox, 137–154. Santa Fe, NM: School of American Research.

Abun-Nasr, Sonia. 2003. *Afrikaner und Missionar: Die Lebensgeschichte von David Asante*. Basel: P. Schlettwein.

Abuosi, Aaron Asibi, and Patience Aseweh Abor. 2015. "Migration Intentions of Nursing Students in Ghana: Implications for Human Resource Development in the Health Sector." *International Migration and Integration* 16: 593–606.

Adams, Kathleen M., and Sara Dickey, eds. 2000. *Home and Hegemony: Domestic Service and Identity Politics in South and Southeast Asia*. Ann Arbor: University of Michigan Press.

Addo, Susan Adole. 2003. "Social Support Systems for the Aged in Ghana: A Study of the Elderly in Accra." MA thesis, University of Ghana.

Addo-Fening, Robert. 1980. "Akyem Abuakwa c. 1874–1943: A Study of the Impact of Missionary Activities and Colonial Rule on a Traditional State." PhD dissertation, University of Ghana.

Adisa, Olumide. 2019. "Why Are Some Older Persons Economically Vulnerable and Others Not? The Role of Socio-demographic Factors and Economic Resources in the Nigerian Context." *Ageing International* 44: 202–222.

Adogame, Afe. 2014. "Reinventing Africa? The Negotiation of Ethnic Identities in the New Religious Diaspora." In *Religion, Ethnicity and Transnational Migration between West Africa and Europe*, edited by Gina Gertrud Smith and Stanislaw Grodz, 12–36. Leiden: Brill.

African Union. 2014. "Draft Protocol to the African Charter on Human and People's Rights on the Rights of Older Persons in Africa." https://au.int/sites/default/files /newsevents/workingdocuments/27995-wd-protocol_older_person_-_english_ -_final.pdf.

Ahearn, Laura. 2001a. *Invitations to Love: Literacy, Love Letters, and Social Change in Nepal*. Ann Arbor: University of Michigan Press.

———. 2001b. "Language and Agency." *Annual Review of Anthropology* 30: 109–137.

Alber, Erdmute. 2011. "Child Trafficking in West Africa?" In *Frontiers of Globalization: Kinship and Family Structures in West Africa*, edited by Ana Marta Gonzales, Laurie de Rose, and Florence Oloo, 71–92. Trenton, NJ: Africa World Press.

———. 2013. "Within the Thicket of Intergenerational Sibling Relations: A Case Study from Northern Benin." In *The Anthropology of Sibling Relations: Shared Parentage, Experience, and Exchange*, edited by Erdmute Alber, Cati Coe, and Tatjana Thelen, 73–96. New York: Palgrave.

———. 2018. "Préparer la Retraite: New Age-Inscriptions in West African Middle Classes." *Anthropology & Aging Quarterly* 39(1): 66–81.

———. 2019. "Heterogeneity and Heterarchy—Middle-Class Households in Benin." In *The Multiplicity of Orders and Practices: A Tribute to Georg Klute*, edited by Thomas Hüsken, Alexander Solyga, and Dida Badi, 29–50. Cologne: Rüdiger Koppe Verlag.

Alber, Erdmute, and Heike Drotbohm. 2015. "Introduction." In *Anthropological Perspectives on Care: Work, Kinship and the Life Course*, edited by Erdmute Alber and Heike Drotbohm, 1–20. New York: Palgrave Macmillan.

Alber, Erdmute, Wenzel Geissler, and Susan Reynolds Whyte. 2004. *African Grandparents and Grandchildren: Lifetimes Intertwined*. Edinburgh: Edinburgh University Press.

Alber, Erdmute, and Tabea Häberlein. 2010. "Ethnologische Generationenforschung in Afrika." In *Verwandtschaft heute. Positionen, Ergebnisse und Perspektiven*, edited by Erdmute Alber, Bettina Beer, Julia Pauli, and Michael Schnegg, 281–304. Berlin: Dietrich Reimer.

Alber, Erdmute, Tabea Häberlein, and Jeannett Martin. 2010. "Changing Webs of Kinship: Spotlights on West Africa." *Afrika Spectrum* 45(3): 43–67.

Allerton, Catherine. 2007. "What Does It Mean to Be Alone?" In *Questions of Anthropology*, edited by Rita Astuti, Jonathan P. Parry, and Charles Stafford, 1–28. Oxford: Berg.

Allman, Jean, and Victoria Tashjian. 2000. *"I Will Not Eat Stone": A Women's History of Colonial Asante*. Portsmouth, NH: Heinemann.

Amenuveve, Vincent. 2015. "Micro-finance Scheme for Bongo Widows." *Daily Graphic*, June 25, 12.

Amselle, Jean-Loup. 2002. "Globalization and the Future of Anthropology." *African Affairs* 101: 213–229.

Anderson, Ben, Matthew Kearnes, Colin McFarlane, and Dan Swanton. 2012. "On Assemblages and Geography." *Dialogues in Human Geography* 2(2): 171–189.

Ani, Abena Asamoabea. 2002. "The Socio-economic Status of the Aged in Ghana: Profile from Large Samples." MA thesis, University of Ghana.

Appadurai, Arjun. 1996. *Modernity at Large: Cultural Dimensions of Globalization*. Minneapolis: University of Minnesota Press.

———. 2013. "The Future as Cultural Fact." In *The Future as Cultural Fact: Essays on the Global Condition*, 285–300. Brooklyn, NY: Verso.

Appiah-Denkyira, Ebenezer, Christopher H. Herbst, Agnes Soucat, and Karima Saleh. 2013. *Toward Interventions in Human Resources for Health in Ghana: Evidence for Health Workforce Planning and Results*. Washington, DC: World Bank.

Apt, Nana Araba. 1991. "The Aged and Disabled in Ghana: Policy Perspectives." Report, Center for Social Policy Research/Social Work Department Library, University of Ghana.

———. 1996. *Coping with Old Age in a Changing Africa: Social Change and the Elderly Ghanaian*. Aldershot: Avebury.

Ardayfio-Schandorf, Elizabeth, and Margaret Amissah. 1996. "Incidence of Child Fostering among School Children in Ghana." In *The Changing Family in Ghana*, edited by Ardayfio-Schandorf, 179–200. Accra: Ghana Universities Press.

Argenti, Nicolas. 2010. "Things That Don't Come by the Road: Folktales, Fosterage, and Memories of Slavery in the Cameroon Grasslands." *Comparative Studies of Society and History* 52(2): 224–253.

Armah, Ayi Kwei. 1971. *Fragments*. Boston: Houghton Mifflin.

Arthur, John A. 2008. *The African Diaspora in the United States and Europe: The Ghanaian Experience*. Burlington, VT: Ashgate.

Astuti, Rita. 2000. "Kindreds and Descent Groups. New Perspectives from Madagascar." In *Cultures of Relatedness: New Approaches to the Study of Kinship*, edited by Janet Carsten, 9–104. Cambridge: Cambridge University Press.

Atobrah, Deborah. 2012/2013. "Caring for the Seriously Sick in a Ghanaian Society: Glimpses from the Past." *Ghana Studies* 15/16: 69–101.

Aulino, Felicity. 2019. *Rituals of Care: Karmic Politics in an Aging Thailand*. Ithaca, NY: Cornell University Press.

Ayernor, P. K. 2012. "Diseases of Ageing in Ghana." *Ghana Medical Journal* 46(2 suppl.): 18–22.

Ayete-Nyampong, Samuel. 2008. *Pastoral Care of the Elderly in Africa: A Comparative and Cross-Cultural Study*. Accra North: Step.

Baah-Boateng, William. 2013. "Determinants of Unemployment in Ghana." *African Development Review* 25(4): 385–399.

Baffour-Awuah, Daniel. 2013. "Ghana Country Report for the 2014 Ministerial Conference on Youth Employment." http://www.adeanet.org/min_conf_youth_skills_employment/sites/default/files/u24/Ghana%20Country%20Report_0.pdf.

Bähre, Erik. 2012. "The Janus Face of Insurance in South Africa: From Costs to Risk, from Networks to Bureaucracies." *Africa* 82(1): 150–167.

Baldassar, Loretta, and Laura Merla. 2014. *Transnational Families, Migration, and the Circulation of Care: Understanding Mobility and Absence in Family Life*. New York: Routledge.

Baldassar, Loretta, Cora Vellekoop Baldock, and Raelene Whiting. 2007. *Families Caring Across Borders: Migration, Ageing, and Transnational Caregiving*. New York: Palgrave.

Barrientos, Armando. 2002. "Old Age, Poverty, and Social Investment." *Journal of International Development* 14: 1133–1141.

Bartle, Philip F. W. n.d. "Who Looks After the Rural Children of West African Urban Migrants? Some Notes on Households and the Non-family in a Dispersed Matrilineal Society." Leiden: Afrika-Studiecentrum.

Behrends, Andrea, Sung-Joon Park, and Richard Rottenburg. 2014. "Travelling Models: Introducing an Analytic Concept to Globalisation Studies." In *Travelling Models in*

African Conflict Management: Translating Technologies of Social Ordering, edited by Behrends, Park and Rottenburg, 1–40. Leiden: Brill.

Berger, Susan. 1981. "Regime and Interest Representation: The Traditional Middle Classes." In *Organizing Interests in Western Europe: Pluralism, Corporatism, and the Transformation of Politics*, edited by Susan Berger, 83–101. Cambridge: Cambridge University Press.

Berlant, Lauren. 2011. *Cruel Optimism*. Durham, NC: Duke University Press.

Bernardi, Bernardo. 1985. *Age Class Systems*. Cambridge: Cambridge University Press.

Biehl, João. 2005. *Vita: Life in a Zone of Social Abandonment*. Berkeley: University of California Press.

Biritwum, Richard, George Mensah, Alfred Yawson, and Nadia Minicucci. 2013. "Study on Global AGEing and Adult Health (SAGE) Wave 1: The Ghana National Report." Geneva: World Health Organization.

Bloom, David E., and Dara Lee Luca. 2016. "The Global Demography of Aging: Facts, Explanations, Future." In *Handbook of the Economics of Population Aging*, edited by John Piggott and Allan Woodland, 3–56. Amsterdam: Elsevier.

Boafo-Arthur, Kwame. 2007. "A Decade of Liberalism in Perspective." In *Ghana: One Decade of the Liberal State*, edited by Boafo-Arthur, 1–20. Dakar: CODESRIA.

Böhmig, Christine. 2010. "Organizing Monies: The Reality and Creativity of Nursing on a Hospital Ward in Ghana." In *Markets of Well-Being: Navigating Health and Healing in Africa*, edited by Marleen Dekker and Rijk van Dijk, 46–78. Leiden: Brill.

Bolten, Catherine E. 2020. *Serious Youth in Sierra Leone: An Ethnography of Performance and Global Connection*. Oxford: Oxford University Press.

Borneman, John. 1992. *Belonging in the Two Berlins: Kin, State, Nation*. New York: Cambridge University Press.

Bourdieu, Pierre. 1977. *Outline of a Theory of Practice*. Translated by Richard Nice. New York: Cambridge University Press.

———. 1986. "The Forms of Capital." In *Handbook of Theory and Research in the Sociology of Education*, edited by John G. Richardson, 241–258. New York: Greenwood.

———. 1989. *Distinction: A Social Critique of the Judgement of Taste*. Translated by Richard Nice. Cambridge, MA: Harvard University Press.

———. 1996. *The State Nobility: Elite Schools in the Field of Power*. Translated by L. C. Clough. Stanford, CA: Stanford University Press.

Bourdieu, Pierre, and Jean-Claude Passeron. 1990. *Reproduction in Education, Society, and Culture*. Translated by Richard Nice. 2nd ed. Newbury Park, CA: Sage.

Bremner, Robert H. 1980. *The Public Good: Philanthropy and Welfare in the Civil War Era*. New York: Knopf.

Brightman, Robert. 2013. "Hierarchy and Conflict in Mutual Being." *HAU: Journal of Ethnographic Theory* 3(2): 259–270.

Brokensha, David. 1972. "Society." In *Akwapim Handbook*, edited by Brokensha, 75–79. Tema: Ghana.

Brown, C. K. 1999. *Caring for the Elderly: Perspectives from Ghana and Japan*. Cape Coast: Catholic Mission Press.

Brown, Phillip. 1985. "Cultural Capital and Social Exclusion." *Work, Employment, and Society* 9(1): 29–51.

Brydon, Lynne. 1979. "Women at Work: Some Changes in Family Structure in Amedzofe-Avatime, Ghana." *Africa* 49(2): 97–111.

Buch, Elana D. 2013. "Senses of Care: Embodying Inequality and Sustaining Personhood in the Home Care of Older Adults in Chicago." *American Ethnologist* 40(4): 637–650.

———. 2015. "Postponing Passage: Doorways, Distinctions, and the Thresholds of Personhood among Older Chicagoans." *Ethos* 43(1): 40–58.

Budniok, Jan, and Andrea Noll. 2018. "The Ghanaian Middle Class, Social Stratification and Long-Term Dynamics of Upward and Downward Mobility of Lawyers and Teachers." In *Middle Classes in Africa: Changing Lives and Conceptual Challenges*, edited by Lena Kroeker, David O'Kane, and Tabea Scharrer, 109–134. New York: Palgrave Macmillan.

Burrows, Olive. 2017. "Universal Social Welfare for Those Over 70 Meant to Foster Inclusivity—PS." *Capital FM*, March 31. https://www.capitalfm.co.ke/news/2017/03/universal-social-welfare-for-those-over-70-meant-to-foster-inclusivity-ps/.

Caldwell, John C. 1967. "Population Change." In *A Study of Contemporary Ghana*, vol 2: *Some Aspects of Social Structure*, edited by Walter Birmingham, I. Neustadt, and E. N. Omaboe, 78–110. Evanston, IL: Northwestern University Press.

———. 1969. *African Rural-Urban Migration: The Movement to Ghana's Towns*. Canberra: Australian National University Press.

Case, Anne, and Angus Deaton. 1998. "Large-Scale Cash Transfers to the Elderly in South Africa." *Economic Journal* 108: 1330–1361.

Case, Anne, and Alicia Mendendez. 2007. "Does Money Empower the Elderly? Evidence from the Agincourt Demographic Surveillance Site, South Africa." *Scandinavian Journal of Public Health* 35: 157–164.

Cattell, Maria G. 1999. "Elders' Complaints: Discourses on Old Age and Social Change in Rural Kenya and Urban Philadelphia." In *Language and Communication in Old Age: Multidisciplinary Perspectives*, edited by Heidi E. Hamilton, 295–317. New York: Garland.

Chen, Melvin. 2015. "Care, Narrativity, and the Nature of *Disponibilité*." *Hypatia* 30(4): 779–792.

Chivers, Sally. 2015. "'Blind People Don't Run': Escaping the 'Nursing Home Specter' in Children of Nature and Cloudburst." *Journal of Aging Studies* 34 (August): 134–141.

Christaller, J. G. [1879] 1990. *Three Thousand Six Hundred Ghanaian Proverbs from the Asante and Fante Language*. Translated by Kofi Ron Lange. Lewiston: Edwin Mellon Press.

Christiansen, Catrine, Mats Utas, and Henrik E. Vigh. 2006. "Navigating Youth, Generating Adulthood." In *Navigating Youth, Generating Adulthood,* edited by Christiansen, Utas, and Vigh, 9–28. Uppsala: Nordiska AfrikaInstitutet.

Citinewsroom. 2018. "Parliament Must Pass Ageing Policy—Prof. Mate Kole." June 15. https://citinewsroom.com/2018/06/parliament-must-pass-ageing-policy-prof-mate-kole/.

Clark, Gracia. 1994. *Onions Are My Husband: Survival and Accumulation by West African Market Women*. Chicago: University of Chicago Press.

———. 2010. *African Market Women: Seven Life Stories from Ghana*. Bloomington: Indiana University Press.

Cliggett, Lisa. 2005. *Grains from Grass: Aging, Gender, and Famine in Rural Africa*. Ithaca, NY: Cornell University Press.

Coe, Cati. 2005. *The Dilemmas of Culture in African Schools: Nationalism, Youth, and the Transformation of Knowledge*. Chicago: University of Chicago Press.

———. 2011. "What Is Love? The Materiality of Care in Ghanaian Transnational Families." *International Migration* 49(6): 7–24.

———. 2012. "How Debt Became Care: Child Pawning and Its Transformations in Akuapem, the Gold Coast, 1874–1929." *Africa* 82(2): 287–311.

———. 2013a. "Disputes over Transfers of Belonging in the Colonial Gold Coast: Pawning or Fosterage?" In *Child Fosterage in West Africa: New Perspectives on Theories and Practices*, edited by Erdmute Alber, Jeannett Martin, and Catrien Notermans, 201–220. Leiden: Brill.

———. 2013b. *The Scattered Family: Parenting, African Migrants, and Global Inequality.* Chicago: University of Chicago Press.

———. 2017. "Returning Home: The Retirement Strategies of Aging Ghanaian Care Workers." In *Transnational Aging and Reconfigurations of Kin-Work*, edited by Parin Dossa and Coe, 141–158. New Brunswick, NJ: Rutgers University Press.

———. 2019a. *The New American Servitude: Political Belonging among African Immigrant Home Care Workers.* New York: New York University Press.

———. 2019b. "'You Are My Slave!' Adjacent Relations of Unfreedom in Care Work and the Racialization of West African Care Workers." In *Diverse Unfreedoms: The Afterlives and Transformations of Post-Transatlantic Bondages*, edited by Sarada Balagopalan, Coe, and Keith Green, 96–116. New York: Routledge.

———. 2020. "Social Class in Transnational Perspective: Emotional Responses to the Status Paradox among Ghanaian Transnational Migrants." *Africa Today* 66(3–4): 161–180.

Coe, Cati, and Erdmute Alber. 2018. "Age-Inscriptions and Social Change: Introduction." *Anthropology and Aging Quarterly* 39(1): 1–17.

Cohen, Lawrence. 1998. *No Aging in India: Alzheimer's, the Bad Family, and Other Modern Things.* Berkeley: University of California Press.

Cole, Jennifer. 2013. "On Generations and Aging: 'Fresh Contact' of a Different Sort." In *Transitions and Transformations: Cultural Perspectives on Aging and the Life Course*, edited by Caitrin Lynch and Jason Danely, 218–230. New York: Berghahn Books.

Cole, Jennifer, and Deborah Durham. 2007. "Introduction: Age, Regeneration and the Intimate Politics of Globalization." In *Generations and Globalization: Youth, Age, and Family in the New World Economy*, edited by Cole and Durham, 1–28. Bloomington: Indiana University Press.

Colen, Shellee, and Roger Sanjek. 1990. "At Work in Homes I: Orientations." In *At Work in Homes: Household Workers in World Perspective*, edited by Sanjek and Colen, 1–13. Washington, DC: American Anthropological Association.

Comaroff, Jean, and John L. Comaroff. 1991. *Of Revelation and Revolution: Christianity, Colonialism and Consciousness in South Africa.* Vol. 1. Chicago: University of Chicago Press.

———. 2001. *Millennial Capitalism and the Culture of Neoliberalism.* Durham, NC: Duke University Press.

Cooper, Elizabeth. 2012. "Sitting and Standing: How Families Are Fixing Trust in Uncertain Times." *Africa* 82(3): 437–456.

Cooper, Elizabeth, and David Pratten, eds. 2015. *Ethnographies of Uncertainty in Africa.* London: Palgrave Macmillan.

Cort, Pia. 2002. *Vocational Education and Training in Denmark: A Brief Description.* Luxembourg: Office for Official Publications of the European Communities.

Daily Graphic. 2018. "Senior Citizens Want NHIS Cover." July 3, 18.

Danely, Jason. 2014. *Aging and Loss: Mourning and Maturity in Contemporary Japan.* New Brunswick, NJ: Rutgers University Press.

Danquah, J. B. [1944] 1968. *The Akan Doctrine of God: A Fragment of Gold Coast Ethics and Religion.* 2nd ed. London: Cass.

Darko, Sammy. 2015. "How Ghana Has Reversed the Exodus of Nurses." *BBC News*, February 27. http://www.bbc.com/news/world-africa-31637774.

de-Graft Aikins, Ama. 2005. "Healer Shopping in Africa: New Evidence from Rural-Urban Qualitative Study of Ghanaian Diabetes Experience." *British Medical Journal* 331(7519): 737–742.

———. 2007. "Ghana's Neglected Chronic Disease Epidemic: A Developmental Challenge." *Ghana Medical Journal* 41(4): 154–159.

de-Graft Aikins, Ama, and Nana Araba Apt. 2016. "Aging in Ghana: Setting Priorities for Research, Intervention and Policy." *Ghana Studies* 19: 35–45.

de Jong, Willemijn, Claudia Roth, Fatoumata Badini-Kinda, and Seema Bhagyanath. 2005. *Ageing in Insecurity: Case Studies on Social Security and Gender in India and Burkina Faso.* Münster: Lit Verlag.

Dekker, Marleen, and Rijk van Dijk, eds. 2010. *Markets of Well-Being: Navigating Health and Healing in Africa.* Leiden: Brill.

De Klerk, Josien. 2016. "Making Sense of Neglect in Northwestern Tanzania." In *Ageing in Sub-Saharan Africa: Spaces and Practices of Care*, edited by Jaco Hoffman and Katrien Pype, 137–158. Bristol: Polity Press.

Dodoo, Samuel, Sophia Adade, Stephen Kpormegbe, Mabel Cudjoe, and Robert D. Agyarko. 1999. "Contributions of Older Persons to Development: The Accra Study." Report, Center for Social Policy Research, Social Work Department Library, University of Ghana.

Doh, Daniel. 2012. *Exploring Social Protection Arrangements for Older People: Evidence from Ghana.* Saarbrücken: Lambert.

Donner, Henrike, and Geert De Neve. 2011. "Introduction." In *Being Middle-Class in India: A Way of Life*, edited by Donner, 1–22. New York: Routledge.

Dossa, Parin, and Cati Coe, eds. 2017. *Transnational Aging and Reconfigurations of Kin-Work.* New Brunswick, NJ: Rutgers University Press.

Douglas, Mary. 1986. *How Institutions Think.* Syracuse, NY: Syracuse University Press.

Dovie, Delali Adjoa. 2018. "Utilization of Digital Literacy in Retirement Planning among Ghanaian Formal and Informal Sector Workers." *Interações: Sociedade e as Novas Modernidades* 34: 113–140. https://doi.org/10.31211/interacoes.n34.2018.a6.

———. 2019. "The Status of Older Adult Care in Contemporary Ghana: A Profile of Some Emerging Issues." *Frontiers in Sociology* 4: 1–12. https://doi.org/10.3389/fsoc .2019.00025.

Dsane, Sarah. 2013. *Changing Cultures and Care of the Elderly.* Saarbrücken: Lambert.

Ducey, Ariel. 2009. *Never Good Enough: Health Care Workers and the False Promise of Job Training.* Ithaca, NY: Cornell University Press.

Dudden, Faye E. 1983. *Serving Women: Household Service in Nineteenth-Century America.* Middletown, CT: Wesleyan University Press.

Economist. 2016. "Nkrumah's Heirs." November 19. http://www.economist.com/news /middle-east-and-africa/21710286-country-should-be-beacon-african-democracy -ailing-nkrumahs-heirs?zid=304&ah=e5690753dc78ce91909083042ad12e30.

Eisenschmid, David. 1866. "Second Quarterly Report, Kyebi." June 25. Afrika: Akim. D-1, 18b. Basel Mission Archives.

Enloe, Cynthia. 2013. *Seriously! Investigating Crashes and Crises as if Women Mattered.* Berkeley: University of California Press.

Ferguson, James. 2009. "The Uses of Neoliberalism." *Antipode* 41(S1): 166–184.

———. 2015. *Give a Man a Fish: Reflections on the New Politics of Distribution.* Durham, NC: Duke University Press.

Ferreira, Monica. 2006. "The Differential Impact of Social-Pension Income on Household Poverty Alleviation in Three South African Ethnic Groups." *Ageing and Society* 26: 337–254.

Fiawoo, D. K. 1978. "Some Patterns of Foster Care in Ghana." In *Marriage, Fertility and Parenthood in West Africa,* edited by C. Oppong, G. Adaba, M. Bekombo-Priso, and J. Mogey, 273–288. Canberra: Australian National University Press.

Finch, Janet, and Jennifer Mason. 1993. *Negotiating Family Responsibilities.* London: Routledge.

Fleck, Ludwig. [1935] 1979. *Genesis and Development of a Scientific Fact.* Translated by Fred Bradley and Thaddeus J. Trenn. Chicago: University of Chicago Press.

Foucault, Michel. 1980. *The History of Sexuality.* New York: Vintage.

Fouron, Georges E., and Nina Glick-Schiller. 2002. "The Generation of Identity: Redefining the Second Generation within a Transnational Social Field." In *The Changing Face of Home: The Transnational Lives of the Second Generation,* edited by Fouron and Mary C. Waters, 168–208. New York: Russell Sage Foundation.

Freeman, Carla. 2000. *High Heels and High Tech in the Global Economy: Women, Work, and Pink-Collar Identities in the Caribbean.* Durham, NC: Duke University Press.

———. 2014. *Entrepreneurial Selves: Neoliberal Respectability and the Making of a Caribbean Middle Class.* Durham, NC: Duke University Press.

Fröhlich, Katrin. 2016. "From Alms to Rights: Boundaries of a Transnational Non-Government Organization Implementing an Unconditional Old-Age Pension." In *Transnational Aging: Current Insights and Future Challenges,* edited by Vincent Horn and Cornelia Schweppe, 248–266. New York: Routledge.

Gal, Susan. 2003. "Movements of Feminism: The Circulation of Discourses about Women." In *Recognition Struggles and Social Movements: Contested Identities, Agencies and Power,* edited by Barbara Hobson, 93–118. Cambridge: Cambridge University Press.

Gambold, Liesl. 2018. "DIY Aging: Retirement Migration as a New Age-Script." *Anthropology and Aging Quarterly* 39(1): 82–93.

Gamburd, Michele Ruth. 2000. *The Kitchen Spoon's Handle: Transnationalism and Sri Lanka's Migrant Housemaids.* Ithaca, NY: Cornell University Press.

Ghana Health Service. 2010. *The Health Sector in Ghana: Facts and Figures.* Accra: Ghana Health Service. https://s3.amazonaws.com/ndpc-static/CACHES/NEWS/2015/07/14//2010+GHS+Facts+and+Figures.pdf.

Ghana News. 2016a. "No Government Jobs in 2017." October 24. http://www.ghanaweb.com/GhanaHomePage/NewsArchive/No-government-jobs-in-2017-480250.

———. 2016b. "List of 25 Unaccredited Nursing Schools in Ghana." August 26. http://www.ghanaweb.com/GhanaHomePage/NewsArchive/List-of-25-Unaccredited-Nursing-Schools-in-Ghana-465243.

———. 2016c. "2016 WASSCE Results Show Improvement—Jinapor." August 13. http://www.ghanaweb.com/GhanaHomePage/NewsArchive/2016-WASSCE-results-show-improvement-Jinapor-462483.

Ghana Statistical Service. 2012. "Ghana 2010 Population and Housing Census." Accra: Ghana Statistical Service.

———. 2015. "National Employment Report." Accra: Ghana Statistical Service.

Gilbert, Michelle. 1995. "The Christian Executioner: Christianity and Chieftaincy as Rivals." *Journal of Religion in Africa* 25(4): 347–386.

Glenn, Evelyn Nakano. 1983. "Split Household, Small Producer and Dual Wage Earner: An Analysis of Chinese-American Family Strategies." *Journal of Marriage and the Family* 45: 35–46.

———. 1992. "From Servitude to Service Work: Historical Continuities in the Racial Division of Paid Reproductive Labor." *Signs* 18(1): 1–43.

———. 2010. *Forced to Care: Coercion and Caregiving in America*. Cambridge, MA: Harvard University Press.

Goffman, Erving. 1986. *Frame Analysis: An Essay on the Organization of Experience*. Boston: Northeastern University Press.

Golomski, Casey. 2015. "Compassion Technology: Life Insurance and the Remaking of Kinship in Swaziland's Age of HIV." *American Ethnologist* 42(1): 81–96.

Goody, Esther N. 1982. *Parenthood and Social Reproduction: Fostering and Occupational Roles in West Africa*. Cambridge: Cambridge University Press.

Goswami, Manu. 2002. "Rethinking the Modular Nation Form: Toward a Socio-historical Conception of Nationalism." *Comparative Studies in Society and History* 44(4): 770–799.

Government of Ghana. 1993. Constitution of the Fourth Republic of Ghana (Promulgation) Law, 1992.

———. 2010. *National Ageing Policy: Ageing with Dignity and Security*. Accra: Ministry of Employment and Social Welfare.

Graw, Knut, and Samuli Schielke, eds. 2012. *The Global Horizon: Expectations of Migration in Africa and the Middle East*. Leuven: Leuven University Press.

Grieco, Margaret, Nana Apt, and Jeff Turner. 1996. *At Christmas and on Rainy Days: Transport, Travel, and the Female Traders of Accra*. Aldershot: Avebury.

Grimm, Carmen. 2016. "Older Persons' Rights: How Ideas Travel in International Development." In *Transnational Aging: Current Insights and Future Challenges*, edited by Vincent Horn and Cornelia Schweppe, 231–247. New York: Routledge.

Guardian. 2020. "'A Lot of Benign Neglect': How Ghana's Social Changes Are Isolating Older People." May 26.

Gupta, Akhil. 2012. *Red Tape: Bureaucracy, Structural Violence, and Poverty in India*. Durham, NC: Duke University Press.

Häberlein, Tabea. 2018. "Complexities of Elder Livelihoods: Changing Age-Inscriptions and Stable Norms in Three Villages in Rural West Africa." *Anthropology and Aging Quarterly* 39(1): 33–47.

Haenger, Peter. 2000. *Slaves and Slave Holders on the Gold Coast: Towards an Understanding of Social Bondage in West Africa*. Basel: P. Schlettwein.

Hagestad, Gunhild O. 1986. "The Aging Society as a Context of Family Life." *Daedalus* 115(1): 119–139.

Hagestad, Gunhild O., and Linda Burton. 1986. "Grandparenthood, Life Context, and Family Development." *American Behavioral Scientist* 29(4): 471–484.

Hall, John R. 1992. "The Capital(s) of Culture: A Nonholistic Approach to Status Situations, Class, Gender, and Ethnicity." In *Cultivating Differences: Symbolic Boundaries and the Making of Inequality*, edited by Michelle Lamont and Marcel Fournier, 257–288. Chicago: University of Chicago Press.

Hamdy, Sherine. 2008. "When the State and Your Kidneys Fail: Political Etiologies in an Egyptian Dialysis Ward." *American Ethnologist* 35(4): 553–569.

Han, Clara. 2012. *Life in Debt: Times of Care and Violence in Neoliberal Chile*. Berkeley: University of California Press.

Hanrahan, Kelsey B. 2018. "Caregiving as Mobility Constraint and Opportunity: Married Daughters Providing End of Life Care in Northern Ghana." *Social and Cultural Geography* 19(1): 59–80.

Hardiman, Margaret. 2003. *Konkonuru: Life in a West African Village*. Accra: Ghana Universities Press.

Hareven, Tamara. 1982. *Family Time and Industrial Time: The Relationship between the Family and Work in a New England Industrial Community*. Cambridge: Cambridge University Press.

Harvey, David. 2005. *A Brief History of Neoliberalism*. Oxford: Oxford University Press.

Heiman, Rachel, Carla Freeman, and Mark Liechty, eds. 2012. *The Global Middle Classes: Theorizing through Ethnography*. Santa Fe, NM: School for Advanced Research Press.

Heintz, J. 2005. "Employment, Gender, and Poverty in Ghana." Working Paper Series no. 92, Political Economy Research Institute, University of Massachusetts.

Held, Virginia. 2005. "The Ethics of Care." In *The Oxford Handbook of Ethical Theory*, edited by David Copp, 537–566. Oxford: Oxford University Press.

Hirsch, Jennifer S. 2003. *A Courtship after Marriage: Sexuality and Love in Mexican Transnational Families*. Berkeley: University of California Press.

Hochschild, Arlie Russell. 2001. "Global Care Chains and Emotional Surplus Value." In *On the Edge: Living with Global Capitalism*, edited by Will Hutton and Anthony Giddens, 130–146. London: Vintage.

Hoechner, Hannah. 2015. "Mobility as a Contradictory Resource: Peripatetic Qur'anic Students in Kano, Nigeria." *Children's Geographies* 13(1): 59–72.

Hoffman, Jaco, and Katrien Pype. 2016. "Introduction: Spaces and Practices of Care for Older People in Sub-Saharan Africa." In *Ageing in Sub-Saharan Africa: Spaces and Practices of Care*, edited by Hoffman and Pype, 1–20. Bristol: Polity Press.

Holdaway, Jennifer, Peggy Levitt, Jing Fang, and Narasimbhan Rajaram. 2015. "Mobility and Health Sector Development in China and India." *Social Science and Medicine* 130: 268–276.

Hollander, Jocelyn. 2004. "The Social Context of Focus Groups." *Journal of Contemporary Ethnography* 33(5): 602–637.

Hondagneu-Sotelo, Pierrette. 1994. *Gendered Transitions: Mexican Experiences of Immigration*. Berkeley: University of California Press.

Howell, Signe. 2006. *The Kinning of Foreigners: Transnational Adoption in a Global Perspective*. New York: Berghahn Books.

Hutchful, Eboe. 2002. *Ghana's Adjustment Experience: The Paradox of Reform*. Geneva: United Nations Research Institute for Social Development.

Ibarra, María de la Luz. 2010. "My Reward Is Not Money: Deep Alliances and End-of-Life Care among Mexicana Workers and Their Wards." In *Intimate Labors: Cultures, Technologies, and the Politics of Care*, edited by Eileen Boris and Rhacel Salazar Parreñas, 117–131. Stanford, CA: Stanford University Press.

Institute of Medicine. 2008. *Retooling for an Aging America: Building the Health Care Workforce*. Washington DC: National Academies Press.

International Organization for Migration. 2009. "Migration in Ghana: A Country Profile, 2009." http://www.iom.int/jahia/Jahia/about-migration/lang/en.

Irwin, Jones. 2010. *Derrida and the Writing of the Body*. New York: Routledge.

ISSER (Institute of Statistical, Social and Economic Research). 2013. "Ghana Social Development Outlook 2012." Legon: Institute of Statistical, Social and Economic Research.

Jafaru, Musah Yahaya. 2018. "Prosecute People Cited in A-G's Report: President Directs at Senior Citizens' Day." *Daily Graphic*, July 2, 32–33.

Kakwani, Nanak, and Kalinidhi Subbarao. 2007. "Poverty among the Elderly in Sub-Saharan Africa and the Role of Social Pensions." *Journal of Development Studies* 43(6): 987–1008.

Kapferer, Bruce. 2010. "Introduction: In the Event: Toward an Anthropology of Generic Moments." *Social Analysis* 54(3): 1–28.

Kar, Sohini. 2018. *Financializing Poverty: Labor and Risk in Indian Microfinance.* Stanford, CA: Stanford University Press.

Kocka, Jürgen. 1981. "Class Formation, Interest Articulation, and Public Policy: The Origins of the German White-Collar Class in the Late 19th and Early 20th Century." In *Organizing Interests in Western Europe: Pluralism, Corporatism, and the Transformation of Politics*, edited by Susan Berger, 63–81. Cambridge: Cambridge University Press.

Kohli, Martin. 2009. "Die Institutionalisierung des Lebenslaufs. Historische Befunde und theoretische Argumente." In *Soziale Ungleichheit. Klassische Texte zur Sozialstrukturanalyse*, edited by Heike Solga, Justin Powell, and Peter A. Berger, 387–400. Frankfurt: Campus.

Kotoh, Agnes Millicent, and Sjaak van der Geest. 2016. "Why Are the Poor Less Covered in Ghana's National Health Insurance? A Critical Analysis of Policy and Practice." *International Journal for Equity in Health* 15: 34. https://doi.org/10.1186/s12939-016-0320-1.

Kroeker, Lena, David O'Kane, and Tabea Scharrer, eds. 2018. *Middle Classes in Africa: Changing Lives and Conceptual Challenges.* London: Palgrave Macmillan.

Kuklick, Henrika. 1979. *The Imperial Bureaucrat: The Colonial Administrative Service in the Gold Coast, 1920–1939.* Stanford, CA: Hoover Institution Press.

Lamb, Sarah. 2009. *Aging and the Indian Diaspora: Cosmopolitan Families in India and Abroad.* Bloomington: Indiana University Press.

———. 2016. "Traveling Institutions as Transnational Aging: The Old-Age Home in Idea and Practice in India." In *Transnational Aging: Current Insights and Future Challenges*, edited by Vincent Horn and Cornelia Schweppe, 178–199. New York: Routledge.

Lamont, Michèle. 1992. *Money, Morals, and Manners: The Culture of the French and the American Upper Middle Class.* Chicago: University of Chicago Press.

Lamont, Michèle, and Annette Lareau. 1988. "Cultural Capital: Allusions, Gaps, and Glissandos in Recent Theoretical Developments." *Sociological Theory* 6(2): 153–168.

Lang, Claudia. 2019. "Inspecting Mental Health: Depression, Surveillance, and Care in Kerala, South India." *Culture, Medicine, and Psychiatry* 43(4): 596–612.

Laslett, Peter. 1980. "The History of Aging and the Aged." In *Family Life and Illicit Love in Earlier Generations*, 174–213. Cambridge: Cambridge University Press.

Laube, Wolfram. 2016. "What Makes Kofi Run? Changing Aspirations and Cultural Models of Success in Northern Ghana." *AnthropoChildren* 6. https://popups.uliege.be/2034-8517/index.php?id=2484.

Laybourn, Keith. 1995. *The Evolution of British Social Policy and the Welfare State, c. 1800–1993.* Keele: Keele University Press.

Leinaweaver, Jessaca B. 2010. "Outsourcing Care: How Peruvian Migrants Meet Transnational Family Obligations." *Latin American Perspectives* 37: 67–87.

Lentz, Carola. 2016. "African Middle Classes: Lessons from Transnational Studies and a Research Agenda." In *Examining the African Middle Classes*, edited by Henning Melber, 17–53. London: Zed Books.

Levitt, Peggy. 1998. "Social Remittances: Migration Driven Local-Level Forms of Cultural Diffusion." *International Migration Review* 32(4): 926–948.

Levitt, Peggy, and Deepak Lamba-Nieves. 2011. "Social Remittances Revisited." *Journal of Ethnic and Migration Studies* 37(1): 1–22.

Livingston, Julie. 2005. *Debility and the Moral Imagination in Botswana*. Bloomington: Indiana University Press.

Locher, Br. 1863. "The Girls Society in Abokobi." *Jahresbericht*, July, 93–95. Basel Mission Archives.

Lopes, Carlos. 2015. "Emerging Africa, Its Middle Class and New Development Challenges." Lecture, International Institute of Social Studies, The Hague, February 12.

Lucht, Hans. 2011. *Darkness before Daybreak: African Migrants Living on the Margins in Southern Italy Today*. Berkeley: University of California Press.

MacLean, Lauren Morris. 2002. "Constructing a Social Safety Net in Africa: An Institutionalist Analysis of Colonial Rule and State Social Policies in Ghana and Côte d'Ivoire." *Studies in Comparative International Development* 37(3): 64–90.

MacLeod, Jay. 1995. *Ain't No Makin' It: Aspirations and Attainment in a Low-Income Neighborhood*. Boulder, CO: Westview.

MacGaffey, Janet, and Rémy Bazenguissa-Ganga. 2000. *Congo-Paris: Transnational Traders on the Margins of the Law*. London: International African Institute in Association with James Currey, Oxford.

Mains, Daniel. 2011. *Hope Is Cut: Youth, Unemployment and the Future in Ethiopia*. Philadelphia: Temple University Press.

Manuh, Takyiwaa. 2006. *An 11th Region of Ghana? Ghanaians Abroad*. Accra: Ghana Academy of Arts and Sciences.

Martin, Jeannett, Christian Ungruhe, and Tabea Häberlein. 2016. "Young Future Africa—Images, Imagination and the Making: An Introduction." *Anthropo-Children* 6.

Marx, Karl. 1963. *The Eighteenth Brumaire of Louis Bonaparte*. New York: International.

Maurus, Sabrina. 2016. "Times of Continuity and Development: Visions of the Future among Agro-Pastoralist Children and Young People in Southern Ethiopia." *AnthropoChildren* 6.

Mauss, Marcel. 2006. "Techniques of the Body (1935)." In *Techniques, Technology, and Civilisation*, edited by Nathan Schlanger, 77–96. New York: Durkheim Press/ Berghahn Books.

Mayer, Annika. 2017. "Old Age—Home? Middle-Class Senior Citizens and New Elderscapes in Urban India." PhD dissertation, University of Heidelberg.

Mazzucato, Valentina. 2008. "Informal Insurance Arrangements in Ghanaian Migrants' Transnational Networks: The Role of Reverse Remittances and Geographic Proximity." *World Development* 37(6): 1105–1115.

Mazzucato, Valentina, Bart van den Boom, and N. N. N. Nsowah-Nuamah. 2008. "Origin and Destination of Remittances in Ghana." In *At Home in the World? International Migration and Development in Contemporary Ghana and West Africa*, edited by Takyiwaa Manuh, 139–152. Accra: Sub-Saharan Publishers.

Mba, C. J. 2010. "Population Ageing in Ghana: Research Gaps and the Way Forward." *Journal of Aging Research* 2010: 672157. https://doi.org/10.4061/2010/672157.

McNay, Lois. 2008. *Against Recognition*. Malden, MA: Polity Press.

McWilliam, H. O. A., and M. A. Kwamena-Poh. 1975. *The Development of Education in Ghana: An Outline*. 3rd ed. London: Longman.

Medick, Hans, and David Sabean, eds. 1984. *Interest and Emotion: Essays on the Study of Family and Kinship*. Cambridge: Cambridge University Press.

Meyer, Birgit. 1999. *Translating the Devil: Religion and Modernity among the Ewe in Ghana*. London: Edinburgh University Press.

Middleton, John. 1979. "Home-town: A Study of an Urban Centre in Southern Ghana." *Africa* 49(3): 246–257.

Miers, Suzanne, and Igor Kopytoff, eds. 1977. *Slavery in Africa: Historical and Anthropological Perspectives*. Madison: University of Wisconsin Press.

Miescher, Stephan. 2005. *Making Men in Ghana*. Bloomington: Indiana University Press.

Millar, Kathleen M. 2014. "The Precarious Present: Wageless Labor and Disrupted Life in Rio de Janeiro, Brazil." *Cultural Anthropology* 29(1): 32–53.

Mohr, Adam. 2013. *Enchanted Calvinism: Labor Migration, Afflicting Spirits, and Christian Therapy in the Presbyterian Church of Ghana*. Rochester, NY: University of Rochester Press.

Moran-Thomas, Amy. 2019. *Traveling with Sugar: Chronicles of a Global Epidemic*. Berkeley: University of California Press.

Muehlebach, Andrea. 2012. *The Moral Neoliberal: Welfare and Citizenship in Italy*. Chicago: University of Chicago Press.

Narotzky, Susana. 1997. *New Directions in Economic Anthropology*. London: Pluto Press.

National Accreditation Board, Ghana. 2016. "Private Nurses Training Colleges." http://www.nab.gov.gh/private-nurses-training-colleges.

Nelson-Cofie, Akosua Mensima. 1998. "Maintaining the Costs and Care of the Elderly in Ghana: Will It Work?" MA thesis, University of Ghana. Available in the Balme Library, University of Ghana.

Newell, Sasha. 2012. *The Modernity Bluff: Crime, Consumption, and Citizenship in Côte d'Ivoire*. Chicago: University of Chicago Press.

Nieswand, Boris. 2011. *Theorizing Transnational Migration: The Status Paradox of Migration*. New York: Routledge.

Ninsin, Kwame A. 2007. "Markets and Liberal Democracy." In *Ghana: One Decade of the Liberal State*, edited by Boafo-Arthur, 86–105. Dakar: CODESRIA.

Nisbett, Nicholas. 2013. "Youth and the Practice of IT Enterprise: Narratives of the Knowledge Society and the Creation of New Subjectivities amongst Bangalore's IT Aspirants." In *Enterprise Culture in Neoliberal India: Studies in Youth, Class, Work and Media*, edited by Nandini Gooptu, 175–189. New York: Routledge.

NVTI (National Vocational and Training Institute). 2010. "Trade Testing Regulations and Syllabus: Health Care, Certificate One." NVTI.

Obiri-Yeboah, D. A., and Hansen Obiri-Yeboah. 2014. "Ghana's Pension Reforms in Perspective: Can the Pension Benefit Provide a House a Real Need of the Retiree." *European Journal of Business and Management* 6(32): 1–13.

Obrist, Brigit. 2016. "Place Matters: The Home as a Key Site of Old-Age Care in Coastal Tanzania." In *Ageing in Sub-Saharan Africa: Spaces and Practices of Care*, edited by Jaco Hoffman and Katrien Pype, 95–114. Bristol: Polity Press.

Olwig, Karen Fog. 2007. *Caribbean Journeys: An Ethnography of Migration and Home in Three Family Networks*. Durham, NC: Duke University Press.

Ong, Aihwa, and Stephen Collier. 2005. *Global Assemblages: Technologies, Politics, and Ethics as Anthropological Problems*. Malden: Blackwell.

Opoku, Darko Kwabena. 2010. *The Politics of Government-Business Relations in Ghana, 1982–2008*. New York: Palgrave Macmillan.

Oppong, Christine. 1974. *Marriage among a Matrilineal Elite: A Family Study of Ghanaian Senior Civil Servants*. Cambridge: Cambridge University Press.

Orozco, Manuel, with Micah Bump, Rachel Fedewa, and Katya Sienkiewicz. 2005. "Diasporas, Development, and Transnational Integration: Ghanaians in the U.S., U.K. and Germany." Report, Institute for the Study of International Migration and Inter-American Dialogue. http://archive.thedialogue.org/PublicationFiles /Ghanaian%20transnationalism.pdf.

Ortner, Sherry B. 2006. *Anthropology and Social Theory: Culture, Power, and the Acting Subject*. Durham, NC: Duke University Press.

Oyěwùmi, Oyèrónké. 1997. *The Invention of Women: Making an African Sense of Western Gender Discourse*. Minneapolis: University of Minnesota Press.

Palmer, J. B. 1860–1867. "Akwapim, Land und Leute, Religion." D-20.4. Basel Mission Archives.

Palmer, Phyllis M. 1989. *Domesticity and Dirt: Housewives and Domestic Servants in the United States, 1920–1945*. Philadelphia: Temple University Press.

Paquette, Danielle. 2020. "U.S. Nurses Face Pay Cuts, Ghana's Get Raises." *Washington Post*, May 25, A10.

Paraprofessional Healthcare Institute. 2016. "U.S. Home Care Workers: Key Facts." https://phinational.org/sites/phinational.org/files/phi-home-care-workers-key-facts .pdf.

Parreñas, Rhacel Salazar. 2004. *Children of Global Migration: Transnational Families and Gendered Woes*. Stanford, CA: Stanford University Press.

Patterson, Orlando. 1982. *Slavery and Social Death: A Comparative Study*. Cambridge, MA: Harvard University Press.

Peil, Margaret. 1981. *Cities and Suburbs: Urban Life in West Africa*. New York: Africana.

Perbi, Akosua A. 2004. *A History of Indigenous Slavery in Ghana: From the 15th to the 19th Century*. Legon: Sub-Saharan Publishers.

Phillips-Cunningham, Danielle T. 2020. *Putting Their Hands on Race: Irish Immigrant and Southern Black Domestic Workers*. New Brunswick, NJ: Rutgers University Press.

Quartey, Peter. 2006. "Migrant Remittances and Household Welfare in Times of Macro-Volatility: The Case of Ghana." Legon: Institute of Statistical, Social and Economic Research, University of Ghana.

Rae-Espinoza, Heather. 2011. "The Children of Émigrés in Ecuador: Narratives of Cultural Reproduction and Emotion in Transnational Social Fields." In *Everyday Ruptures: Children, Youth, and Migration in Global Perspective*, edited by Cati Coe, Rachel R. Reynolds, Deborah A. Boehm, Julia Meredith Hess, and Heather Rae-Espinoza, 115–138. Nashville, TN: Vanderbilt University Press.

Raffety, Erin L. 2017. "Fostering Change: Elderly Foster Mothers' Intergenerational Influence in Contemporary China." In *Transnational Aging and Reconfigurations of Kin Work*, edited by Parin Dossa and Cati Coe, 85–101. New Brunswick, NJ: Rutgers University Press.

Ranger, Terence. 1983. "The Invention of Tradition in Colonial Africa." In *The Invention of Tradition*, edited by Eric Hobsbawm and Ranger, 211–262. Cambridge: Cambridge University Press.

Resnick, Danielle. 2019. "Strong Democracy, Weak State: The Political Economy of Ghana's Stalled Structural Adjustment." In *Ghana's Economic and Agricultural Transformation: Past Performance and Future Prospects*, edited by Xinshen Diao, Peter Hazell, Shaishidhara Kolavalli, and Danielle Resnick, 49–96. Oxford: Oxford University Press. https://doi.org/10.1093/oso/9780198845348.003.0003.

Reverby, Susan. 1987. *Ordered to Care: The Dilemmas of American Nursing, 1850–1945.* Cambridge: Cambridge University Press.

Riis, Hans Nicolaus. 1854. *Grammatical Outline and Vocabulary of the Oji-language, with Especial Reference to the Akwapim-Dialect: Together with a Collection of Proverbs of the Natives.* Basel: Bahnmaier.

Riley, Matilda White, and John W. Riley Jr. 1986. "Longevity and Social Structure: The Added Years." *Daedalus* 115(1): 51–75.

Rollins, Judith. 1990. "Ideology and Servitude." In *At Work in Homes: Household Workers in World Perspective*, edited by Roger Sanjek and Shellee Colen, 74–88. Washington, DC: American Anthropological Association.

Roth, Claudia. 2007. "'Tu ne peux pas rejecter ton enfant!': Contrat entre les Generations, Sécurité Sociale et Vieillesse en Milieu Urbain Burkinabe." *Cahiers d'Études Africaines* 185(1): 93–116.

———. 2008. "'Shameful!' The Inverted Intergenerational Contract in Bobo-Dioulasso, Burkina Faso." In *Generations in Africa: Connections and Conflicts*, edited by Erdmute Alber, Sjaak van der Geest, and Susan Reynolds Whyte, 47–69. Berlin: Lit Verlag.

———. 2014. "The Strength of Badenya Ties: Siblings and Social Security in Old Age—The Case of Urban Burkina Faso." *American Ethnologist* 41(3): 547–562. https://doi.org/10.1111/amet.12094.

Rytter, Mikkel. 2011. "Money or Education? Improvement Strategies among Pakistani Families in Denmark." *Journal of Ethnic and Migration Studies* 37(2): 197–315.

Sagner, Andreas. 2000. "Ageing and Social Policy in South Africa: Historical Perspectives with Particular Reference to the Eastern Cape." *Journal of South African Studies* 26(3): 523–553.

———. 2001. "'The Abandoned Mother': Ageing, Old Age, and Missionaries in Early and Mid-Nineteenth Century South-East Africa." *Journal of African History* 42(2): 173–198.

Sahlins, Marshall. 1980. *Historical Metaphors and Mythical History.* Ann Arbor: University of Michigan Press.

Sanjek, Roger. 1990. "Maid Servants and Market Women's Apprentices in Adabraka." In *At Work in Homes: Household Workers in World Perspective*, edited by Sanjek and Shellee Colen, 35–62. Washington, DC: American Anthropological Association.

Sassen, Saskia. 1998. "The Informal Economy: Between New Developments and Old Regulations." In *Globalization and Its Discontents*, 153–172. New York: New Press.

———. 2006. *Territory, Authority, Rights: From Medieval to Global Assemblages.* Princeton, NJ: Princeton University Press.

Schauert, Paul. 2015. *Staging Ghana: Artistry and Nationalism in State Dance Ensembles.* Bloomington: Indiana University Press.

Scherz, China. 2014. *Having People, Having Heart: Charity, Sustainable Development, and Problems of Dependence in Central Uganda.* Chicago: University of Chicago Press.

Schielke, Samuli. 2012. "Living in the Future Tense: Aspiring for World and Class in Provincial Egypt." In *The Global Middle Classes: Theorizing through Ethnography*, edited by Rachel Heiman, Carla Freeman, and Mark Liechty, 31–56. Santa Fe, NM: School for Advanced Research Press.

Schultheiss, Katrin. 2001. *Bodies and Souls: Politics and the Professionalization of Nursing in France, 1880–1922.* Cambridge, MA: Harvard University Press.

Scott, James C. 1985. *Weapons of the Weak: Everyday Forms of Peasant Resistance.* New Haven, CT: Yale University Press.

Segalen, Martine. 2016. "On *Papies* and *Mammies*: The Invention of a New Parent in Contemporary European Kinship." Paper, Max Planck Institute, Halle, May 27.

Senah, Kodjo Amedjorteh. 1997. *Money be Man: The Popularity of Medicines in a Rural Ghanaian Community*. Amsterdam: Het Spinhuis.

Sewell, William H. 2005. *Logics of History: Social Theory and Social Transformation*. Chicago: University of Chicago Press.

Shipton, Parker. 2007. *The Nature of Entrustment: Intimacy, Exchange, and the Sacred in Africa*. New Haven, CT: Yale University Press.

Sill, Ursula. 2010. *Encounters in Quest of Christian Womanhood: The Basel Mission in Pre- and Early Colonial Ghana*. Boston: Brill.

Skocpol, Theda. 1992. *Protecting Soldiers and Mothers: The Political Origins of Social Policy in the United States*. Cambridge, MA: Harvard University Press.

Spronk, Rachel. 2014. "Exploring the Middle Classes in Nairobi: From Modes of Production to Modes of Sophistication." *African Studies Review* 57(1): 93–114.

Stacey, Clare L. 2011. *The Caring Self: The Work Experiences of Home Care Aides*. Ithaca, NY: Cornell University Press.

Stack, Carol, and Linda M. Burton. 1993. "Kinscripts." *Journal of Comparative Family Studies* 24(2): 157–170.

Stambach, Amy. 2017. "Introduction." In *Anthropological Perspectives on Student Futures: Youth and the Politics of Possibility*, edited by Stambach and Kathleen Hall, 1–16. New York: Palgrave Macmillan.

Standing, Guy. 2011. *The Precariat: The New Dangerous Class*. London: Bloomsbury.

Steinberg, Jonny. 2015. *A Man of Good Hope*. New York: Vintage.

Stevenson, Lisa. 2014. *Life Beside Itself: Imagining Care in the Canadian Arctic*. Berkeley: University of California Press.

Stucki, Barbara. 1995. "Managing the Social Clock: The Negotiation of Elderhood among Rural Asante of Ghana." PhD dissertation, Northwestern University.

Subramanian, Ajantha. 2015. "Making Merit: The Indian Institutes of Technology and the Social Life of Caste." *Contemporary Studies in Society and History* 57(2): 291–322.

Swidler, Ann. 2001. *Talk of Love: How Culture Matters*. Chicago: University of Chicago Press.

Takyi-Boadu, Charles. 2018. "Gov't Fetes Senior Citizens." *Daily Guide*, July 3, 6.

Thelen, Tatjana. 2015. "Care as Social Organization: Creating, Maintaining and Dissolving Significant Relations." *Anthropological Theory* 15(4): 497–515.

Thelen, Tatjana, and Cati Coe. 2019. "Political Belonging through Elder Care: Temporalities, Representations, and Mutuality." *Anthropological Theory* 19(2): 279–299.

Tonah, Steve. 2009. "The Challenge of Ageing in Rural and Urban Ghana." In *Contemporary Social Problems in Ghana*, edited by Tonah, 125–146. Legon: Department of Sociology, University of Ghana.

Turner, Jeff, and Edward Kwakye. 1996. "Transport and Survival Strategies in a Developing Economy: Case Evidence from Accra, Ghana." *Journal of Transport Geography* 2(3): 161–168.

Twum-Baah, K. A. 2005. "Volume and Characteristics of International Ghanaian Migration." In *At Home in the World? International Migration and Development in Contemporary Ghana and West Africa*, edited by Takyiwaa Manuh, 55–77. Accra: Sub-Saharan Publishers.

United Nations, Department of Economic and Social Affairs, Disability Division. 2008. "Convention on the Rights of Persons with Disabilities." https://www.un.org /development/desa/disabilities/convention-on-the-rights-of-persons-with-disabilities .html.

United Nations, Department of Economic and Social Affairs, Population Division. 2013. "World Population Ageing 2013." ST/ESA/SER.A/348. http://www.un.org /en/development/desa/population/publications/pdf/ageing/WorldPopulation Ageing2013.pdf.

United Nations, Population Division. 2012. "World Population Prospects: The 2010 Revision." http://esa.un.org/unpd.

United Nations Population Fund. 2012. *Ageing in the Twenty-First Century: A Celebration and a Challenge.* New York: UNFPA.

U.S. Department of Health and Human Services. 2003. "The Future Supply of Long-Term Care Workers in Relation to the Aging Baby Boom Generation." Report to Congress. https://aspe.hhs.gov/pdf-report/future-supply-long-term-care-workers -relation-aging-baby-boom-generation.

Vail, Leroy, ed. 1989. *The Creation of Tribalism in Southern Africa.* London: James Currey.

Van der Geest, Sjaak. 1997. "Money and Respect: The Changing Value of Old Age in Rural Ghana." *Africa* 67(4): 534–559.

———. 1998. "*Yebisa Wo Fie:* Growing Old and Building a House in the Akan Culture of Ghana." *Journal of Cross-Cultural Gerontology* 13: 333–359.

———. 2001. "'No Strength': Sex and Old Age in a Rural Town in Ghana." *Social Science and Medicine* 53: 1383–1396.

———. 2002a. "'I Want to Go!' How Older People in Ghana Look Forward to Death." *Ageing and Society* 22(1): 7–28.

———. 2002b. "Respect and Reciprocity: Care of Elderly People in Ghana." *Journal of Cross-Cultural Gerontology* 17: 3–31.

———. 2002c. "From Wisdom to Witchcraft: Ambivalence towards Old Age in Rural Ghana." *Africa* 72(3): 437–463.

———. 2003. "Grandparents and Grandchildren in Kwahu, Ghana: The Performance of Respect." *Africa* 74(1): 47–61.

———. 2004a. "Dying Peacefully: Considering Good and Bad Death in Kwahu-Tafo, Ghana." *Social Science and Medicine* 58: 899–911.

———. 2004b. "'They Don't Want to Listen': The Experience of Loneliness among Older Peoples in Kwahu, Ghana." *Journal of Cross-Cultural Gerontology* 19(2): 77–96.

———. 2016. "Will Families in Ghana Continue to Care for Older People? Logic and Contradictions in Policy." In *Ageing in Sub-Saharan Africa: Spaces and Practices of Care,* edited by Jaco Hoffman and Katrien Pype, 21–42. Bristol: Polity Press.

Van der Geest, Sjaak, Anke Mul, and Hans Vermeulen. 2004. "Linkages between Migration and the Care of Frail Older People: Observations from Greece, Ghana, and the Netherlands." *Ageing and Society* 24(3): 431–450.

Van Dongen, Els. 2008. "Memories and Intergenerational Conflicts in South Africa." In *Generations in Africa: Connections and Conflicts,* edited by Erdmute Alber, Sjaak van der Geest, and Susan Reynolds Whyte, 183–206. Berlin: Lit Verlag.

Van Eeuwijk, Peter. 2016. "Older People Providing Care for Older People in Tanzania: Against Conventions—but Accepted." In *Ageing in Sub-Saharan Africa: Spaces and Practices of Care,* edited by Jaco Hoffman and Katrien Pype, 71–94. Bristol: Polity Press.

Vaughan, Megan. 1983. "Which Family? Problems in the Reconstruction of the History of the Family as an Economic and Cultural Unit." *Journal of African History* 24(2): 275–283.

Vavrus, Frances. 2003. *Desire and Decline: Schooling and Crisis in Tanzania.* New York: Peter Lang.

Wang, Jing, and Bei Wu. 2016. "Domestic Helpers as Frontline Workers in China's Home-Based Elder Care: A Systematic Review." *Journal of Aging and Women* 29: 294–305. https://doi.org/10.1080/08952841.2016.1187536.

Wendland, Claire L. 2010. *A Heart for the Work: Journeys through an African Medical School.* Chicago: University of Chicago Press.

Whyte, Susan Reynolds. 2020. "Whose Aspirations? Intergenerational Moves and Materialities in Eastern Uganda." Paper, Aspiring in Later Life Workshop, Max-Planck Institute, Göttingen.

Williams, Raymond. 1973. *The Country and the City.* Oxford: Oxford University Press.

———. 1977. *Marxism and Literature.* Oxford: Oxford University Press.

World Bank. 2011. *Migration and Remittances Factbook 2011.* 2nd ed. Washington, DC: World Bank.

———. 2019a. "Personal Remittances, Received (% of GDP)." https://data.worldbank.org/indicator/BX.TRF.PWKR.DT.GD.ZS.

———. 2019b. "GDP Growth (% Annual)—Ghana." https://data.worldbank.org/indicator/NY.GDP.MKTP.KD.ZG?end=2018&locations=GH&start=1961&view=chart.

———. 2019c. "Government Expenditure on Health, Total (% of Government Expenditure)—Ghana." https://data.worldbank.org/indicator/SE.XPD.TOTL.GB.ZS?locations=GH.

———. 2019d. "Domestic General Government Health Expenditure (% of General Government Expenditure)—Ghana, Tonga." https://data.worldbank.org/indicator/SH.XPD.GHED.GE.ZS?locations=GH-TO.

World Health Organization. 2015. *World Report on Ageing and Health.* Geneva: World Health Organization.

———. 2017. *Towards Long-Term Care Systems in Sub-Saharan Africa.* Geneva: World Health Organization.

Wouterse, Fleur, and Mahamadou Tankari. 2015. "Household Out-of-Pocket Expenses on Health: Does Disease Type Matter?" *Journal of African Economics* 24(2): 254–276.

Yarrow, Thomas. 2008. "Paired Opposites: Dualism in Development and Anthropology." *Critique of Anthropology* 28(4): 426–445.

Yeates, Nicola. 2009. *Globalizing Care Chains and Migrant Workers: Explorations in Global Care Chains.* New York: Palgrave Macmillan.

———. 2012. "Global Care Chains: A State-of-the-Art Review and Future Directions in Care." *Global Networks* 12(2): 135–154.

Index

About the Author

CATI COE is a professor of anthropology at Rutgers University. She has published widely on nationalism and schooling, transnational families, and care work as a niche employment field for African immigrants. Her books include *Transnational Aging and Reconfigurations of Kin Work* (coedited with Parin Dossa, 2017) and *The New American Servitude: Political Belonging among African Immigrant Home Care Workers* (2019).